THE

CHINA

RENAISSANCE

The Rise of Xi Jinping
and the 18th Communist Party Congress

THE
CHINA
RENAISSANCE

The Rise of Xi Jinping
and the 18th Communist Party Congress

By the writers, artists and editors of the
South China Morning Post

Edited by Jonathan Sharp

SCMP BOOKS

World Scientific

Published by

World Scientific Publishing Co. Pte. Ltd.

5 Toh Tuck Link, Singapore 596224

USA office: 27 Warren Street, Suite 401-402, Hackensack, NJ 07601

UK office: 57 Shelton Street, Covent Garden, London WC2H 9HE

British Library Cataloguing-in-Publication Data
A catalogue record for this book is available from the British Library.

THE CHINA RENAISSANCE

The Rise of Xi Jinping and the 18th Communist Party Congress

Copyright © 2013 by South China Morning Post Publishers Limited

ISBN 978-981-4522-86-1 (pbk)

Printed in Singapore by Mainland Press Pte Ltd.

Foreword

In November 2012, an ageing generation of Chinese leaders headed by Communist Party Chief Hu Jintao stepped aside and handed power to the fifth generation led by Xi Jinping. While the 18th Communist Party Congress and the transfer of state posts at the parliament meeting the following March went off smoothly, the year of transition was anything but orderly. Any Chinese transfer of power would be expected to yield its share of behind the scenes jockeying and intrigue — the traditional secrecy of the party's political process virtually ensures it. But 2012 featured for the first time overt campaigning for high office more resembling American democracy than Chinese communism. It also saw the downfall of one of the country's most popular leaders involved in that campaigning, Bo Xilai, undone by a web of corruption, betrayal and murder. A protégé of Hu Jintao saw his political career self-destruct in another scandal.

From the start of 2012, the *South China Morning Post* embarked on an ambitious project to chart the transfer of power and pull the veil of secrecy from a new generation of Chinese leaders who will run the country for the next decade. The result was unparalleled coverage and a series of exclusives that kept the newspaper well ahead on the story. To list but a few: the *Post* was first among international media in reporting the line-up of the seven men who would form the elite Politburo Standing Committee — that story was published before the secretive Congress even opened; the newspaper also was first with the news that Hu would retire from all of his posts, including the military commission chairmanship, despite speculation he might hang on as past leaders have done; the newspaper also led the way on the saga of one of Hu's aides, Ling Jihua, whose career ambitions were clipped after the cover up of a Ferrari crash that killed his son. Along the way, we also profiled all of the other senior leaders who would rise in the new leadership.

Xi completed the transition in March by taking on the presidency, and the stakes could not be higher. If Hu's decade saw China grow from an economy roughly the size of Italy to surpass Japan by the time he stepped down, then Xi's decade is expected to see China grow to rival the United States as the top economic power in the world. Shanghai has grand ambitions of becoming a global financial centre, but critical reforms to the markets and the renminbi currency must take place for it to get there. China is modernising its military to ensure it can protect its security in Asia if not project its presence beyond the region. Yet at home it still grapples with the threat of unrest — seeing thousands of mass protests each year — and developing country problems related to its growth for growth's sake strategy that has left its air, land and water-ways poisoned by pollution. Who are the people that will guide China through its challenges at home and on the global stage? Through our profiles of dozens of rising stars and movers and shakers over the past year, the *South China Morning Post* has provided the most complete portrait to date of the leaders who will control the halls of power of the world's most populous country over the next decade.

The book profiles the 25 members of China's new Politburo, starting with Xi and six other standing committee members. We look at senior Cabinet officials and financial leaders who will be overseers of China's economy and architects of its regulatory transformation, as well as top leaders running the country's domestic, military and foreign affairs. We also chart the most dramatic political episode of the transition, the collapse of Bo Xilai, and the challenge the sieve-like Weibo poses for a party accustomed to secrecy and control of information. Finally, we reveal the sixth generation of leaders — those who are expected to assume power when Xi's generation is ready to retire in 2022. There are many unknowns as the new leaders set out to chart the course of Chinese history over the next decade. This book, by the reporters and editors of the *South China Morning Post*, aims to provide the reader with a comprehensive primer on the men, and the handful of women, who are going to be charting that course.

Wang Xiangwei
Editor-in-Chief, the *South China Morning Post*
March 2013

Contents

THE

CHINA

RENAISSANCE

The Rise of Xi Jinping
and the 18th Communist Party Congress

CHAPTER 1

From Strongman to Consensus Rule

*by **Cary Huang***

China's Communist Party may have long since moved on from its violent legacy of bloody purges and ruthless power grabs that punctuated the early decades of the People's Republic. But the level of intrigue and infighting that permeated the months leading up to and during the 18th Communist Party Congress in November 2012 showed that in China the transfer of power is just as contentious as ever. As a sign of the uncertainties bedevilling the handing over to the so-called fifth generation of Chinese leaders, not even the date of the congress of the world's largest political party — in charge of the globe's most populous nation and its second largest economy — was made public until a mere six weeks before the opening.

The era when China was effectively run according to dictates or whims of strongmen such as Mao Zedong and Deng Xiaoping has long since passed. Nowadays the Communist Party of China strives to project an image of "consensus-building" among a "collective leadership".

However, whatever the effort to provide a smoothly scripted process, the bitter feuding that was clearly apparent in the run-up to the 18th party congress may well have been just as intense as any that occurred at previous such junctures, at least since the 1966–76 Cultural Revolution.

Tensions were bound to run high at the latest conclave, particularly as almost 60 per cent of the 205 members of the Central Committee were being replaced, 14 of 25 members of the Politburo were relinquishing office and seven out of nine members of the inner sanctum of power, the Politburo Standing Committee, would retire. Only twice previously in the history of the Chinese Communist Party had so many leadership positions become available at the same time at a party congress.

Before the death of the last strongman, Deng, in 1997, decisions were taken by leaders within a very small circle, often indeed by a sole individual. The top figures, Mao before his death in 1976, and to a lesser extent Deng in the 1980s and 1990s, could more or less choose to stay in power until they died no matter what capacity they held, appoint anyone they favoured to any powerful position, and depose anyone whom they disliked or deemed incompetent.

Mao Zedong

In the post-1949 period, Mao loomed almost monolithically large, steering China through revolution and governance — often equally disastrously — implementing drastic land reforms, launching the Great Leap Forward that led to horrific famine, and unleashing the infamous Cultural Revolution.

During his reign, Mao ousted his anointed successor, Liu Shaoqi, after launching the Cultural Revolution. Liu died in squalor in prison. His second anointed successor, Lin Biao, died in a plane crash in 1971 after fleeing a failed court coup. Following the purge of the Gang of Four led by Mao's widow Jiang Qing in 1976 and the rise of Deng, ruthless Communist Party power struggles continued in an almost forgotten chapter of China's history.

In the post-Mao period, Deng heralded the "second revolution", establishing his credentials as a reformer *par excellence* through reforms and open doors — de-collectivisation of agriculture, recognition of private entrepreneurship, creating Special Economic Zones and easing up on the micro-management of people's everyday lives. Deng served as "paramount leader"— even without any formal party or state position — until his death.

Deng also wrested control of China from a third anointed Mao successor, Hua Guofeng, and then proceeded to depose his own two chosen protégés, Hu Yaobang and Zhao Ziyang, after both expressed sympathy with students demanding democracy. Zhao's ousting came just prior to the bloody military crackdown on student-led demonstrations in Tiananmen Square on June 4, 1989.

Deng Xiaoping

Deng's departure marked the end of an era of the one-man dominance, the most important change in the communist-ruled nation's political landscape. In the post-Deng era, however, decisions to choose incoming leaders are all made behind closed doors in secret Communist Party gatherings. And any hint of uncertainty can spark an explosion of speculation, virtually ensuring that no leadership transition unfolds without drama.

And drama there was aplenty in the months preceding the 18th party congress, with the spectacular fall from grace of Communist Party aristocrat and Politburo member Bo Xilai, party chief in the huge Chongqing municipality.

Professor Steve Tsang, director of the University of Nottingham's China Policy Institute, said the changes in the political arena since 1997 were meant to institutionalise the succession process and make it much more predictable and therefore stable, including long spells of apprenticeship for those earmarked for the top political and management posts.

"There has always been scope for balancing or horse trading for membership in the rest of the Politburo Standing Committee, but Bo's efforts to force his way into the Standing Committee by his maverick approach in Chongqing changed the dynamics," Tsang said.

Starting from the 1980s, Deng attempted to establish a set of rules to govern elite interactions and power succession. He re-institutionalised the party congress, and introduced age and term limits for leading government cadres. As time passed, some implicit and explicit rules seemed to have been established. In fact, rules such as age and term limits now effectively rule out the possibility of top leaders staying in power for too long, resulting in a much more predictable elite turnover. For instance, at the 16th party congress in 2002, the number four leader, Li Ruihuan, retired aged 68 after having served two terms. Since then, 67 has become the oldest age for anyone to start a new term in the Politburo and its elite Standing Committee. At the 17th party congress in 2007, all Politburo members aged 68 or above retired, and the same rule applied at the 18th party congress.

"The age limit has therefore greatly curbed the rise of charismatic leaders and figures with sultanistic tendencies. It is also now a critical criterion when the Party identifies future leaders," said Zhengxu Wang, a senior fellow and deputy director of the University of Nottingham's China Policy Institute. Thus the process to groom top leaders has been planned and prepared for years ahead. A number of promising leaders are identified early on and appointed to ministerial or provincial leadership positions in their early and mid-50s before they are eventually "elected" to become a member of the top decision-making Politburo and the Standing Committee.

For example, newly-promoted top leaders Xi Jinping and Li Keqiang were elevated to the Standing Committee at the 17th party congress in 2007 at the ages of 54 and 52, respectively.

Despite intense factional fighting to promote their members into top positions at the 18th party congress, no one would have doubted that Xi and Li had been assured of their top positions. Xi and Li were referred to as the incoming Xi–Li administration even before they were installed as number one and number two, respectively, at the conclave.

Before his death, Deng ruled there should be a core of the collective leadership in the Communist Party hierarchy. He said that Mao was the core of the first generation of leadership while he himself was that of the second generation. When Deng selected Jiang Zemin to succeed him as the core of the third generation, Jiang was at first regarded as a transitional leader, but amazed everyone when his protégés gained a majority in the Politburo and Standing Committee when he retired. While he was alive, Deng also picked Hu Jintao to succeed Jiang to become the core of the fourth-generation leadership.

The power handover from Jiang to Hu was a milestone in Chinese politics, since the change occurred without a major political crisis. It was an unprecedented peaceful transition of power.

However, the Jiang–Hu handover was pre-dictated by Deng. Nowadays, no figure has the same clout as Mao and Deng. So the Hu–Xi power transition was still the first test for a power transition without the presence of an all-powerful strongman.

Despite the intense internal fighting, the latest party congress did make progress in terms of institutionalising the power succession. It also featured for the first time overt campaigning more akin to American democracy than Chinese communism.

However, Cheng Li, of the John L. Thornton China Center at the Brookings Institution in Washington, said that like many other things happening in China, changes in the Chinese leadership were a paradox of hope and fear. "The growing pluralistic thinking in Chinese society and increasing diversity among political elites not only make consensus-building in the leadership very difficult, but also cause serious concerns about leadership unity and elite cohesion." Indeed, the larger implications of the latest power transition suggested there was still little transparency or very small room for intra-party democracy. It also showed that the last major communist-ruled nation refused to accept any Western concept of democracy and constitutional rule, despite its devolving into a rule-by-consensus system.

CHAPTER 2

The Hu–Wen Decade
Glorious, Golden and Lost

It was an era of glittering achievement for China under President Hu Jintao and Premier Wen Jiabao, so said the state media. But critics begged to differ, saying that despite the undoubted success stories, the country was subject to rising social, economic and environmental woes, plus growing mistrust between the people and government and lost opportunities for reform.

Stability but Stagnation

by **Shi Jiangtao**

In a bid to drown out discordant assessments of the previous decade, the party propaganda machine was at full throttle in the months prior to the 18th party congress, lavishing praise on China's accomplishments under President Hu Jintao and Premier Wen Jiabao. It's been 10 long, hard but glorious years, state media declared, a "Golden Decade" that saw the per capita gross domestic product soar to US$5,432 from US$1,135 in 2002 and the size of the Chinese economy grow to be the second largest in the world, behind only the United States.

Hu Jintao

Naturally, that's how Hu wanted to be remembered, along with his two pet slogans — the "scientific concept of development" and "building a harmonious society" — enshrined in the party constitution.

In one of his last key speeches in the run-up to the 18th party congress, Hu claimed victory over a "string of severe challenges" along "an extremely bumpy road" since becoming the party's general secretary in November 2002.

While appearing anxious to secure his own legacy before he stepped down from the pinnacle of power, Hu was also aware that many people took such self-promotion, one of the trademarks of the self-perpetuating communist regime, with a pinch of salt. He sounded a note of caution in the speech, delivered to a group of senior central and local government cadres, many of them poised for key roles after the party congress.

"We are confronting unprecedented opportunities and we have to deal with unprecedented challenges in view of the current domestic and international situation," Hu said. "We must not be afraid of any risks, or be confused by any distractions." Hu also warned against the dangers of stagnation and ossification of thinking — terms that critics at home and abroad have used to describe Hu's era and China.

While even his critics were impressed by the glittering economic success of the Hu–Wen decade, they disagreed with party apologists over who should be given credit for the nation's increased prosperity. State media listed China's economic strides amid the global downturn as the biggest achievement of the Hu administration. But several China specialists in the United States and Professor Zhu Lijia from the Chinese Academy of Governance said Hu and Wen mostly benefited from the efforts of their predecessors, including former president and party chief Jiang Zemin and former premier Zhu Rongji, whose bold reforms ushered in a period of rapid growth that culminated in the present economic miracle. "The accumulated effect of reform and opening up in the past two decades has helped the country's economy onto the fast track and it doesn't necessarily mean the current administration has done a better job than the previous one in terms of economic policies," Professor Zhu said.

Professor Roderick MacFarquhar from Harvard University said one main contribution of Hu and Wen had been their attempt to "move away from helter-skelter investment in coastal provinces" and seek more balanced development, especially for central and western China. He said that was something that was neglected by the "catchphrase of the Deng-ist era ... some people will get rich before others".

But analysts also said the "Golden Decade" hailed by state media was an overstatement, glossing over acute social, economic and environmental woes that had yet to be properly addressed, and inherent defects of one-party rule such as unbridled government power and secretive political manoeuvring. "This is the golden era of Chinese GDP growth and an explosion of productivity, and the era in which China, on aggregate, became a wealthy country," said Professor Kerry Brown, a specialist in Chinese politics at the University of Sydney. "But it is also an era of deepening social and structural issues, of political stagnation, and of the failure to properly solve the problems of all-round growth."

Professor Zhu warned that the authorities' celebration of the golden era overlooked enormous dangers and challenges that could paralyse material prosperity overnight and plunge the country into a full-blown crisis. "It is more of a stagnant decade, if not a decade of retrogression," he said. "The mistrust between the people and the government has reached boiling point, with public confidence in the authorities crumbling amid constant suppression of public opinion. Tough questions have been raised one after another in the past decade, but we have yet to see any of them sincerely addressed."

Despite the rapid economic growth, an infrastructure boom in big cities and a string of populist policies aimed at improving people's well-being, economist Mao Yushi said the authorities had failed to tackle difficult issues such as rebalancing growth and conservation in the controversial 4 trillion yuan economic stimulus package in 2008, or ending the state monopolies which posed a threat to China's nascent market economy. "Apart from joining the World Trade Organisation in 2001 [which happened before Hu and Wen took office], we haven't seen much progress in economic reform since the turn of the century. Instead, we have witnessed the phenomenon of *guojin mintui* [literally the state advancing as the private sector retreats]."

Professor Yuan Weishi, a historian at Sun Yat-sen University in Guangzhou, agreed that Hu had failed to live up to public expectations, with the so-called fourth-generation leadership making little headway in political reform and claiming too much credit for other successes. He said everyone in the country should be given credit for the modest progress in education, health care and social welfare the country had seen in the past 10 years, not just Hu and Wen. "It is regrettable that Hu and Wen did not consciously take any steps to push ahead with political reform, which was still considered an alien, destabilising force not to be reckoned with," he said.

Hu's open — albeit belated — handling of the severe acute respiratory syndrome (SARS) outbreak in 2003 at the start of his reign stirred up expectations of political openness and hopes he was a closet liberal, but that turned out not to be the case. His inability to take bold, substantial moves and his lack of appetite for economic and political reform were widely believed to result from his unadventurous personality.

Widely seen as a diffident apparatchik with an ultraconservative track record who excelled at political cunning and tactical manoeuvring, Hu was billed by many as exemplifying the communist regime's mediocrity. Unlike his predecessors, MacFarquhar said, Hu did not appear to be a risk-taker and that impaired his ability to act decisively on many important issues.

Zhu said Hu, among the first generation of technocrats educated and trained after the party took power, appeared more interested in maintaining the status quo than embracing changes that involved risks.

As proof, analysts pointed to his deliberate vagueness and addiction to propaganda clichés and fancy but ambiguous slogans.

In 2007, in his opening address at the 17th party congress, he mentioned the word democracy more than 60 times. But instead of ushering in a new era of political openness and democratic reform, he was widely seen as a hardline autocrat who had imposed censorship, limited political freedom and trodden on civil rights. Analysts were not surprised that Hu often resorted to party clichés and vapid ideological grandstanding, given his past experience as a political tutor at Beijing's elite Tsinghua University, where he indoctrinated students in Marxist theory. Rumour had it that a speech he made at a closed-door party conclave in 2004 was more revealing of his thinking. He said the country should learn from North Korea and Cuba in terms of their ability to silence dissent and restrict freedom.

As the fourth-generation leader anointed by late patriarch Deng Xiaoping, Hu clearly knew the high stakes involved in maintaining a brisk economic growth rate for China's "market economy with socialist characteristics" — the source of the party's legitimacy for most Chinese after the bloody 1989 Tiananmen Square crackdown on pro-democracy advocates and the Soviet Union's collapse in 1991.

And obviously he had his own reasons for not pushing ahead with long-stalled political reforms, which most analysts agreed were the root cause of stagnation and discontent. Paraphrasing a term Deng once used, Hu unveiled his ultimate motto, *bu zheteng*, slang for "don't rock the boat", in a 2008 speech marking the 30th anniversary of the launch of reform and opening up. It was understood as an attempt to defuse criticism from both advocates of political reform and those opposed to market-driven reform, and was widely seen as showing his true colours as an orthodox Marxist with a Taoist approach to maintaining the status quo.

Zhu said that for Hu, the status quo meant first and foremost the party's monopoly on power and he tended to see grievances and growing disobedience resulting from an avalanche of social woes, such as a yawning wealth gap, rising food and housing prices, corruption and pollution, and calls for Western-style democracy, as threats to his leadership. "We must be clearly aware that development is of overriding importance and that stability is our overriding task," Hu often stressed. "If there is no stability, then nothing can be done, and whatever achievements we have made will be lost."

Dr Elizabeth Economy, director of Asia studies at the New York-based Council on Foreign Relations, said that whether by design or circumstance, Hu had left virtually no imprint on the outside world. Speaking before Hu stepped down, she said: "It appears less that the current leadership accomplished great things than that the country transformed without a strong leader at the helm. Even the Chinese economy — arguably one of the great success stories of the past decade — is reportedly plagued by 'vested interests' and reform has been stalled for much of Hu's tenure. I think the greatest tragedy of Hu's tenure will be his — and the rest of the Chinese leadership's — failure to make significant progress on their effort to construct a 'harmonious society'."

Analysts said Hu and Wen failed to redress the imbalances of the previous 20 years of "go-go" economic growth. Environmental protection, public health and social security continued to run a distant second to the imperatives of heavy investment and rapid economic growth. Sydney University's Brown called the decade an era of managed contention because, although Hu had talked a great deal about a harmonious society, the visible signs of disharmony had increased. "His greatest failure is his inability to show political courage in addressing some of the structural needs for more accountability in the party and more transparency, and to move towards greater predictability in the political environment through rule of law," Brown said.

Analysts also said that Hu had failed to present a clear image of a rising China or communicate a consistent message about China's vision of the world. "The evolution in Chinese foreign policy from Deng Xiaoping's low-profile approach to a far more assertive stance, for example, seems less a function of Hu's leadership than a lack of direction or certainty about what kind of power China should be," Economy said.

Although the hosting of the Olympics in Beijing and other international events has been listed among Hu's achievements, economist Mao said costly efforts to polish China's international image had failed to achieve satisfactory results due to domestic political stagnation. He said Beijing's suppression of free speech and its ruthless clampdown on dissent and rights activists over the past decade had effectively nullified its efforts to show the country's economic power and to repair its image as a brutal, dictatorial regime. "China has clearly been increasingly marginalised and isolated due to its refusal to recognise universal values and grant its people democratic rights," Mao said. "The Olympics may have helped a little, but it could not solve real problems."

Professor Cui Weiping, from the Beijing Film Academy, lamented that Hu's reign could be best characterised as an era of maintaining stability, resulting in a drastic deterioration of human rights and growing antagonism between the people and government. "The main feature of the era is that all those who are aggrieved are being guarded against and treated as targets of surveillance," Cui wrote on her microblog. "As a result, the enemies of the state are everywhere to be found and they could be anyone, especially those underprivileged workers and peasants."

MacFarquhar noted the widespread frustration and disillusionment among political activists and intellectuals. "I believe a lot of intellectuals thought he would be presiding over a much more liberal atmosphere or intellectual life. But in fact most people will tell you there has been a retreat from what there was under Jiang Zemin."

Professor He Weifang, a law expert from Peking University, said the Hu leadership had turned a deaf ear to widespread public appeals for greater democracy and social justice. "The past 10 years have seen virtually no progress in the rule of law. We have seen, on the contrary, setbacks and even backpedalling." That failure was laid bare by the appointment of Wang Shengjun, a career bureaucrat with no legal education or court experience, as the head of the Supreme People's Court, and the blatant lawlessness and regular political interference seen in high-profile court cases across the country. The law expert said the stalling of judicial reform was clearly the result of a lack of progress on political reform. "We have yet to see any preparations for ideological or judicial reform."

Although Hu took the reins from Jiang in 2002 in what was widely seen as the first peaceful transition of power in China, Hu appears to have done little since to make the murky transition process more transparent and accountable. An example both He and MacFarquhar noted was the removal of former Chongqing party chief Bo Xilai, a Politburo member who campaigned almost openly for a seat on the Politburo Standing Committee until he fell from grace in 2012, sparking the worst political crisis in decades.

Despite swirling rumours and conspiracy theories damaging the party's image and the prospects for a smooth leadership transition, Beijing continued its embarrassing silence for a lengthy period due to prolonged behind-the-scenes political manoeuvring and wrangling. A similar, intense power struggle within the top echelon of power was also laid bare in 2006 when former Shanghai party boss Chen Liangyu, a leading member of the so-called "Shanghai Gang", Jiang's power base, was sacked ahead of the 17th party congress. "It certainly looks as if they had real difficulties coming to decisions as to how to handle the case of Bo," MacFarquhar said.

In an era of burgeoning environmental awareness and internet-based social activism, there were also more protests over pollution, land rights, civil rights and labour rights, threatening the social stability that was Hu's overriding priority. "We have seen direct confrontations between the authorities and a public increasingly aware of their rights," Professor Yuan said. "Frankly, we can't pin our hopes on the authorities, who have been reluctant to relax their controls all along. Only adequate public pressure can help them realise that there is no turning back on democratic reform."

Economy said the extraordinary growth in civil society activism, largely fuelled by the surging number of internet users, seemed to catch the authorities by surprise. The government "seems woefully unprepared for how to deal with the new transparency and accountability demanded by the Chinese people and advanced via the internet", she said.

Intriguingly, after 10 years in power, people still asked "Who is Hu?". Even as he was about to step down, Hu remained an enigmatic cipher, largely unknown even to his cronies and acolytes. Hu's bland, wooden image was offset by Wen's positioning of himself as an affable champion of ordinary people and, from time to time, an advocate of political reform, but a veil of secrecy still shrouded the government.

MacFarquhar said Hu was a difficult man for foreign leaders to relate to, because he was so tightly buttoned up. "I think the reason why that is the case is because that's how he got to the top, by not opening himself up for criticism. He was very diligent and very much stuck to the party line. That, of course, endeared him to his superiors and eventually led to him being general secretary and president."

Yuan attributed glaring differences between Hu and Jiang to their different educational background and personalities. "Jiang received his college education before the founding of the People's Republic, when the Communist Party used slogans of democracy and freedom to woo the public and garner support. In comparison, Hu was largely influenced by Soviet-style education when he was trained to be a hydraulic engineer and worked as a political instructor at Tsinghua."

He Weifang said Hu and other members of the fourth-generation leadership had mostly been brought up and educated in the worst of times in China and lacked the vision to make substantive changes. "They know almost nothing about modern, constitutional government, or human rights and freedom."

* * *

People's Champion or Chameleon?

by *Cary Huang*

Wen Jiabao won praise and criticism in equal measure during his decade-long rule as premier. Sympathisers and admirers said he was a true reformer and the "people's premier". Opponents questioned his sincerity because he often failed to live up to his reformist pledges and meet public expectations.

When Wen Jiabao was made premier and given custody of the world's largest developing economy, he was seen as a cautious and skilful technocrat with an uncanny ability to adapt to fast-shifting political winds and maintain the trust of different Communist Party factions.

Leaving office aged 70, he had an image as the most outspoken state leader of his time, thanks to his calls for political reform.

Wen Jiabao

They made him a lonely voice in the communist leadership, regardless of his sincerity.

In one of his last major speeches, Wen showed he was still willing to take risks, once again calling for political reform to uphold democracy and the rule of law. Wen frankly summarised his cabinet's achievements and failures over the previous decade, including mismanagement of the economy and stagnating institutional reform that left the government without checks and balances.

Wen also used his last annual press conference, at the end of the 2012 session of the National People's Congress, to apologise for his mistakes, and he used his last cabinet meeting to acknowledge his frustration with the system and his failure to bring about any meaningful change.

Professor Liu Kang, a China-watcher and director of Duke University's China Research Center, said Wen had worked hard to cement two legacies — as "a political reformer" and "a people's premier". Wen called for political reform in a series of speeches, mostly during trips overseas, appearing more like a dissident or a human rights campaigner than a communist leader by saying that "democracy, rule of law, freedom and human rights are shared values pursued by humanity over the long course of history, the products of a common civilisation".

Critics accused him of using his last two years in office to cultivate his public image before retirement — or deliberately playing the role of an outspoken reformer in an effort to balance the communist leadership's conservative image. But sympathisers said Wen did really represent a dissenting voice within the top leadership because many other members of the Politburo and its Standing Committee argued the opposite on countless occasions.

Many analysts said Wen's remarks echoed increasingly loud calls for political reform from within and outside the ruling party, with many

lower-ranking officials and academics in government think tanks joining the chorus.

Professor Zhang Ming, a political scientist at Renmin University in
Beijing, said the fact that Wen often made his bold calls during overseas
trips, and those remarks were sometimes censored inside China, suggested he was out of step with other senior leaders. Then president Hu
Jintao and other party leaders repeatedly ruled out Western-style
democracy and made it clear the leadership did not envision a fundamental overhaul of one-party rule.

Professor Steve Tsang, director of the China Policy Institute at the
University of Nottingham, said: "It got to the point that one has to ask
whether Wen was really committed to political reform, which most
China hands, including myself, thought he was, at least of a kind, when
he took power a decade ago. Having been premier for 10 years and yet
delivered so little in a policy area that he said he was committed to does
come across as odd or highly incompetent or disingenuous."

Even in the less politically contentious field of economic management, Wen's record was mixed. Quantitatively, he could lay claim to
being the most outstanding head of government in China's history due
to the exceptional economic growth during his reign. But qualitatively,
Wen failed to live up to public expectations and reach the goals he set
for himself when he came to office in 2003.

Wen oversaw the continuation of one of the most remarkable economic transformations in history, taking China from the world's sixth-
largest economy to number two. It also became the world's wealthiest
nation in terms of foreign reserves, the world's largest exporter, car
producer and consumer, and home to the world's longest high-speed
rail system.

He presided over the world's largest poverty eradication campaign
and succeeded in lifting tens of millions of people out of misery, with
per capita income growing from US$800 to about US$5,000 in the

decade. Since 2010, the country also replaced the US to become the biggest single contributor to global economic growth.

But Wen also came to office with pledges to tackle an unbalanced economic structure, reduce income disparity and alleviate environmental destruction. Zhang said Wen would leave behind severe environmental damage, a deteriorating economic structure and an ever-widening wealth gap. Some bloggers said that under Wen's rule, disparity, pollution and corruption had become the worst in the history of the People's Republic.

He also failed to continue the reform momentum set by his predecessor Zhu Rongji in reducing bureaucrats' economic power, breaking up state monopolies in many highly profitable sectors and deregulating state controls on prices. Tsang said Wen had little to show for his decade in power. "The economy looks robust but the major problems that needed to be tackled are still there. The task of re-balancing the economy has just got bigger and more difficult in the past decade. This is one of the main legacies of Wen."

Wen also tasted defeat in his decade-long fight to tame skyrocketing property prices, losing to a coalition of businessmen and local officials. Housing prices in urban areas soared, with almost ten-fold gains in Beijing and Shanghai over the decade. Wen used his last cabinet meeting to reiterate the government's determination to continue the fight. But Winnie Cheng Yun, research director at Hong Kong real estate agency Centaline Group, said he was just talking the talk with regard to taming property prices.

Wen worked hard on his populist image as a grandfatherly premier who cared for the underprivileged, earning nicknames including "grandpa Wen" and the "people's premier". He was usually the first top official to arrive at the scene of a disaster. In the aftermath of the devastating earthquake in Sichuan in 2008, Wen travelled around the quake zone, comforting distraught victims.

His sole visit to Hong Kong won him plaudits because he chose to visit Amoy Gardens, the housing estate hit hard by the severe acute respiratory syndrome (Sars) outbreak in 2003. Residents credited him with helping restore confidence in the estate at a time when even taxi drivers were reluctant to drop passengers off there.

He also routinely ushered in the New Year by visiting remote, cold and backward places, using the occasion to send out a caring message. But Wen's image was tainted by a *New York Times* report in 2012 on the wealth allegedly accumulated by his relatives. And in the book *China's Best Actor: Wen Jiabao*, dissident author Yu Jie dismissed Wen's image as a reformist "people's premier", saying he deserved an Oscar for the political role he had played.

Tsang said new Communist Party chief Xi Jinping, who succeeded Hu Jintao as president, was comfortable in his own skin and, unlike Hu, was at ease rubbing shoulders with ordinary people, which meant "there will not even be a legacy in the double act that marked the Hu–Wen partnership. Wen's successor, Li Keqiang, is unlikely to inherit a new 'uncle Li' image that 'grandpa Wen' associated with the premiership."

Liu said that as Wen became frustrated and gave up hope of a substantive overhaul of the system, he had chosen instead to "shape the verdict of posterity" — like many emperors and mandarins before him.

* * *

The Price of Growth

by *Cary Huang*

China's new leaders can be under no illusions: the country's rise to superpower status has been extraordinary — but at a heavy cost.

When the Communist Party's fourth-generation leaders entered the Great Hall of the People for its 18th party congress, they had a lot to congratulate themselves on, including a decade of rapid economic growth under President Hu Jintao and Premier Wen Jiabao. But they left behind huge challenges for the next leaders under President Xi Jinping and Premier Li Keqiang. Chief among those challenges is squaring pragmatic capitalism with one-party rule by what is, in name, a Marxist party.

Nowadays, the Communist Party — the world's largest political party with more than 80 million members — claims that its rule is legitimised by its ability to make the world's most populous nation prosperous. Since taking office in 2002, the Hu–Wen leadership oversaw the continuation of one of the most remarkable economic transformations in history.

Zhuang Jian, senior economist with the Asian Development Bank's China Resident Mission, said the government had succeeded in steering the economy out of the 2008 crisis and was on track to do the same with the European debt crisis. He also said improvements had been made in housing, medical care and social welfare — although more needed to be done — as well as energy conservation and environmental protection. Zhuang's view appeared to be supported by official data. Statistics suggested the government hit or exceeded all eight obligatory targets in the 11th five-year plan (2005–2010): population control; energy and water consumption per unit of gross domestic product; reduction in emissions of two major pollutants; area of cultivated land; urban social security coverage; and rural co-operative medical coverage.

However, analysts at home and abroad said the Hu–Wen administration generally failed to live up to expectations on economic reform and social development. When they came to power, Hu and Wen called for a reorientation of China's development strategy, away from cut-throat economic growth and towards sustainable, balanced and people-oriented growth. But some analysts said the decade's growth

leap was achieved at excessive cost, with environmental damage, a deteriorating economic structure and an ever-widening rich-poor gap.

The Hu–Wen government came to power at a time when hopes for
reform were high following China's admission into the World Trade
Organisation. Hu quickly made three key policy goals, calling for a scientific concept of development, people-oriented policies and building a
harmonious society. Under Hu's pronouncements, the administration was
tasked with improving the country's economic structure and boosting
socio-economic equality, creating a society that was prosperous and free
of conflict. The idea was to restructure the economy in order to achieve
more balanced and sustainable, consumption-driven growth, which
would be made possible by a fairer distribution of wealth. The country
also wanted to cut its over-reliance on exports and capital investment.

But critics said the administration reached few of the goals set by
Hu, particularly in economic reform. Those goals included curbing
widespread official corruption, reducing bureaucrats' economic power,
breaking up state monopolies in many highly profitable sectors, deregulating state controls on prices, and restructuring the banking and
financial markets.

Jianguang Shen, chief economist at Mizuho Securities China, said
there were three unresolved issues left up to the new, fifth-generation
leaders. The country's economic structure was less balanced, state influence had risen while the private sector had suffered, and income disparity had increased. Shen said the government had failed to shift growth
away from a dependency on fixed-asset investment and towards private
consumption, reduce its trade surplus or increase the service sector's
share in the national economy. "The investment ratio rose further, while
the consumption ratio dived. The current account surplus reached
record highs and the share of services remained stagnant."

Fixed-asset investment accounted for 49.2 per cent of gross
domestic product in 2011, the highest level ever recorded outside

Soviet-style economies. And the imbalance continued to worsen, with urban fixed-asset investment growing 20.4 per cent in the first half of 2012, while nominal GDP grew 11 per cent, suggesting that investment's share of GDP might have topped 50 per cent.

State-owned enterprises (SOEs) experienced tremendous growth during the decade due to the inherent advantage of having government backing, but private firms faced more obstacles. Despite their poor quality management and services, four state-owned banks — Industrial and Commercial Bank of China, China Construction Bank, Bank of China and Agricultural Bank of China — became the world's largest financial institutions in terms of profits and market capitalisation, surpassing American and European lenders.

Meanwhile, income inequality between urban and rural residents worsened significantly. In a report in 2011, the Labour Ministry warned that the wealth gap had widened in the previous decade, with incomes in urban areas three times higher than those in rural areas, and the average income of the top 10 per cent of earners 20 times higher than that of the bottom 10 per cent. Zhang Lifan, a political affairs analyst, said increasingly widespread discontent had many looking back nostalgically to the previous administration led by president Jiang Zemin and premier Zhu Rongji.

Zhu, a reform-minded and no-nonsense economic czar, took a tough stand against corrupt officials, fostered a market-based economy, brought China into the WTO, overhauled state-owned enterprises and restructured the banking system. Liu Kang, director of Duke University's China Research Center, said: "Generally speaking, the Hu-Wen administration is more conservative in both politics and economic policies than previous administrations." Liu said that despite the economic progress, the Communist Party was facing a more severe challenge — that of challenges to the legitimacy of its rule. He cited social tensions, ideological conflicts, widespread corruption and internal power struggles as ongoing challenges, adding: "Things have only deteriorated, rather than improved, and citizens have thus become less satisfied and happy than a decade ago."

* * *

Ten Years of "a Bumpy Road"

November 2002: Hu Jintao becomes party general secretary at 16th party congress.

November 2002–June 2003: SARS deaths in Guangdong province covered up until disease spreads across nation and sparks global panic. Epidemic kills 348 in China. Health Minister Zhang Wenkang and Beijing mayor Meng Xuenong sacked in April.

March 2003: Hu becomes president and Wen Jiabao becomes premier.

July 2003: Half a million march in Hong Kong on July 1, protesting against anti-subversion legislation. City government shelves proposal.

October 2003: Yang Liwei becomes China's first astronaut aboard Shenzhou V.

October – November 2004: Tens of thousands of villagers in Sichuan's Hanyuan county protest against planned Pubugou Dam on Dadu River, clash with armed police in biggest protest since Hu took power.

March 2005: National People's Congress ratifies anti-secession law endorsing use of "non-peaceful means" of reunification if Taiwan moves towards independence.

April 2005: Lien Chan, honorary chairman of Taiwan's Kuomintang, meets Hu in Beijing, the first meeting in more than half century between leaders of civil war adversaries.

November 2005: Massive benzene leak from Jilin city chemical plant contaminates Songhua River, leaving millions without drinking water for days. Environment Minister Xie Zhenhua sacked.

January 2006: Central government eliminates centuries-old rural taxes.

May 2006: Building of main structure of Three Gorges Dam on Yangtze River completed, 11 years after it began.

September 2006: Shanghai party boss and Politburo member Chen Liangyu sacked over corruption.

March 2007: Landmark property law protecting private ownership rights passed by National People's Congress.

April 2007: Wen makes "ice-melting" visit to Japan, the first by a Chinese premier in seven years.

June 2007: Thousands rally in Xiamen, Fujian province, successfully blocking petrochemical project because of health and environmental concerns.

March 2008: Nineteen people killed in rioting in Lhasa that spreads to other areas with large Tibetan populations.

May 2008: Magnitude-8 earthquake devastates Sichuan and neighbouring provinces, killing more than 87,000 people.

August 2008: Beijing Olympics.

September 2008: Infant formula adulterated with melamine kills six children and makes nearly 300,000 ill with kidney ailments.

November 2008: Beijing launches 4 trillion yuan stimulus package to help China ride out global financial crisis.

July 2009: Thousands of Uygurs clash with Han Chinese in Urumqi, Xinjiang. At least 197 people killed.

December 2009: Rights activist Liu Xiaobo jailed for 11 years for inciting subversion of state power. In 2010, Liu wins Nobel Peace Prize.

December 2009: Wen attends UN climate talks in Copenhagen, where China, world's largest carbon polluter, is accused of torpedoing treaty on emissions.

June 2010: Beijing and Taipei sign Economic Co-operation Framework Agreement — most significant agreement between them since 1949.

August 2010: China replaces Japan as world's second largest economy.

February 2011: Railways minister Liu Zhijun sacked for corruption.

July 2011: Forty die and at least 192 injured when two high-speed trains collide in Wenzhou, Zhejiang province.

September 2011: Thousands riot in Wukan village, Guangdong province, over seizure of farmland by officials. Provincial authorities intervene and promise elections for a new village committee — hailed as milestone for grass-roots democracy.

March 2012: Bo Xilai sacked as Chongqing party chief after attempted defection in February of municipality's former police chief. Biggest political crisis in more than two decades sees Bo suspended from Politburo and Central Committee in April after wife, Gu Kailai, named main suspect in November murder of British businessman Neil Heywood. Gu given suspended death sentence in August.

April 2012: Blind rights activist Chen Guangcheng escapes house arrest in Shandong province and flees to US embassy in Beijing, helped by fellow activists. Chen and his family allowed to leave for US in mid-May.

April 2012: Chinese and Philippine vessels engage in stand-off at Scarborough Shoal (Huangyan Island) in South China Sea. Territorial disputes with Vietnam and Japan escalate.

June 2012: Thousands march in Hong Kong demanding inquiry into mysterious death of June 4 activist Li Wangyang.

September 2012: Bo Xilai expelled from Communist Party, faces criminal prosecutions. Date for 18th party congress announced.

November 2012: Xi Jinping becomes party general secretary at 18th party congress.

CHAPTER 3

Change Agent or Steady as She Goes?

The era of Xi Jinping dawned at the 18th Communist Party Congress. Xi replaced Hu Jintao as party general secretary, marking the climax of the once-a-decade leadership succession. He also became chairman of the powerful Central Military Commission and in March 2013 he succeeded Hu as president. With all three of the nation's top posts in his grasp and the leadership transition complete, analysts fixated on whether Xi would be the transformative leader that reformists longed for, or would he simply reprise the risk-averse policies of his predecessors designed to preserve stability and — above all — one-party rule.

by *Cary Huang*

The stakes could hardly have been higher for Xi Jinping, the 59-year-old son of a respected revolutionary leader and unsurprisingly anointed at the 18th Communist Party Congress to be China's chief standard bearer through the next decade. Not only did he face a host of challenges on the domestic and international policy fronts, as is commonplace for incoming leaders of any major nation, but there were also lingering uncertainties among his own Communist Party retinue about Xi himself. What did he really think? What was his preferred course to steer the world's most populous nation and the planet's second-largest economy? The prolonged intrigue and jockeying among rival factions in the months leading up to the congress raised inevitable doubts about the strength of the supposed consensus backing him in the Beijing corridors of power. And Xi's sudden disappearance from public view for two weeks shortly before the congress sparked intense speculation even about the state of his health. In the event, the transfer of power from predecessor Hu Jintao proved to be orderly, and analysts said the smooth transition indicated that Xi was a strong leader who had settled power struggles among different factions in the party.

"Exactly who is Xi?" asked the *South China Morning Post's* headline in a profile of Xi published shortly before the congress opened in November 2012. It was a pertinent question. It was being asked not just by the curious-minded world at large but also by many of his fellow communist apparatchiks, who knew little about Xi apart from his enviable pedigree as the "princeling" son of a revolutionary leader. Despite his meticulous grooming for the country's

Xi Jinping

top job over the previous five years, Xi remained unsettlingly something of an enigma.

However, in the months that followed the congress, Xi's actions and pronouncements on some of China's most intransigent problems, and his projection of an informal meet-the-people style that sharply differentiated him from his predecessors, helped to dispel — at least in part — the mystery surrounding him. A Beijing-based political analyst said Xi was shaping up to be a very different leader from Hu, whose leadership was considered weak. "Xi's style is more like a strongman leader than Hu."

Following the congress, Xi lost little time in mounting an attack on corruption, saying in stark terms that this was a make-or-break issue as the party's very existence depended on curbing the party's deeply ingrained graft. He promised to crack down on senior and low-ranking corrupt officials and restrict officials' power by "confining them in the cage" of a regulatory system. Dozens of officials were duly arrested or sacked. He also called for respect for China's often-ignored constitution, signalled limited judicial reform, and launched a high-profile attack on official perks and extravagance. Another motif of his early pronouncements was an expansive clarion call for "the great renaissance of the Chinese nation and the Chinese dream", although he gave no detailed account of the phrase's meaning.

Reformists were further encouraged when the party's new security czar, Meng Jianzhu, pledged that the dreaded re-education through labour system, modelled on the Soviet gulags and regarded internationally and by many in China as one of the darkest stains on China's human rights record, would be halted.

Xi also quickly established himself as a strong commander-in-chief after he assumed the chairmanship of the Central Military Commission. Within less than three months, he managed to inspect major military regions and visit the troops of all armed forces of the People's Liberation Army. Winning the trust of the 2.3 million-strong PLA, Xi wasted no time in assuring them through various speeches that strengthening the military was a centrepiece of his plans to rejuvenate the country.

A fundamental issue, crucial for the outside world as much as for the future of the Chinese Communist Party itself, was how Xi, his newly promoted number-two Premier Li Keqiang and their team would handle the nation's economy. China's phenomenal growth in the past three decades served not just to underpin the party's right to rule but also became an increasingly influential factor in global economic health. As the head of China's sovereign wealth fund, Lou Jiwei, said soon after the 18th party congress: "China's economy supports a very large part of global demand."

Hopes of a continued and perhaps increasingly liberal economic course were raised when in Xi's first trip outside Beijing following the congress, he toured the southern economic powerhouse of Guangdong province. This was a step that resonated with reform advocates in China as it recalled a famed "southern tour" by the late paramount leader Deng Xiaoping in 1992, which reinvigorated economic reforms that have driven China's remarkable growth.

Xi also seemed to be shaping up to be a firm, if not hawkish, advocate of China's interests on the international stage. He was widely seen as taking personal charge of Beijing's territorial disputes with Tokyo over the Diaoyu Islands — known as Senkaku in Japan — and said China would never "waive its legitimate rights" on the world stage, despite vowing to stick to its peaceful development path.

Reflecting the more open style of leadership he adopted, Xi allowed his inspection trips to villages to be broadcast live on microblogging websites of the state media. He was seen chatting with farmers, visiting local groceries, and eating a meal in a canteen with soldiers, all contributing to his skyrocketing popularity which was evidenced by an online fan club dedicated to him.

While many analysts welcomed the early domestic initiatives by Xi as clear signals of a more liberal approach, others cautioned against jumping to early conclusions that he would turn out to be a decisive agent of change. Many preferred to see the early moves as the beginning of a process of familiarisation, in which Xi took stock of the multiple problems China faced. These challenges were indeed daunting, including widening discontent and social unrest over issues such as land confiscation by officials and unemployment, growing resentment over income and wealth inequality, and pressing demographic issues, including an ageing population.

Professor Liu Kang, director of the China Research Center at Duke University, said Xi had acted quickly because he was "eager to show that he is a different leader". Exploring Xi's possible agenda, analysts cited three post-congress speeches by Xi touching on "the people's livelihoods", "Chinese dreams" and "governing the country according to the constitution". The speeches were interpreted by some as his manifesto, ushering in the new era. Others cautioned that similar talk by former leaders often ended up going nowhere.

In one speech, Xi emphasised that "all citizens are equal before the law" and that "freedom should be guaranteed". He admitted that "supervising mechanisms and systems ensuring the constitution's implementation have not been perfect" and that "judicial and law enforcement problems concerning people's immediate interests are still evident". He then said that fully implementing the constitution was "the primary task and the basic work in building a socialist nation ruled by law".

Professor Ma Guoxian, director of Shanghai University of Finance and Economics' Public Policy Research Centre, said Xi's speeches had the following major themes: calls for the revival of market-oriented reform, which many think stalled under former leaders Hu Jintao and Wen Jiabao; measures to attack bureaucratic formalism among officials; and calls for the rule of law, which Ma saw as a prerequisite for political reform. "Things are changing fast, which has already brought some hopes rarely seen for years."

He said Xi and his Politburo colleagues were practising a new style of work, compared with the party's predecessors. "The new leaders are all different in their mindset, behaviour and language."

Professor Gu Su, a constitutional law specialist at Nanjing University, said Xi's introduction of several considerable changes in such a short time reflected his reformist bent. He said Xi's Guangdong tour, harking back to one made by Deng, highlighted the new leader's desire to send out a reformist message. Gu also cited Xi's emphasis on the rule of law, new regulations to reform the extravagant work style of senior officials, dealing swiftly with corruption allegations against senior officials, and an obvious change in the style of language used by leaders, replacing rhetoric with down-to-earth talk.

Among a raft of events early in Xi's leadership, analysts singled out a row breaking out in January 2013 between reporters at Guangzhou's progressive *Southern Weekly* newspaper and local propaganda officials over censorship, calling it the first real test of Xi's administration. The standoff was defused, apparently after decisive intervention from the top, and this was read as reflecting Xi's acknowledgment of the symbolic importance of the dispute, with some saying it might also signal that some relaxing of press curbs was on the way. "The result was a surprisingly mild approach, including mediation by a high-level government official and a vague promise for less censorship in the future," said Douglas Young, a visiting scholar teaching journalism at Fudan University in Shanghai.

Unlike in the past, when protests were put down with an iron fist, the new leadership chose to negotiate a way out, tacitly giving an assurance that the party propaganda official at the centre of the conflict would be replaced. Young said the unusually tolerant tack could well reflect a new attitude by Xi and the rest of the leadership, who had "come to realise the media can serve many important functions beyond its traditional role as a propaganda machine".

Professor Steve Tsang, head of Contemporary Chinese Studies at the University of Nottingham, said that while Xi had "made the right noises", he was yet to be convinced that Xi would actually deliver on his pledges. "Overall, he has taken initiatives to project a more positive image, but what he has so far done is not, or at least not yet, convincing." Zhang Lifan, a political affairs analyst formerly with the Chinese Academy of Social Sciences, said Xi was just trying to "build his personal image and win back waning public support of communist rule at a critical juncture". Zhang added that Xi and his administration had to deal with many tough challenges, with China confronting an unstable and complex situation domestically and globally which was unlike anything seen in recent memory.

One of the more pressing issues on the domestic agenda, namely the rancid clouds of smog stifling Beijing and spreading across northern China, was a direct in-the-face reminder to Xi, his fellow leaders and to Chinese people rich and poor, of how the country's pell-mell economy has poisoned China's air, land and waterways. This strategy of growth for growth's sake may have propelled China into the ranks of the world's economic superpowers, lifted tens of millions out of poverty and indeed created millions of millionaires, but it also left its major urban and industrial centres literally gasping for breath.

*   *   *

Xi's Chinese Dream

by *Cary Huang*

Chinese communist leaders have a favourite phrase or slogan, often seen as something that defines their rule. Xi Jinping is no exception.

Former president Jiang Zemin had his "theory of the three represents" (the Communist Party represents advanced productive forces, advanced culture and the interests of the broad masses) and "relatively prosperous society". His successor Hu Jintao used a "harmonious society" and "scientific concept of development"; and Xi Jinping, just weeks after being installed as party general secretary, has his "Chinese dream" and "Chinese renaissance".

During a visit to an exhibition in Beijing following the 18th Communist Party Congress, Xi first revealed his vision of rule in the coming decade by saying, "to realise the renaissance of the Chinese nation is the greatest dream for the Chinese nation in modern history".

Xi spoke of the Chinese dream and Chinese renaissance, or *fu xing* in Putonghua, on several occasions since then, including in his first speech after being declared president in the March 2013 session of the National People's Congress. The phrases caught the imagination of officials, the media and millions of Chinese internet users. He said China is "closer to the goal of achieving the great rejuvenation of the Chinese nation".

But what was not so clear was how Xi defined the Chinese dream and Chinese renaissance. Even before the 18th party congress, hopes were high that Xi — the son of a revolutionary leader who helped oversee the nation's post-Mao economic transformation — could bring about meaningful change to the nation, which faces unprecedented challenges in its quest to realise its dream of modernisation.

Many believed the new leader was trying to mobilise domestic support for his agenda of continuing reform and opening up by inspiring people towards a Chinese Dream — the title of a 1987 play about a Chinese couple dreaming of success in the United States.

"It serves to galvanise the people's support and rally the public around the new administration's economic and political agenda," said Liu Kang, director of the China Research Center at Duke University in the US.

"The Chinese dream is about solving China's problems," said Zheng Bijian, a leading party theorist and former executive vice-president of the Central Party School.

Kerry Brown, a professor of Chinese politics at the University of Sydney, said he saw the Chinese renaissance "mostly in the context of a peaceful rise, and China returning to a status it once enjoyed before modernity set in. For a China dream, I guess the emotional message is to the fore."

Some interpreted it as a call to implement an ambitious programme, set by the 18th party congress to realise the goals of "completing the building of a moderately prosperous society when the party celebrates its 100th birthday in 2021, and the building of a prosperous, strong, democratic, culturally advanced, harmonious and modernised socialist country when the new China marks its 100th anniversary in 2049".

Professor Steve Tsang, director of the University of Nottingham's China Policy Institute, said it was not yet clear how much of Xi's Chinese dream was replicated in the Chinese renaissance.

Shortly after Xi's remarks, internet users began to compare the Chinese dream with the American dream — a set of ideals which includes the opportunity for prosperity and success, and an upward social mobility achieved through hard work. Like the American dream, the rapid rise of China's economy in three decades allowed a new middle class to dream about the symbols of success and affluence in clothing, homes, furniture, cars, computers and mobile phones.

But for the first pilgrims who sailed to America on the Mayflower, the American dream started with their voyage to a new world across the sea, where they could escape from religious persecution. This spirit was formalised in the Declaration of Independence one and a half centuries later, which proclaims all men to be equal and endowed with certain inalienable rights.

Historian James Truslow Adams popularised the phrase "American dream" in his 1931 book, *The Epic of America*. He wrote: "It is not a dream of motor cars and high wages merely, but a dream of social order in which each man and each woman shall be able to attain to the fullest stature of which they are innately capable, and be recognised by others for what they are, regardless of the fortuitous circumstances of birth or position."

Martin Luther King, Jr. wove it into the civil rights movement in his celebrated "I have a dream" speech, in which he saw an upgrading of one's personality as the utmost ideal of the American dream.

The Chinese dream is more a vision of the world's longest-surviving civilisation taking its place in the world, in pursuit of a version of

Chinese exceptionalism that will steer country and people to fulfil their collective destiny.

Brown said the Chinese dream echoed the American dream in that it acted as a cultural counterbalance of sorts. But he said the vision was contaminated by a sense that a new political elite, desperate for support from the public, had few means to win over the people except through appeals to nationalism and by making them richer. "For hearts and minds stuff, the party still leaves people cold."

Tsang said: "The Chinese dream is not the dream of the people of China freely articulated by them. It is 'the Chinese dream' to be articulated on their behalf by Xi and the Communist Party."

In China, the idea of a renaissance and what it would represent was also widely discussed online, with suggestions ranging from "social justice", "less corruption" and "a better life" to "freedom and democracy".

Historians point to many periods they consider to have represented a Chinese renaissance, such as the Song dynasty (960–1279), together with the Tang dynasty (618–907) and the Han dynasty (206 BC– AD 220). All were times of economic growth, artistic achievement and numerous scientific advances.

The idea of a modern Chinese renaissance was popularised by political leaders and intellectuals throughout the last century. A group of Peking University professors gave the name "renaissance" to a monthly magazine. The May Fourth Movement, the 1919 upsurge in nationalism and re-evaluation of cultural institutions that helped usher in modern China, was also described by intellectual Hu Shi as the Chinese renaissance due to its striking similarities to Europe's Age of Enlightenment in the 17th and 18th centuries, which is also described in Putonghua as a renaissance.

The May Fourth Movement was based on the Western ideas of democracy and science, while the Age of Enlightenment advanced the notion that modernism was centred on individualism, rights and science, a uniquely Western heritage.

Almost all non-Western civilisations, including China, attempted to import the political, social and economic values of modernism to rebuild their own cultures in order to achieve modernisation. But while historians agree that various periods of Chinese history deserve the "renaissance" title, they say they all also shared one defect: the absence of a conscious recognition of their historical mission.

The communist revolution was also intended to achieve a "Chinese renaissance", promising "a prosperous, free and democratic new China". While prosperity eventually arrived under Deng Xiaoping's economic reforms, democracy and freedom remain elusive. Many observers felt Xi was tapping more deeply into that nationalistic vein than his recent predecessors, perhaps recognising that the traditional communist ideology no longer has popular appeal.

"As the new Chinese leadership begins to write the script for the next act of their country's reform, it appears as if Xi Jinping is finding nationalism an irresistible ingredient in his effort to galvanise his people," said Orville Schell, a veteran China watcher co-writing a book on China's modern quest for wealth and power.

Leaders know that nationalism aimed at foreign powers is a powerful undercurrent in Chinese society. Just weeks before Xi took power, anti-Japanese protests erupted in Chinese cities over a territorial dispute.

Xi's brand of modernism, analysts said, could mix bolder economic policies with anti-corruption campaigns, a vigorous military build-up and a muscular foreign policy. The combination is reminiscent of the Self-Strengthening Movement in the late 19th century, when some reformist political leaders and intellectuals sought reforms to revive a weakening Qing dynasty (1644–1911) harassed by Western powers and Japan.

But Gregory Kulacki, China project manager and senior analyst with the Union of Concerned Scientists, does not believe Xi's statement represents a dramatic departure from past practice. "Those concerned about Xi's choice of words should watch [state broadcaster] CCTV's six-part series from 2007, *The Road to Renaissance*," said Kulacki, who lived and worked in China for more than two decades.

The documentary tells the familiar story of an ancient civilisation, fractured by the dissolution of its traditional culture and exploited by Western imperialists, that is now in the process of restoration under the leadership of the Communist Party.

Rejecting alarmist rhetoric that suggested Xi's statement was aimed at transforming the People's Republic into a 21st-century version of the Third Reich or late Meiji Japan, Kulacki said the aims of the Chinese renaissance were modest: to achieve the status of a "basically modern" nation.

Brown said that with the catchphrases, "there's an attempt to dabble with idealism but in a controlled way, to leverage off ideas of some sort of historic roots to China's new uber-modernistic aspirations and identity". But he warned that Xi's dictums ran "the risk of surrendering to impractical idealism in ways Hu's 'scientific development' and 'harmonious society' never did".

Tsang said the Chinese renaissance had more to do with promoting China's stature in the world than any idea of liberating the minds of the people. "This is about advancing the re-emergence of China, which had a great civilisation and the capacity to be looked up to in ways beyond what the US has so far managed. Nothing is wrong in wanting China to be great. But it must be uncomfortable for the rest of the world, particularly China's neighbours, to see a new general secretary who wants to be identified as the man who reasserts China's illustrious past — which, despite Chinese rhetoric was primarily the result of establishing hegemony. What it all boils down to is that we will have to get used to a more assertive China under the leadership of Xi."

*   *   *

Shunning the Easy Road

by *Shi Jiangtao*

The South China Morning Post *delved into the mysteries surrounding Xi Jinping's background by examining his early assignments in rural Hebei province and his work in the affluent coastal provinces of Fujian and Zhejiang that were the foundation for his rise to power.*

Xi Jinping kick-started his political career with a bold move. At the age of 29, Xi turned his back on a life of privilege as a "princeling" son of a party elder in Beijing to accept a posting 250 kilometres away in an obscure, dusty town in Zhengding county, Hebei province.

His father, Xi Zhongxun, an ex-guerilla leader close to Mao Zedong, was at the height of his powers, serving as secretary of the party's Central Committee secretariat. Under his wing, the younger Xi seemed to have a guaranteed, easy road to success. He had earned a degree in chemical engineering from Tsinghua University and was working as secretary to General Geng Biao, the defence minister at the time.

But he struck out on his own, moving to Zhengding in 1982 to work as the county's deputy party chief. Within a few months, he had risen to the rank of party chief, and three years later was transferred to Xiamen, in Fujian province. Xi would recall his time in rural politics fondly, saying it had laid a solid foundation for his future career. "[Zhengding] is the place that I often miss ... it was there where I began to learn how to become a leading cadre," he said when he revisited the town in 2005. "I felt so humbled and nervous, as it was for me like a tiger trying to swallow the sky. I may have accumulated a certain amount of valuable knowledge before, but I had little practical experience. I had to learn everything from the very beginning. It was an unusual three years."

His words offered few, if any, clues as to why he gave up the relative comfort of his privileged life to go to the middle of nowhere. Zhengding has a history as a regional political and religious centre spanning more than 1,000 years. But it was largely bypassed by China's economic boom. It finally emerged into the media spotlight as the place where the man in line to be the nation's next leader got his political start.

"Everyone is so proud that Xi used to work here, although it was nearly two decades ago," said Chen Fei, a restaurant owner. "But it's a pity that his stay happened before he rose to power. Obviously we have not benefited much from it." Jia Yonghui, whose father, the late novelist Jia Dashan, was a friend of Xi, said the future leader did rather well in Zhengding considering his princeling pedigree and lack of experience. Xi had a good reputation in the county, he recalled. "Xi was famous for his willingness to make friends with experts and specialists, such as my father. He often said it was not that bad for leading officials to admit there were things they did not know as long as they have real experts to count on."

The elder Jia was promoted under Xi to head the county's cultural bureau in 1982 and they continued their friendship even after Xi's departure for Fujian. "When my father was critically ill, Xi, then deputy party chief of Fujian, visited him in a Beijing hospital in early 1997. A few weeks later, Xi made a detour to Zhengding on his way back to Fujian and paid his final visit to my father shortly before he died that year," Jia said.

Details about Xi's years in Zhengding remain sketchy — seemingly deliberately so. Most contemporaries and former government officials were reluctant to talk about him, especially his time in Zhengding. They either declined to be interviewed or said they had been warned against making any comments about Xi. However, state media hailed Xi's apprenticeship in Zhengding as a courageous move and testament to both his thirst for practical leadership skills and his ability to stay close to the people at the grassroots level.

In an article published by the *Shijiazhuang Daily* in 2011, Wang Youhui, who was deputy county chief when Xi was in Zhengding, lavished praise on the future leader. Wang recalled Xi as a mild-mannered and easy-going man who resembled an old-fashioned military cook in his green uniform when he first arrived. "Although he was the offspring of a senior cadre, he kept a very low profile. He had been to the countryside, suffered hardships, and behaved like a regular person who knew how to befriend others. Despite his plain appearance, he often displayed an admirable temperament, apparently the result of good education and maturity." Xi was also popular among retired cadres because he took care of their interests and heeded their concerns, he said.

Both Jia and Wang said one of Xi's main accomplishments was his promotion of tourism as a pillar of the local economy. Xi decided to spend more than 3.5 million yuan building an imperial palace modelled after one in the novel *A Dream of Red Mansions*. The palace has become one of the county's best known tourist attractions.

Some say Xi's decision to start his political career in Zhengding was a calculated one which turned out well and paved the way for his later rise. "Xi wanted to pursue a political career in the provinces, but he obviously did not want to drift too far from Beijing, the power base of his father, and that's why he chose Zhengding, which was close to the capital," said an acquaintance of Xi.

Citing an unnamed professor who was a childhood friend of Xi, a leaked US embassy cable said Xi's move to Zhengding was part of an ambitious career plan to expand his own power base and seek promotion. According to the professor, Xi believed staying with General Geng would eventually shrink his power base, which would ultimately rest on his father's and Geng's networks and political support. In the long run, "Going to the provinces was his 'only path to central power'."

While being a princeling may have helped him get on the fast track to success, Xi's political pedigree earned him the animosity of political rivals, including those of his father. According to one widely circulated rumour, former Hebei provincial party chief Gao Yang did not like the way Xi was parachuted into Zhengding and refused to promote him to a more senior position in the province. Gao reportedly openly criticised the elder Xi for seeking political favours from Gao for his son. When Gao, a president of the central party school in the late 1980s, died at the age of 100 in 2009, Xi, the incumbent president of the school, skipped the funeral of his former superior. That led to further speculation about their rivalry.

*   *   *

The Tide Turns

by *Minnie Chan*

> The leader-in-waiting had setbacks early in his long sojourn in Fujian province, but he learned fast.

Xi Jinping fine-tuned his political antennae during 17 years spent as an official in the southeastern province of Fujian.

An official in the provincial capital Fuzhou who worked under Xi said he always harboured grand ambitions. "On the surface, Xi looked like a mediocre leader who would like to play it safe. But actually, he was an ambitious politician who wanted to make something big out of his life. When he was still young, he had already made up his mind to enter the Communist Party's central leadership. But I dare say even Xi himself didn't expect that he would become China's supremo one day."

Xi's father Xi Zhongxun was well known for being a strong supporter of economic reform and the special economic zone (SEZ) pilot schemes in Guangdong province at the outset of China's opening up to the world championed by Deng Xiaoping. Xi Jinping's first job in Fujian was to take care of Fujian's SEZ in Xiamen, just five kilometres from Taiwan's Quemoy Island. He tried to learn from his father in supporting Xiamen's development, but failed.

Xi was suddenly ordered to go to Xiamen in 1985 to replace deputy mayor An Li, the daughter-in-law of then party chief Hu Yaobang. An was forced to resign because her extravagant lifestyle and arrogance upset officials and residents. "After An's resignation, provincial party chief Xiang Nan asked party general secretary Hu Yaobang to send another person to fill the vacancy," the Fuzhou official said, adding that Hu chose Xi because of his princeling background and rustic, low-profile personality.

In 2000, Xi told a documentary programme on state broadcaster CCTV that Fujian "was not the well-developed place I imagined before I headed there", and recalled a difficult, 236-kilometre trip from the provincial capital to Xiamen. "In June 1985, I went to Xiamen, spending eight hours to get there [by car] from Fuzhou due to the poor transportation network." A biography of Xi published by Taipei-based China Times Publishing in 2012 said that, after the long journey, Xi decided to build a highway linking Xiamen and Fuzhou. "Many Xiamen comrades told me that their city was like 'a beautiful young girl wearing a shabby dress'," the book, *Xi Jinping — the Chinese Communist Party's New Leader Who Is Standing at a Historical Crossroads*, quoted Xi as saying. The new deputy mayor also planned to give Xiamen a makeover.

However, Xi left Xiamen three years later after losing out in the race to become the city's mayor. And most of his plans to reshape the city were rejected by the province's new leadership after Xiang Nan was forced to resign in 1987 to take responsibility for a fake medicine scandal. Insiders believed Xiang's resignation as party chief was actually a form of political punishment after he lost out in a political struggle between local and non-local officials in the province.

After Xiamen, Xi became a district party head in Ningde, a relatively poor city in a remote corner of northeastern Fujian. Another official in Fuzhou, working in the province's cultural department, said that when Xi was in Ningde, local officials and residents asked him to use his connections as a princeling to help them upgrade the small district into a prefectural-level city. "But Xi turned down their request and instead launched an environmental protection campaign with the slogan 'Returning green mountains and rivers to our people' that moved many big graves built along a key road connecting Ningde to the outside world." The cultural official said Xi was prepared to "offend rich and powerful people who harmed the public interest", with most of the tombs built by rich local families with special backgrounds or official connections. "Xi's assertiveness made many powerful families and local officials very unhappy."

The official added that environmental protection had become one of Xi's priorities ever since, with a desert control project in Longyan's Changding county when he was acting Fujian governor in 1999 being one notable achievement. "But none of us realised the importance of such a progressive and innovative environmental protection concept more than a decade ago, with most local officials just trying to create some 'image projects' to pave the way for further promotion."

In 2000, an environmentally friendly Ningde was formally upgraded to a prefectural-level city when Xi became Fujian's governor. Another of Xi's achievements was his success in attracting overseas capital to Fuzhou when he was the city's party head from 1998 to 2000. One of the projects saw Hong Kong tycoon Li Ka-shing brought in to take part in the renovation of the Three Lanes and Seven Alleys, a historic residential area dating back to the Ming and Qing dynasties.

Several people who worked under Xi in Fujian said it was hard to notice any flaws with him, even as a controversial and spectacular smuggling case ensnared at least 700 central government and local officials. Xi's time in Fujian coincided with the rise and fall of Lai Changxing, who established the notorious Yuanhua Group in Xiamen in the 1990s and became China's most-wanted fugitive in 2000. Fleeing to Canada, Lai fought a long but ultimately vain battle against extradition and was deported back to China in July 2011 on promises he would not be executed.

At his trial in Xiamen in April 2012, Xinhua reported that his smuggling operations evaded 14 billion yuan in customs duties from 1996 to 1999 and that he paid at least 64 government officials nearly 40 million yuan in bribes. He was sentenced to life imprisonment.

A source close to the Fujian provincial government said Xi was not touched by the scandal. "No evidence shows Xi, Fujian's number two leader after Jia Qinglin, had a connection with A-Xing [Lai]," he said. "During the mid-1990s, the golden time of A-Xing's Yuanhua Group, almost all the provincial government officials, including our party head Jia, were so proud of making friends with A-Xing, and all of us were keen on showing off our relationship because it signified that you were in the club. But Xi was a rare senior official who tried to keep his distance from A-Xing."

He said Xi's work in the early 1980s as one of the secretaries of defence minister Geng Biao had been invaluable in cultivating his "political sense and awareness" and paving the way for entry to the party's upper echelons. "As a defence minister's secretary, he had opportunities to sit in on many meetings of the Communist Party's Politburo and read many of the party's confidential documents," the provincial official said. "Those privileges made him understand that his key mission in Fujian was neither colluding with influential people nor racing to compete with neighbouring Guangdong and other coastal provinces in terms of economic development, but another, political, task — to do the united-front work on Taiwan."

Shi Bing, head of the Fuzhou bureau of the Hong Kong-based newspaper *Ta Kung Pao*, said that when Xi was Fujian governor, local media asked him why there was a huge development gap between Fujian and Guangdong, which was governed by his father in the late 1970s. "I remember Xi's answer: 'When the starting pistol for our country's reform and opening-up race fired, Guangdong ran out immediately, while Fujian was still tying its shoes ... and it is my job to lay a good foundation for Fujian'."

That foundation included taking steps to maintain Fujian's status as China's province with the most forest cover (more than 60 per cent), attracting capital and improving local infrastructure, Shi said. Sze Chi-ching, a Hong Kong-based entrepreneur originally from Fujian who has been Xi's friend since 1985, said it was unfair to blame Xi for Fujian's lacklustre economy. "The central government didn't want to develop Fujian because it had been designated as a war front, due to tension between Beijing and Taipei. Meanwhile, when Guangdong pulled out all the stops for economic development [in the 1980s and 1990s], Fujian was still busy with political struggles, with many able-minded cadres from Beijing and other provinces being excluded by local people and leftists. It was a great pity."

Many middle-aged officials in Fuzhou said Xi had been one of the "outside officials" and he was given a hard time during his 17 years in the province. "But as a leader with a princeling background, Xi's simple life and selflessness made an impression on the local officials and people," a provincial foreign affairs official said. "When Xi was in Xiamen and Ningde, he still put on green military uniforms, the clothes he wore in Zhengding, Hebei. He started wearing Western-style suits when he became party head of Fuzhou because he needed to dress up when meeting overseas entrepreneurs at investment promotion functions."

Sze said Xi had a humble personality and always remembered friends. "He lived in a public dormitory and washed his own clothes when he was deputy mayor of Xiamen. He also dined at a public canteen and never visited fancy restaurants. He has never forgotten old friends like me ... when he was moved to Zhejiang and Shanghai, he still managed to find time to meet me ... it made me feel that he is still my little brother."

The Fuzhou foreign affairs official said Xi had taken steps to maintain a clean image, "just like Taiwanese leader Ma Ying-jeou. For example, he didn't allow his brothers and sisters to run businesses in Fujian when he was there," the official said. "He told us that he once warned them: 'I will not provide any help if you guys have problems in Fujian'." The official said Xi's mother, Qi Xin, played a key role in removing "family obstacles" and persuading his brother and sisters, who all became entrepreneurs, to support Xi's political career. "That's why his younger brother, Xi Yuanping, agreed to withdraw all his businesses in Shanghai after Xi was appointed the municipality's party chief in 2007."

*   *   *

Doing the Business

by *Louise Ho*

> Xi Jinping's time in Zhejiang province was a period when private firms and innovation flourished. So to find clues about how Xi Jinping might manage the world's second-largest economy, Zhejiang is a good place to start looking.

The three and a half years Xi Jinping spent at the helm of one of China's richest provinces are regarded as a transformative period, during which

Zhejiang expanded its private sector and moved towards cleaner, more innovative industries.

After arriving in the autumn of 2003, Xi, as governor and party secretary, set about encouraging factories and heavy industry to move further inland to make way for privately funded research and development facilities. The campaign paid off: R&D investment by private industry increased four-fold to 31.6 billion yuan in 2007, from 5.6 billion yuan in 2003.

Xi also embraced Zhejiang's reputation for supporting private industry in a nation where the majority of large businesses were still state-run. "Xi Jinping's achievement in Zhejiang was impressive, especially in promoting the development of the private economy — which shows he is an open-minded leader," said Dr Cheng Li, a China expert working at the US-based think tank the Brookings Institution.

Zhejiang was already ranked the nation's fourth-largest provincial economy when Xi arrived after 17 years in neighbouring Fujian province. The new party secretary was well aware that the private enterprise that blossomed in the 1980s after Deng Xiaoping's "opening up" reforms was responsible for much of its growth.

He set about developing plans to continue that success. One was to encourage traditional labour-intensive industries to relocate to provinces further inland where land and labour were more abundant, while supporting and attracting more innovative businesses to Zhejiang. Xi did this because of land shortages and soaring labour costs in Zhejiang, said Shi Jinchuan, head of the Centre for Research of the Private Economy at Zhejiang University. "It was the right policy direction because it brought into play Zhejiang's advantages while at the same time pushing the innovation process for Zhejiang companies."

The private economy started to bloom in Zhejiang in the late 1970s and early 1980s. The province, which was left out of the industrial investment programmes of an earlier era, was among those best equipped to adapt quickly to a new environment. "Many of the businessmen in Zhejiang started from scratch, but they worked very hard and became wealthy," Xi said in December 2003. He noted that one-third of China's 500 biggest companies were based in Zhejiang.

To gain a better understanding of private business, Xi visited many big private companies. The first one he went to was Geely, headquartered in Hangzhou and the only car maker in the province. Soon afterwards, Xi introduced nine measures to support Geely, including encouraging Zhejiang taxi companies to use Geely vehicles. Geely became one of China's top car makers.

The province's gross domestic product continued to expand at a brisk pace during Xi's tenure, growing to 1.8 trillion yuan from 939 billion. His support for private industry was strong enough to weather an onslaught from more conservative elements in the Communist Party, who blamed speculation by private businessmen for driving up property prices. Xi resisted calls to roll back economic reforms, said Yao Xinbao, a professor of journalism at Shanghai's Jiao Tong University. Xi felt the rights of entrepreneurs were recognised by law and they were instrumental to the nation's economic development, he said. "Xi was able to stand firm to his belief. The development of private business was at its best during Xi's time in Zhejiang."

To promote private business, Xi Jinping had another plan: to work more closely with Shanghai, the nation's financial centre, and Jiangsu province, Zhejiang's neighbour. Xi's philosophy was to let Shanghai lead Zhejiang and Jiangsu in the development of the Yangtze River Delta. "Xi had a vision of how Zhejiang should be positioned in the Yangtze River Delta," said one correspondent who worked in Zhejiang for a Hong Kong newspaper when Xi was party boss. There were arguments at the time over who should be in charge of developing the Yangtze delta, because each of the three areas had its own advantages, she said. For example, Shanghai was powerful in finance, Zhejiang had a strong economy and Jiangsu had a lot of investment from Taiwan.

Xi did not mind letting Shanghai take charge. In a plan to establish an international shipping centre for the region, Xi decided to let Shanghai manage Yangshan, a deep-water container port in the south of Shanghai's Hangzhou Bay. Construction started in 2002 and it began operation in 2005.

In March 2007, Xi was appointed Shanghai party chief. He replaced Han Zheng, who had served as acting party secretary after former party secretary Chen Liangyu was removed for misappropriating money from the Shanghai social security fund.

Shanghai has always had close economic ties with Zhejiang, and his experience of leading Zhejiang helped Xi secure the top job in China's financial powerhouse, said Li of the Brookings Institution. When Xi arrived in Shanghai, he had the important task of getting the city through the social security fund scandal and had to flex his political muscle at a critical time, analysts said. Jiao Tong University's Yao said Xi ignored approaches from some influential Americans to let a US company build what would eventually become Shanghai Tower — designed by San Francisco-based architectural firm Gensler. Xi decided that such an iconic tower — slated to become the second-tallest building in the world — had to be built by a Chinese firm. "It shows Xi is resolute and decisive," Yao said.

Xi's time in Shanghai was brief. Seven months after arriving, Xi was promoted to the Politburo Standing Committee.

*   *   *

Star in Her Own Right

by **Minnie Chan**

China's first lady, Peng Liyuan, is a dazzling singer whose profile long eclipsed that of her husband Xi Jinping. She brings a touch of glamour not normally associated with the wives of China's top leaders.

Such was Peng Liyuan's fame, and so little known was her husband, that the joke among many Chinese used to be: "Who is Xi Jinping? Ah yes, he is Peng Liyuan's husband."

And whether Peng, following her husband's elevation, would withdraw behind the cloak of virtual anonymity that surrounded the wives of Xi's predecessors, Hu Jintao and Jiang Zemin, or would project an image more akin to that of spouses of Western leaders was a topic of intense speculation among her huge following of fans. Peng has been admired by hundreds of millions in China for her performances on state broadcaster CCTV's New Year's Eve shows. The gala has been the most watched TV programme in China, attracting more than 700 million viewers.

Peng, born in 1962 in Shandong province, has been a legend of contemporary Chinese folk singing since she was just 18 years old. She was one of the first people in China to obtain a master's degree in ethnic music and has been recognised as a "national first-degree performer".

She adopted a lower profile when her husband was promoted to vice-president in 2008. But in 2012, Peng appeared to be trying to step out of Xi's shadow as she geared up for her new role. In late May of that year she promoted the World No Tobacco Day with software magnate and philanthropist Bill Gates and in June she was appointed a World Health Organisation goodwill ambassador in the campaign against tuberculosis and HIV.

In May 2008, after a devastating earthquake hit Sichuan, eight of the nine members of Politburo Standing Committee visited the worst-hit areas of the western province. However Xi was not among them. He headed to less-damaged counties in neighbouring Shaanxi instead, provoking some criticism that the country's leader-in-waiting was cold-blooded and unwilling to face danger.

His wife, in contrast, immediately visited many stricken parts of Sichuan for special charity performances, and spoke about her family's quake relief efforts. She said she had donated 200,000 yuan to victims and that their only child, daughter Xi Mingze, just 16 at the time, had volunteered to work in one of the worst-hit areas for a week.

Peng was the youngest civilian to be given the rank of major general in the People's Liberation Army, owing to her background in the military's performing arts troupes.

Wang Yuncheng, a former head of the publicity office in Shishi, Fujian province, said that when Xi was party secretary of the provincial capital, Fuzhou, in the early 1990s, Peng's performances and speeches won much applause and helped polish Xi's image. Wang met Peng in 1992 and said she was very approachable. "She wore no make-up when dining with us and looked like a common woman," he said. "She told us that since both she and Xi were very busy, their only daughter, who was just a few months old at the time, had been left behind with her parents."

Wang said that as a father of two, he could feel Peng's self-reproach when talking about her family life. "Peng said it was a luxury for the couple to meet once a month when Xi was party head of Fuzhou," he said. "She talked to us so nicely, without any official airs. I was so proud to receive her and am so happy that we will have such a natural and graceful first lady."

Professor Zhang Ming, a political scientist at Renmin University in Beijing, said Peng had helped bolster and soften Xi's public image in a country that, stimulated by the new social media, had become increasingly hungry for news about its leaders and their personal lives. "I hope her outspokenness will change China's past conservative traditions, which have shaped coverage of all first families, with anything about their activities being a state secret."

"In China's modern history, Soong May-ling [the wife of Kuomintang leader Chiang Kai-shek] was the most high-profile and successful first lady. But if Peng follows her style, it might arouse controversy. That's because China is very different from Western countries, because Chinese are not used to idolising women, unlike the British, who adored Princess Diana. On the contrary, we even can't accept that a princess can outshine her crown prince husband."

For three decades or so, leaders' spouses played no political role at all in China — a convention some analysts link to the legacy left by Jiang Qing, the third wife of Mao Zedong, who was arrested after his death as the ringleader of the Gang of Four radicals.

Liu Yongqing, Hu Jintao's wife, rarely appeared and almost never spoke in public. Wang Yeping, the wife of Jiang Zemin, Hu's predecessor, was described by local and overseas media as "an invisible and silent first lady". Peng, however, once broke the silence surrounding the family lives of China's leaders by talking about her relationship with Xi before his promotion to the Politburo Standing Committee in 2007.

"When he comes home, I've never thought that there's some leader in the house," she told the state-run *Zhanjiang Evening News* in Guangdong. "In my eyes, he's just my husband. When I get home, he doesn't think of me as some famous star. In his eyes, I'm simply his wife."

Renmin University's Zhang said that to make sure that she did not outshine her husband, Peng had tried to shift the public's focus from her well-known voice to her philanthropic career — a similar path to that trodden by many first ladies in the West. "I think the Chinese would prefer it if Peng did not learn from Soong or US first lady Michelle Obama. In fact, it would be good enough if she just imitated

Chow Mei-ching, the wife of Taiwan's leader Ma Ying-jeou, who is well-known for her common touch."

Xi met Peng, who was more famous than him at the time, at a friend's home in Xiamen in 1986. She told the *Zhejiang Daily* in September 2007: "In our first encounter, I found his dress was out-moded and severely plain, while [his face] looked older than his real age." However, Peng said she was attracted to Xi, then 32, when he began to talk. "Jinping didn't ask me how much I earned for every per-formance, like other common people...He just asked me, 'How many skills are involved in singing?' And he didn't even realize how famous I was and that I was the original performer of one of his favourite songs." They married on September 1, 1987, a year after their first date.

CHAPTER 4

Sent-Down Youth Rise Up

On November 2, 2012, the *South China Morning Post* broke to the world the names of the seven men forming the Standing Committee of the Chinese Communist Party Politburo, the elite at the pinnacle of power of the world's most populous nation. The *Post*'s exclusive story hit the print and digital newsstands even before the start of the congress, at which the seven, led by Xi and wearing identical dark suits, walked to the centre of the stage in Beijing's Great Hall of the People. We examine the ideological leanings and backgrounds of this all-powerful group in China and profile the six men standing side by side with Xi, plus the wife of Premier Li Keqiang.

Will Xi Surprise the Naysayers?

by **Wang Xiangwei**

As soon as Xi Jinping and the six other top Communist Party officials walked into the media limelight at noon on November 15, 2012, many overseas analysts and media organisations immediately labelled China's new leadership line-up as being "conservative" and dominated by the "old guard". They expressed concerns that, with such a line-up, Xi could find himself hamstrung in his efforts to carry out political and economic reform that was needed to put the country on a path to more sustainable growth.

Their concerns appeared to stem partly from the observation that former president Jiang Zemin again managed to outmanoeuvre his successor Hu Jintao in filling seats on the Politburo Standing Committee with his protégés and allies — accounting for five of the seven members. Moreover, they pointed to the fact that Li Yuanchao and

Wang Yang, two relatively younger leaders known for their liberal views and reformist outlook, failed to make the cut, even though they were seen as Hu's close allies. The unspoken suggestion was that Jiang's allies and protégés were largely hardliners, while Hu's supporters were liberals and reformists.

People really should have taken these findings by so-called China pundits with a pinch of salt. First of all, their sweeping characterisations lacked a solid basis. There was a good reason that the 10-year reign by Hu and premier Wen Jiabao was referred to as "the lost decade", for its lack of meaningful economic and political reform. By comparison, many Chinese were now nostalgic for Jiang's 13-year reign, in which the country joined the World Trade Organisation and undertook major economic reform that paved the way for the lift-off during Hu's era. In fact, many people argued that, during the Hu–Wen decade, the opposite had happened — not only through reform being stalled, but also rolled back in many ways, with the state sector consolidating its hold on the economy.

Secondly, Chinese officials with liberal leanings, in the eyes of so-called China observers, were not the same as the ones defined by Western standards. Liberal Chinese officials might be seen calling for more transparency and accountability in the government, for the need to uphold the rule of law, and even for more efforts to promote civil society. But their goal was to maintain the dictatorial rule of the Communist Party and to toe the party line, including by muzzling the media and showing intolerance for political dissent.

In fact, the prevailing view among China's elites seemed to be that undertaking a new round of reform was the only way forward, and even its most liberal-minded economist, Wu Jinglian, said the 18th party congress had put reform back on the agenda, and that now implementation was the key. It went without saying that for reform to

SENT-DOWN YOUTH RISE UP

proceed, the country needed a stronger leader. The question was: would Xi fit the profile?

There were reasons for optimism. The fact that Xi took over the leadership of the party and the military at the same time, and assumed the presidency as scripted at the following March meeting of the National People's Congress, gave him a strong mandate. There was the fact that he was a close ally of Jiang, which meant it would be much easier for Xi to get support from other leaders in addressing vested interest groups or pushing for reform.

Much was written about the leadership's decision to reduce the size of the Politburo Standing Committee from nine to seven, to reduce political wrangling in the hope of reaching faster decisions. More importantly, the move was aimed at allowing the top leaders to focus on strategic issues and challenges. Over the previous 10 years, the nine committee members functioned like the line managers often seen in multinationals — responsible for only their own portfolios, and failing to spend time on the big picture.

But a deeper layer of meaning was that the decision was also aimed at bolstering Xi's authority. One prevailing concern was how Xi dealt with the possible intervention of the party elders. For the first time in the party's history, Xi had to face a situation in which he had two retired party chiefs, Jiang and Hu, breathing down his neck. There were also about 20 retired Politburo Standing Committee members who could influence the policy agenda through their own supporters. But the speculation from the corridors of power in Beijing suggested that the party elders, including Jiang and Hu, had reached a consensus to give Xi a freer hand in making his own decisions.

If that were true, it was a major boost for Xi's power. It would also explain why we saw a confident and relaxed Xi giving an inspirational speech televised live on the day of the leadership's unveiling. He abandoned slogans and instead vowed to fight corruption while promising good jobs and better lives for Chinese people.

As one traditional Chinese saying goes, a hero is nothing but a product of his time. In his time, Xi would need strong leadership to fulfil his promises.

* * *

Generation of Hope

by **Verna Yu**

> The Chinese say that people must first know a bitter taste before they understand sweetness, and no political group in modern China knows this better than the country's so-called fifth generation of leaders.

During the brutal chaos of the 1966–76 Cultural Revolution, many of the figures handed the keys to power at the 18th Communist Party Congress were just teenagers who were Red Guards and later became "sent-down youth" packed off to the countryside to live in poverty and "learn from the peasants".

Nearly all went on to experience the heady intellectual spring at Chinese universities in the 1970s and 1980s. The crackdown on pro-democracy protesters in and around Tiananmen Square in 1989 was a watershed — for some it meant jail and exile, while others survived to ascend the ranks of the party bureaucracy to witness, and enjoy the fruits of modernisation. Given their background, it was not surprising that many Chinese regarded the new leadership as the brightest to date — compassionate yet practical, visionary yet resilient.

Take, for example, Premier Li Keqiang. He was remembered by contemporaries at Peking University as a quick-witted and outspoken law student who excelled in debates amid the liberal campus atmosphere at the time. "He was sharp, passionate and an independent thinker," recalled Dr Wang Juntao, a fellow student who nominated him to the post of student federation chairman.

Three decades on, their fates could not be more different. Li is the country's premier and ranked second in the party's hierarchy, while Wang, the chairman of the US-based China Democracy Party, is living in exile after having been jailed for being the "black hand" of the 1989 Tiananmen pro-democracy movement.

It was these kinds of early encounters with people from different political and intellectual backgrounds that raised hopes that the new leadership would have more modern views on governance and a broader world outlook than the older generation, analysts said.

"This leadership will probably be very different from the Hu Jintao generation," said Professor Michel Bonnin, a researcher at the Paris-based École des Hautes Études en Sciences Sociales' Centre for the Study of Contemporary and Modern China. "These people were at university when universities were absorbing Western ideas and there was a freer atmosphere on campus." But it was also their first-hand experience of hardship in the countryside that raised expectations that the new leaders would have greater sympathy with the poor. As "educated youth", or *zhi qing*, many were sent to farms where they experienced the grinding poverty of the rural poor. It is hard to imagine that this would fail to have an impact on their lives, making them sensitive to the plight of ordinary people and having a realistic view of the country's problems.

Bonnin, who wrote *The Lost Generation: The Rustication of Urban Educated Youth in China, 1968–1980*, believes the new generation of leaders, having lived through the horrors of the Cultural Revolution and also tasted the liberal atmosphere of the 1980s, would have realised that the country's problems would need to be solved through the rule of law and political reform.

"It is a mistaken idea that, since these people were Red Guards in the Cultural Revolution era, they will be Maoists. Going down to the countryside made them reflect upon reality and ... they are against empty slogans. I think these people who went through the Cultural Revolution will try to modernise China in the direction of the rule of law. They will understand that this is the only resolution — and the Maoist methods of mobilisation and propaganda are not good for solving China's problems."

Historian Yuan Weishi believed the new leaders' understanding of the grass roots, coupled with their more modern outlook, would distinguish their style of rule from the current generation. "The new generation is different from the last one. Their mentality is less authoritarian. They understand people from the bottom level and they have more knowledge and ideas of what the world is about — this will have an impact on their governance."

But even if they realised that political reform was a necessary step to tackle social inequality, a growing wealth gap and rampant corruption, Yuan worried that they would still lack the resolve to push through these initiatives for fear that liberalisation might unleash social instability and, for some, jeopardise lucrative vested interests in the commercial sector. "Failing to make big-enough steps will be detrimental to China's development. We will have to wait and see whether they have the courage and vision to carry them through. When they assume authority, their priority will be to ensure that their positions are secure."

Analysts feared some of the new leaders might have evolved into the sort of officials they once abhorred. It was no secret that many Chinese officials and their relatives traded on their connections and lineage to wield influence in politics and business, and accumulated astonishing wealth. Many had acquired foreign passports, sent their children abroad and stashed hundreds of millions of dollars offshore.

Public resentment over corruption and cronyism among politically powerful families had grown as the income gap in China continued to widen, threatening the rule of the party. Bloomberg news and information service reported in June 2012 that the extended family of President Xi Jinping had business interests in various commercial sectors including investments in companies with total assets of US$376 million. It was reported that the family of disgraced Chongqing party chief Bo Xilai — who was ousted in March 2012 and expelled from the Communist Party for crimes including corruption — accumulated at least US$136 million in assets.

Analysts said this complex network of vested commercial interests would be a key obstacle in the political reform plans of the next leadership. "Political reform will also touch on their vested interests and the regime's inertia is not something that a handful of people can change ... when you're part of the regime, you can't afford not to participate in the game," veteran China watcher Ching Cheong said.

Bonnin agreed: "People have the feeling that [the leaders' vast wealth] has not been legally or morally acquired, and they will resist change because they're afraid that if there is rule of law and democracy, they will be accused."

Historian Zhang Lifan said the humble past of the new generation of leaders, and their understanding of the poor, did not guarantee that they would advocate reform. "You cannot always rely on past experience to judge future performance. The key is what they will be like once they have tasted power."

Wang, who knew Premier Li well at university, said he was not sure if Li was still bold enough to carry out reforms, given the years he spent in the conservative bureaucracy while he rose to the top. "If [Li] can survive in the party, he could have changed. At a critical juncture, when the circumstances force the party to embark on reforms, he might do it, but he is not a bold person who would launch initiatives on his own."

Zhang said the party's overall priority would always be its political survival, so leaders must first ensure that any reform did not threaten their power. "If they do [undertake reform], it will be for the sake of maintaining their ruling position ... so the party can remain in power," Zhang said. "They will act only under the condition that they will be safe. They must remain loyal to the interests of the party. This is the bottom line, and cannot be crossed."

Profiles

Li Keqiang

by *Cary Huang*

Li Keqiang was among the first group of students admitted to university after late paramount leader Deng Xiaoping ordered the resumption of the university entrance exam in 1977 following the chaos of the Cultural Revolution, and is probably the best-educated premier the People's Republic of China has ever had.

At prestigious Peking University, Li studied the ideas of leading British judges and mixed with democracy advocates, leading

Li Keqiang

some to hope his premiership would herald significant political change in the world's last major communist-ruled nation. Li is the first senior central

government leader to hold a PhD in economics and master's and bachelor's degrees in law, all earned at a university that was a hot spot of dissent. His liberal studies background contrasted strongly with the engineering backgrounds of those who had recently run China. He studied law under Professor Gong Xiangrui, an expert on Western constitutional law who had studied in Britain in the 1930s. Li followed that with a PhD in economics under Li Yining, the Chinese market reform guru.

Professor Kerry Brown, of the China Studies Centre at the University of Sydney, said Li was the first lawyer to become a member of the party's supreme Politburo Standing Committee and he would be the first lawyer to become premier. "He typifies the new leaders inasmuch as he is not a technocrat, has a PhD from Peking University and had a long period of training in the provinces before elevation to executive vice-premier in 2008."

Li is one of the few top leaders fluent in English, surprising observers during a visit to Hong Kong in 2011 when he broke with protocol and addressed an event at the University of Hong Kong in English. His wife, Cheng Hong, is a linguistics professor and an expert on American literature who has translated several modern American works into Chinese.

Brown praised Li for having an engaging public manner, something he said was shown in Li's visit to Hong Kong. "He is not afraid of using English in public, though the heavy treatment of protesters and journalists [by police] at the time caused much criticism."

Most of the Chinese leaders over the previous couple of decades were engineers-turned-bureaucrats, trained in an education system heavily influenced by the Soviet Union. But Li, like many of his contemporaries, brought a markedly different mindset to the problems facing the nation.

Li rose through the Communist Youth League, a power base of former party chief Hu Jintao, before taking on senior postings in big, tough provinces — challenges that marked him for higher things. He started his political career as secretary of the Youth League at Peking University and went on to become a member of the secretariat of the League's central committee in 1985, when Hu headed the secretariat. He was appointed president of the League's Chinese Youth Political Academy in 1993 and also headed the League's secretariat from 1993 to 1998.

In 1999, Li became China's youngest governor — and the first with a PhD — when he was appointed to head the central province of Henan at the age of 43. He became Henan party secretary in 2003 and Liaoning province party boss in 2004. He won promotion to the central leadership in late 2007, becoming a member of the Politburo Standing Committee, and was made executive vice-premier in March 2008.

When he studied at Peking University from the late 1970s, calls for free speech and democracy were sprouting amid the ideological disillusionment with Mao Zedong's Cultural Revolution. Li reportedly plunged into campus politics as reformist ideas galvanised students, befriending freethinkers who went on to become dissidents in exile, and helping to translate *The Due Process of Law* by famed English jurist Lord Denning.

Former classmate and prominent dissident Wang Juntao, who went into exile in the United States in 1994 after being sentenced to 13 years in jail for supporting the 1989 Tiananmen Square democracy movement, was surprised that Li had remained in the bureaucracy for so many years because he had expressed his dislike for the bureaucratic way of doing things. "On campus, Li Keqiang was a student with an active mind and sharp words," Wang wrote in a memoir. "He has his own independent thinking and preferences. But he will not challenge authority on major issues. He is also a person who wants to have big personal accomplishments."

Another exiled dissident, Hu Ping, recalled that in 1980 Li, then a member of the official student union, backed controversial campus elections contested by Hu and other pro-democracy activists. Party conservatives were aghast at the radical experiment. "After the election, I talked to him about elections, democracy and the political future of China," Hu Ping told overseas media.

At the university, Li attached himself to Professor Gong Xiangrui, whose classes became a seedbed for exotic, liberal ideas. Gong had earned his PhD at the London School of Economics and was also a student of Qian Duansheng, a Harvard professor in the 1930s who was the founder of constitutional law studies in contemporary China and also a key drafter of several Kuomintang and Communist constitutions. Gong organised Li and two other students to translate *The Due Process of Law.* "As a student of Gong at an age when a person's value framework is set and as a translator of the great British work, he must have deep belief in the rule of law and modern constitutional systems," another of Gong's former students said.

But China watchers said Li's past experiences did not mean he would be a harbinger of radical liberalisation, with accounts by party insiders also depicting him as a political chameleon who has stayed within the system and paid his dues as a functionary.

Li, born in 1955 into a traditional Chinese bureaucrat's family, underwent systematic training in Chinese philosophy and culture before he was admitted to university. His father was a county magistrate who later became the official in charge of relics and historical records in Anhui province. The younger Li was taught to recite many classical Chinese works when he was a child. A former China Youth League official described Li as cautious and prudent. "He's seldom the first to speak up or lose his composure in conversations or meetings. And he also never lost his temper, at least in my memory."

Cheng Li, the director of research and a senior fellow with the John L. Thornton China Center at the Brookings Institution in Washington, said Li's policy priorities were those of a new generation. "Li Keqiang has drawn attention for his strong interest in new-issue areas such as affordable housing, food safety, public health care, climate change, and clean and renewable energy," Li wrote in an essay about China's latest leaders. "Not one of these issues was a priority for the Chinese leadership 10 years ago."

Hu Yifan, China economist with Hong Kong-based securities firm Haitong International, said that given Li's background in economics, hopefully "he could have a good understanding of China's economy and set up medium- and long-term strategies to facilitate economic transformation", something the departing leadership had not achieved. Like his predecessor Wen Jiabao, Li was at the centre of reports about his family's business interests. Research by Cheng Li showed that his brother, Li Keming, held a key position in the tobacco industry as deputy director of the State Tobacco Monopoly Administration. This was particularly ironic as Li Keqiang had been in charge of China's public health since 2008, Cheng Li wrote in his paper, *The Political Mapping of China's Tobacco Industry and Anti-Smoking Campaign.*

Brown said that as a protégé of Hu Jintao and with his experience in the provinces, Li had proved he was "able to handle and avoid crises", citing several career setbacks including the controversy over the spread of Aids in Henan through the buying of tainted blood.

Though seen as a rising political star, Li was not named as Hu Jintao's heir-apparent at the 17th party congress in 2007, losing out to rival Xi Jinping, a "princeling" supported by former president Jiang Zemin. It was not his first such setback. To the surprise of many observers, he failed to be elected to the party's Central Committee at the 14th party congress in 1992, even though he was first secretary of the Youth League's central committee. And two parts of his portfolio as vice-premier — housing and food safety — were massive sources of embarrassment for Beijing.

Brown said Li had proved himself to be economically reformist and liberal, although his attitude on socio-political issues was less clear. In an indication of Li's priorities, he said soon after the 18th party congress that China's rapid GDP growth must translate into higher income for ordinary people. "If our GDP growth does not help income growth of the people, it will be a meaningless exercise no matter how high the rate," Li was quoted by the *People's Daily* as saying. "It's not favourable for development, or for stability."

* * *

Cheng Hong

by Keith Zhai

Like many who lived through the 1966–76 Cultural Revolution, Cheng Hong, wife of Premier Li Keqiang, felt she'd had enough excitement to last a lifetime.

It was in 1995, while she was a visiting scholar in the US at Brown University, Rhode Island, that these thoughts crystallised. Cheng revealed how she developed her interest in writings on nature and ecology during her stay in New England in her book *Tranquillity Is Beyond Price*, published a decade later. It perhaps helps explain why Cheng, a professor of English at the Capital University of Economics and Business in Beijing, remained little known among ordinary Chinese. Even among the generally low-profile wives of China's elite, Cheng has stood out as something of a recluse.

"Cheng comes back to our university on an extremely rare basis, and most of our staff members are not in contact with her," said a professor from the same English department. "She was still teaching English and American literature for postgraduate students when her husband was the top leader of Liaoning province. But ever since Li Keqiang assumed his role inside the central Politburo, she has given up any course workloads."

Three professors from the department confirmed that Cheng had rarely been seen on campus since the early 2000s. The university, established in 1956, is considered to be among the second tier of higher education institutes in the capital, ranking behind more famous universities.

It has become almost routine for relatives of top leaders to become wealthy during their family members' leadership. But people interviewed by the *South China Morning Post* said Cheng was a serious scholar with no business interests. One professor said Cheng was once put forward by university officials to become dean of the department, but she refused. "Cheng is a dedicated scholar who prefers to concentrate on her work. She treats others with sincerity and courtesy," said the professor, who also taught English literature in the department.

The university website listed Cheng as one of its "renowned scholars" and said she was a member of the institute's academic committee. One graduate of the English department described Cheng as a strong, competent teacher of English literature and a researcher who had made an impact in her chosen field. She was also considered one of the leading Chinese scholars of American nature writing, having published two books on the subject and translated several books from English to Chinese.

"Her studies definitely played a role in popularising nature literature in China," said one literary critic based in Guangzhou. "None of the wives of high-level officials have such English ability and writing skills. Cheng's books are beautifully written."

American author Terry Tempest Williams praised Cheng, translator of her book *Refuge: An Unnatural History of Family and Place*. Cheng "represents [my] vision through her translation with great beauty. *Refuge* is ultimately a project of peace. I understand that her translation of *Refuge* is a translation of great care, insight and sensitivity to both the language and spirit of my book," Williams said.

In *Tranquillity Is Beyond Price*, Cheng writes about the 19th century naturist and philosopher Henry David Thoreau, paying tribute to his best-known book, *Walden, a reflection on the tranquillity of living amid nature*, based on Thoreau's experience of living for two years in a cabin he built in rural Massachusetts.

Cheng has twice visited Walden Pond, where Thoreau built his cabin. The first time was in 2000, as she was about to finish her doctorate at the Chinese Academy of Social Sciences. It proved disappointing, as the site was overrun by tourists. But after a second visit, on a still autumn day with the tourists gone, she wrote: "When the original nature and the simple happiness are gradually gone, it seems Thoreau is even more remembered by many, and people want to follow his steps, to pursue pristine nature, a free mind, and a sound mind and body."

She did not discuss another of Thoreau's works: his 1849 essay *Civil Disobedience*, an argument for individual resistance to civil government in moral opposition to an unjust state.

* * *

Zhang Dejiang

by Fiona Tam

When Chongqing party chief Bo Xilai dramatically fell from grace in 2012 and left a power vacuum in the booming metropolis, Zhang Dejiang was just the man Beijing needed to step in and clean up the chaos.

Once installed, Zhang quickly moved to reorganise the government and reassure

Zhang Dejiang

Hong Kong, Taiwanese and overseas investors who worried about instability in the mega-city of nearly 30 million. Holding the high-profile post as Chongqing party secretary while retaining his title as vice-premier made Zhang an odds-on favourite to gain a seat on the supreme seven-man Politburo Standing Committee at the 18th party congress. Furthermore, Zhang's close association with the party's more conservative wing — he studied economics in North Korea — would send a signal that the hardliners were not on the way out despite seeing Bo, one of their champions, disgraced.

Such a promotion also let his long-time patron, former president Jiang Zemin, keep a vital ally on the party's supreme policy-making body. The relationship between the two men dates back to March 1990, when the Korean-speaking Zhang accompanied Jiang on an important solidarity mission to Pyongyang amid China's international isolation in the wake of the 1989 Tiananmen crackdown on pro-democracy protesters.

Zhang, who at the March 2013 session of the National People's Congress became chairman of that body and therefore China's top legislator, developed a reputation for rigid efficiency during his rise over two decades from provincial party boss to vice-premier, even if his heavy-handed tactics sometimes led critics to accuse him of being ruthless.

The "princeling" son of former People's Liberation Army general Zhang Zhiji, Zhang was born in Liaoning province in 1946 and spent two years at Kim Il-sung University. He returned to China in 1980 and held a variety of posts. Eventually Zhang landed in the Yanbian Korean Autonomous Prefecture in Jilin province, where his success in stemming the tide of illegal immigration from North Korea caught the eyes of leaders in Beijing. Jiang tipped him for the trip to Pyongyang and appeared to have been much impressed with the ambitious cadre.

Afterwards, the president summoned Zhang to Beijing and asked him to turn Yanbian into a "model prefecture" for the nation. Deemed successful, Zhang was promoted to party boss in Jilin in 1995 and Zhejiang province in 1998 before ultimately assuming control of the manufacturing powerhouse of Guangdong province in 2002. It was in Guangdong that Zhang logged some of his biggest achievements — steering the province through a period of explosive economic growth. But his iron-fisted style also landed him at the centre of numerous controversies.

Zhang drew the heaviest criticism for his response to the SARS outbreak in 2003, which observers argued was made worse by the province's lethargic response to early cases and the suppression of news reports about the disease. Those who violated orders were dealt with harshly. In 2004, the editor-in-chief and general manager of the upstart *Southern Metropolis News*, the first newspaper to expose the SARS outbreak, were prosecuted on corruption charges. While the editor was acquitted, the general manager was jailed for four years.

The newspaper had already suffered a reported clampdown by authorities in 2003 after publishing a story about the death of a 27-year-old graphic designer who failed to produce a residency permit when questioned by Guangzhou police. An autopsy showed Sun Zhigang had been beaten before his death. The coverage helped spur national outrage over the government's practice of detaining migrant workers in cities and returning them home, even if they had not broken the law.

Zhang also drew fire for violent crackdowns on social unrest during his tenure. In 2005, police were believed to have killed 20 people in Dongzhou village in the Shanwei municipal region when they fired into a crowd protesting against inadequate land compensation. That same year, hundreds of police raided Guangzhou's Panyu district to put down protests against village officials. Reporters and rights lawyers were reportedly beaten by thugs while police looked the other way.

But analysts say such episodes did little to damage Zhang's standing in Beijing, as Guangdong continued to prosper under his leadership and "mass incidents" were kept in check. The province's per capita gross domestic product surged 80 per cent during his tenure. "Although he has been accused of mishandling the SARS outbreak, including restricting the flow of information to the public, Beijing won't regard it as a mistake," said Professor Steve Tsang, director of the China Policy Institute of the University of Nottingham. "Zhang's initial response to SARS was the default option for every communist official on the mainland."

Tsang said Zhang's rigid leadership style was common among party leaders, especially those considered members of Jiang's "Shanghai gang". "Like the rest of the Shanghai gang, Zhang's administration style focuses on rapid economic development and an iron-fist government, paying no attention to social injustice. Their initial response to major crisis is high-pressure control."

Nonetheless, Zhang's ill-fated effort to create a pan-Pearl River Delta regional co-operation project including Hong Kong and Macau was seen as a poorly managed overreach by Beijing. He was passed over for a seat on the Politburo Standing Committee at the 17th party congress in 2007; his subsequent appointment as vice premier was widely seen as a consolation prize.

Zhang's crisis management style was again called into question in 2011 after a high-speed train crash in Wenzhou claimed 40 lives and badly damaged the reputation of the high-speed rail system. As the vice-premier in charge of energy, telecommunications and transport, Zhang reportedly brought the search-and-rescue effort to an abrupt halt and ordered officials to rush the trains back into service. Professor Yang Kai-huang, of Ming Chuan University, who is head of the Taiwan-based Mainland China Studies Association, believed such decisive action actually endeared Zhang to party elders. They might want people like him around to deal with future problems.

"The Communist Party expects to encounter lots of uncertainty and difficulty in the coming decade ... and it'll need candidates with strong political compliance," Yang said. "Zhang Dejiang is that kind of candidate who always carries out the central government's decision." That was likely one of the reasons Zhang was chosen to take over Chongqing in March 2012, following Bo's removal.

Professor Dong Liwen from Central Police University in Taiwan, said Zhang's history showed he was more of a pragmatic opportunist than the hardline conservative other observers had portrayed him to be. "Opportunism is one of the common political characteristics of the Shanghai gang," Dong said. "To maximise their political interests, their ideology is always swaying between that of the leftists and the rightists, combining hard and soft tactics."

*　*　*

Yu Zhengsheng

by *Minnie Chan*

Yu Zhengsheng, former Shanghai party chief and a "princeling" promoted to the Politburo Standing Committee at the 18th party congress, has a knack for using both the carrot and the stick.

Yu, born in 1945 and one of the Politburo's most senior members, developed his sound political judgment after enduring many political crises, including managing to survive during the 1966–76 Cultural Revolution despite his blue-blood pedigree. "Yu is a fairly open-minded leader who is willing to compromise with local officialdom when moving into a new environment," Hong Kong-based political

Yu Zhengsheng

commentator Ho Leong-leong said, citing the differences that Yu adopted in his working style during his spells in Shandong and Hubei provinces and in Shanghai. "Shanghai is a very different place, as the municipal government has been dominated by natives, and Yu, once an iron-fisted leader in Hubei, has become a more low-profile and easygoing party chief since becoming head of the city in late 2007."

In January 2008, just two months after Yu arrived in Shanghai and was busy preparing for a meeting with then British prime minister Gordon Brown, more than 2,000 residents protested outside the main government headquarters against plans to build a high-speed maglev rail line from Shanghai to Hangzhou. Yu immediately promised to postpone the project and hold a further round of discussions.

Ho said Yu's good relationship with Mayor Han Zheng, whose future had appeared uncertain following the downfall of disgraced Shanghai party chief Chen Liangyu in 2006, had helped ensure that many of his high-profile tasks, including running the 2010 World Expo, progressed smoothly. "I think Yu tried to protect Han from having his connections with his former boss Chen checked by the upper level, resulting in the Shanghai-native mayor working closely with the new party head," Ho said.

Ma Guoxian, an economist and political observer at Shanghai University of Finance and Economics, said Yu had "a clear political mindset, especially when dealing with some sensitive issues like the Cultural Revolution". Ma cited Yu's cautious response to disgraced Chongqing party secretary Bo Xilai's anti-triad crackdown and "red song" campaign as a case in point. In a rare, high-profile lecture to 5,000 student party members at Shanghai Jiao Tong University on June 20, 2011, at the height of Bo's campaign to promote the singing of songs in praise of the Communist Party, Yu said a "personal mistake" by Mao Zedong was to blame for the Cultural Revolution and the wrong direction taken by the party.

"[Mao] made a serious personal mistake ... he launched the Cultural Revolution ... as an attempt to prevent workers and farmers from being reduced to an underclass in our society," Yu told the students. "But he shouldn't have sought such a wrong way out."

Yu said at least six members of his family died during the decade of nationwide political struggle, with his younger sister committing suicide when she was at high school. His mother, one of the party's revolutionary vanguards, became schizophrenic during seven years in jail.

As a senior politician in the communist hierarchy, Yu defied his patrician roots to scale the political heights. He was born into an aristocratic family in Shaoxing, Zhejiang province, with many members of the family serving as officials during the late Qing dynasty or in the Kuomintang regime. His great-uncle Yu Da-wei served as Taiwan's defence minister in 1954, and among his cousins was Yu Yang-ho, the son-in-law of former Taiwanese president Chiang Ching-kuo.

Other family members had a party pedigree. Yu's father, Yu Qiwei, also known as Huang Jing, was at one point married to Mao Zedong's third wife, Jiang Qing, and introduced her to the party. Yu Qiwei was also the first mayor of Tianjin following the establishment of the People's Republic and head of the Ministry of Machine-building Industry in the 1950s.

Yu Zhengsheng's mother, Fan Jin, was a former general director of the *Beijing Daily*, and his wife, Zhang Zhikai, is the daughter of the late Zhang Zhenhuan, a former vice-chairman of the Commission of Science, Technology and Industry for National Defence.

Yu Zhengsheng graduated from the missile engineering department of the Harbin Military Institute and spent 16 years as a cadre in the Ministry of Electronics Industry, with his last two years as a deputy department head under Jiang Zemin. His career progressed despite the defection to the US in 1985 of his older brother, Yu Qiangsheng, a senior intelligence officer in the Ministry of State Security, while the younger Yu was deputy party secretary of Yantai in Shandong province.

Yu Zhengsheng went on to serve as mayor and party chief of Qingdao, and as a member of the Shandong party Standing Committee. He became construction minister in 1998 and was promoted to be Hubei province party secretary in 2001. In 2002 he became director of the provincial party Standing Committee and was appointed to the Politburo.

No matter where he was placed, Yu always displayed a solid capacity to govern. While mayor of Qingdao, he sold the city government's central offices to an overseas developer and moved the administration into the countryside to boost rural development — a decision that was well received. When he was party head of Hubei from 2002 to 2007, Yu launched several pilot reforms covering party affairs, the urban and rural tax systems, civil servants' benefits and other areas despite strong opposition. In the provincial capital, Wuhan, Yu cancelled 500 highway passes for provincial government vehicles, ordering that all official cars should pay highway tolls, the *People's Daily* said. Yu also cut all kinds of cash allowances for provincial officials, replacing them with a 400-yuan monthly subsidy, it said.

But he adopted a more low-profile and humble approach after moving to Shanghai in 2007. Shanghai University's Ma said Yu was more flexible on some less sensitive issues, like mass protests, and was willing to listen to public opinion. "Yu is very skilful when dealing with political crises, because he's not like other conservative leaders who have grown used to forcing the public to accept their own thinking." Ma cited the example of Yu's handling of a high-rise fire in Shanghai in November 2010 that claimed 58 lives. One week after the fire, thousands of Shanghai residents united in a rare expression of mass public grief to mourn the victims. Yu and Han then made a public apology, acknowledging that they should be blamed for the weak supervision of the city's chaotic construction industry. "His quick and friendly reaction successfully assuaged public anger over the municipal government's dereliction of duty," Ma said.

As expected, as part of China's leadership handover in 2012–13, Yu was selected to head the top government advisory body, the Chinese People's Political Consultative Conference, a companion body to the top legislature, the National People's Congress.

* * *

Liu Yunshan

by **Raymond Li**

Liu Yunshan, head of the Communist Party's Publicity Department and newly elevated to the Politburo Standing Committee, faced daunting propaganda policy challenges arising from the new media, analysts said.

In the past, Liu had often been seen in public as a sidekick to propaganda czar Li Changchun and for nearly 10 years he largely served as an enforcer following orders from his superiors to come down hard on dissent.

Liu Yunshan

Prior to the 18th party congress, Liu spared no effort in touting departing president Hu Jintao's campaign under the banner "Go to the grass roots, renew the manner, and change the writing style" to make propaganda more relevant to a public growing weary of the constant burnishing of the party's deeds. The campaign promoting Hu's propaganda policy was apparently an effort by Liu to boost his political capital in the intense jockeying for top posts. Having risen to the highest ranks, Liu was expected to assume a major role in ideological control in the following five years. However, analysts said he would face greater challenges from social

media, an emerging civil-society movement empowered by the internet and deepening disdain for the party's rule and its ideological control.

Qiao Mu, an associate professor at Beijing Foreign Studies University who has studied the propaganda department, noted that Liu's promotion to the central government was as secretive as the department he leads.

A widely circulated and censored blog article by Qiao, which recounted his first visit to the Publicity Department in 2011, offered a rare glimpse into the secrecy surrounding it. He observed that the address and phone numbers of the department were not listed in street directories or phone books. Qiao said Liu's role in ideological control was significantly weakened in 2002 when the Politburo Standing Committee was enlarged from seven to nine members. He said Liu, who would otherwise have served as an architect of ideological control, had been relegated to the role of coordinator among censors such as the State Council Information Office and State Administration of Radio, Film and Television.

Qiao said that the propaganda department under Liu's control had been operating "like a fireman", rushing in wherever there was a problem with the media. He pointed to the crackdown targeting management at the Guangzhou-based *New Express* and *Oriental Morning Post* in Shanghai in July 2012 for writing about sensitive topics. "When someone, or the department he leads that once dealt with strategy development and vision building, is preoccupied with micromanagement, it no longer holds the clout it used to have," Qiao said.

He said Liu could claim credit for boosting the international presence of state-owned media over the past several years to cultivate China's so-called soft power. Liu was tasked with overseeing a budget of about US$8 billion for overseas expansion of the media, including opening branches of state broadcaster CCTV in the United States and Africa and the launch of a US edition of the *China Daily*.

Qiao said a TV commercial promoting China that made its debut on a giant screen in New York's Times Square ahead of Hu Jintao's visit to the US in January 2011, and an earlier campaign for "made-in-China" products, made a big impression. However, other efforts, such as the rapid expansion of Confucius Institutes worldwide, had only caused unease.

Qiao said Liu and his department would face daunting challenges from internet-based new media, as he had failed to put in place a sound strategy for the development of the web. The introduction of a licensing regime for internet service providers and a requirement for microbloggers to register with their real names underscored how little Chinese censors know about the internet. They were trying to control cyberspace as they controlled traditional media.

Liu, born in 1947, a native of Xinzhou in Shanxi province, began his career as a schoolteacher in Inner Mongolia's Tuzuo Banner region after he graduated from the Jining Normal School in 1968. Like many Chinese propaganda officials who cut their teeth at state-owned news organisations, Liu worked at the regional branch of the Xinhua News Agency in Inner Mongolia. He was later transferred to the region's Youth League, where he rose through the ranks to become a deputy party secretary for Inner Mongolia and party secretary for Chifeng in 1993.

In a sudden promotion to the central government that year, Liu was appointed a vice-minister of the publicity, or propaganda, department. The appointment prompted intense speculation about Liu's "princeling" background and his ties to party elders and to Hu Jintao. One account attributed his promotion to his parents' ties to Bo Yibo, a revolutionary elder and father of the now disgraced former Chongqing party secretary, Bo Xilai.

Overseas Chinese media reports generally credited Hu for Liu's promotion. Liu served as the chief of the Inner Mongolia branch of the

Youth League between 1982 and 1985 when Hu was head of the Youth League. Liu became director of the Publicity Department and a member of the Politburo in 2002.

Liu's tertiary education consists only of a bachelor's degree from the Central Party School earned by distance learning between 1989 and 1992. There has been little public information about Liu's family. His son, Liu Lefei, became chief executive of Citic Private Equity Funds Management in December 2008. The junior Liu previously served as the chief investment officer at insurer China Life, overseeing nearly one trillion yuan in assets. He is among the many offspring of senior officials who have struck gold in businesses with strong government ties.

Peking University's Jiao said the biggest challenge lay in the fact people like Liu Yunshan no longer took pride in what they did. "All they have been doing in propaganda work has been centred on maintaining stability to serve their self-interest," he said. "The longer they stay in power, the more their families will benefit."

*   *   *

Wang Qishan

by *Cary Huang*

Wang Qishan, elevated to the Politburo Standing Committee at the 18th party congress, would need all his legendary qualities of problem solving, crisis management and troubleshooting in order to succeed as the new leader of the crackdown on corruption, analysts said.

Wang, who built up a reputation as the point man for China's economic integration

Wang Qishan

with the global economy, was once seen as Li Keqiang's closest rival in the race to become the next premier. Li won that race but, as widely expected at the 18th party congress, Wang joined the seven-man Standing Committee and in addition took up the highly challenging mission to lead China's top discipline watchdog.

"Ethics of the party determine its survival or demise," Wang told a symposium just two weeks after he became secretary of the party's Central Commission for Discipline Inspection. Soon after the party congress closed, new party chief Xi Jinping himself stressed the vital nature of the anti-corruption drive, telling a Politburo study session: "A great deal of facts tell us that the worse corruption becomes, the only outcome will be the end of the party and the end of the state."

Analysts described Wang as an apt choice for the anti-corruption campaign, noting that he knew how financing works, having run the China Construction Bank. However, swiftly changing hats following the party congress and demonstrating his versatility, Wang flew to Washington, to attend the 23rd session of the China–US Joint Commission on Commerce and Trade.

Analysts said that whatever role he played, Wang brought decades of experience in economics and banking and a long record of success-ful troubleshooting. Symbolism can matter a great deal Chinese poli-tics, and Wang's similarities to his political mentor, former premier Zhu Rongji, helped boost his popularity among party officials and ordinary citizens. With similar personalities, working styles and political careers, Wang and Zhu, a respected reformist, even shared many nicknames, including "fire-brigade captain".

Both have been described as straight-talking, dynamic and decisive, rare traits in Chinese officialdom, where talking the talk while doing nothing is the safest path to promotion.

Since his elevation to the Politburo at the 17th party congress in 2007 and his promotion to vice-premier in March 2008, Wang played a crucial role in steering China's economy through the global financial crisis in 2008 and the ongoing European sovereign-debt crisis. Talking about a way out of the global financial crisis, Wang spoke of the need for two hands: not just Adam Smith's invisible hand of the marketplace, but also the hand of government. In negotiations with foreign leaders, he stressed the need for government support.

Since the emergence of the crisis, Wang strengthened his influence among government economic agencies and played a significant role in spearheading macroeconomic policies. "Wang emulates Zhu's style, and this symbolism has boosted his popularity within and outside the establishment," said a senior banking official who worked under Wang.

Wang was born in 1948 in the coastal city of Qingdao, Shandong province, where his father worked as an urban-planning engineer. During the turmoil of the Cultural Revolution, Wang, like many young people and intellectuals, was sent to the countryside. He lived in the impoverished county of Yanan, Shaanxi province, from 1969 to 1971. Wang, who studied history at Northwest University in Xian, Shaanxi's capital, worked at a provincial museum before going to Beijing in 1979. There he studied at the Chinese Academy of Social Sciences, the government's leading think tank, where he began research on rural economic reform. That led to his first job in finance: working for a rural trust-and-investment company.

While he is generally considered a reformist official, he is also a "princeling" — the son of a former leader and hence well-connected. Wang's father was party chief of Shanxi province and his father-in-law, Yao Yilin, was a vice premier.

As well as earning a reputation as a troubleshooter, ready to come to the rescue in any emergency, Wang proved his technocratic mettle in key positions in regional governments and central government agencies. However, he owed his rise primarily to Zhu, who promoted him to be deputy governor of the central bank from 1993 to 1994, when Zhu was its governor. Zhu later made Wang head of the China Construction Bank from 1996 to 1997.

Zhu also gave Wang the task of dealing with the financial mess in Guangdong province in the late 1990s. As provincial vice-governor from 1998 to 2000, he oversaw the cleaning up of the troubled trust sector following the 1998 collapse of Guangdong International Trust and Investment and the restructuring of Guangdong Investment, the two government investment arms.

Zhu later called on Wang to head the central government's Economic Restructuring Office. Then, in a brief stint as Hainan's provincial party chief, Wang overhauled the island's economy, transforming it into an all-season holiday destination after years of being plagued by rampant property speculation and widespread corruption.

He was parachuted into Beijing during the 2003 SARS scare to clean up the city's image after mayor Meng Xuenong was sacked for covering up the crisis. He ordered daily public updates and status reports, helping China regain international credibility after months of government reticence and obfuscation. "He didn't want to hear the sweet music. He was ready to do some straight talking," said Dr Hendrik Bekedam, the World Health Organisation's representative in China at the time. He said Wang gave WHO officials unprecedented access to data about the disease.

As mayor of Beijing, Wang took aim at over-the-top billboards for expensive housing projects, and told Beijingers to stop bad habits such as spitting, shouting and pushing, in time for the 2008 Olympics. He was one of three executive presidents of the Beijing Organising Committee for the Olympic Games.

A Guangdong official said Wang had impressed those who had worked with him and even those who had met him only briefly, irrespective of whether they liked him or not. Wang also boasts good ties in the West, which could serve him in good stead if, as expected, he takes on responsibility for high-level economic talks with Washington and Brussels.

He developed relations with some of the world's most important financial and banking leaders over the years, including former US treasury secretary Henry Paulson, who called Wang a friend. "He's a man of enormous capabilities," Paulson said. "He understands markets, he understands people. He knows how to communicate. I don't speak Chinese, he doesn't speak English, but he's very easy for me to communicate with."

Professor Kerry Brown, of the China Studies Centre at the University of Sydney, said: "[Wang] has been the face of China to the US, and therefore to much of the world, through heading the strategic economic dialogue. He's shown in his dealings over a difficult time with the US that he can be pragmatic but hard edged."

Harley Seyedin, president of the American Chamber of Commerce in South China, who identified Wang as a rising star in a 1994 newspaper commentary, said Wang had proved his "ability to produce optimal outcomes" in various positions over the past two decades. "I am supremely confident he will help build a future characterised by sustainable economic growth, increased integration with the global economy and a continuation of the opening up that has been a cornerstone of China's success for the past 30 years."

Perhaps he is the man to break new ground, as his mentor did more than a decade previously. He does not appear to be afraid of the challenge, once telling *The Wall Street Journal*: "Frankly speaking, we are heading on a path never tried before."

*   *   *

Zhang Gaoli

by *Teddy Ng*

Former Tianjin party chief Zhang Gaoli has usually preferred to work away from the spotlight, but analysts predicted that could change after his elevation to the all-powerful Politburo Standing Committee. He was also named one of four vice-premiers as part of the new government led by President Xi Jinping and Premier Li Keqiang.

His preference to remain low key was tested in September 2012 when Tianjin hosted the World Economic Forum, which

Zhang Gaoli

saw global business leaders and domestic officials flock to the northern port city.

While Zhang had rarely made public comments about his personal views and was largely known for his economic policies, in the months leading up to the 18th party congress there were signs he was throwing off his old image, being seen as more eager to engage with the public and the media.

In February 2012 he participated in a discussion with internet users, saying authorities should respond to the suggestions the public put forward. At a press conference held on the sidelines of the National People's Congress in March 2012, Zhang was relatively garrulous in response to questions about his governing style.

"We need to produce tangible results and let the public benefit," Zhang said. "You are performing only when the public says you are doing well." Compare that to a press conference in 2011 when he referred most answers to Tianjin Mayor Huang Xingguo.

Zhang's change in his public approach led to suggestions he was overhauling his personal image to better gain the public's trust ahead of the leadership reshuffle. Although Zhang remained tight-lipped about his future political career, in the months before the 18th party congress he rejected outright the possibility of becoming a member of the elite Standing Committee. "Anything about the 18th party congress is just speculation," he said in March 2012.

"I am a poor kid. My responsibility is to remain faithful to my job, working honestly for the public and serving the people wholeheartedly." When Chiang Pin-kung, chairman of the Straits Exchange Foundation, jokingly said in May 2012 he hoped Zhang could visit Taiwan before being "promoted", Zhang replied: "I hope I can step back from the front line."

Political observers said Zhang stood a good chance of promotion not simply because of his policy achievements but also due to his close ties with former leaders such as Jiang Zemin, who still wielded considerable behind-the-scenes influence. "Zhang keeps a low profile all the time, and there is little negative news about him," said political commentator Li Datong, former editor at the *China Youth Daily*, prior to the party congress.

Hong Kong-based political commentator Johnny Lau Yui-siu said Zhang was experienced enough for the job. "Zhang has not committed any big mistakes over the past years, and that is more important than doing significant works to further advance his political career," he said.

Zhang, born in 1946 in Fujian province, graduated from Xiamen University in 1970 and went on to work in the oil industry, the power base of former vice-president Zeng Qinghong. He started as a worker in a petroleum company in Maoming, Guangdong province, before becoming its general manager and then deputy party secretary of the city in 1984. Four years later, he was appointed deputy governor of Guangdong province. In 1998, he was made deputy party secretary of Guangdong, and party secretary of Shenzhen, before moving to Shandong province in 2001.

One of Zhang's significant achievements while he was in Guangdong was hosting the first China Hi-Tech Fair in Shenzhen in 1998. During his tenure in Guangdong, Zhang reportedly paid regular visits to Xi Zhongxun, the father of Xi Jinping, who has succeeded Hu Jintao as president and party chief. There was also speculation Zhang and Jiang Zemin had established close ties, as Jiang made a speech in Maoming in 2000 promoting the "Three Represents" as the guiding principle of the party. The "Three Represents" generally refer to social productive forces, cultural development and political consensus.

Zhang spent about a year in Shandong in 2001 as deputy party secretary and acting governor and was promoted to party secretary and governor a year later. In 2003, he was made chairman of the provincial People's Congress Standing Committee. While in Shandong, Zhang focused on the province's economic growth.

In 2007, Zhang was moved to Tianjin and appointed a member of the Politburo. Explaining the move, He Guoqiang, then director of the party organisation department, said Zhang had extensive experience in developing coastal areas. Shortly after Zhang's move to Tianjin, Song Pingshun, former chairman of the municipality consultative conference, committed suicide amid a graft investigation. Zhang said Song had allegedly received bribes and kept mistresses.

Zhang continued to focus on economic development in Tianjin, building the city's financial and aviation businesses. During his tenure, the supercomputer Tianhe-1 was installed in Tianjin. The GDP of Binhai New Area, located east of the city, grew to exceed that of Shanghai's Pudong district, and the municipality attracted visits by many state leaders. In April 2012, Hu said during his tour of the municipality that it should explore new development opportunities.

About six months later, Xi said at a party cadre meeting that he gave "high marks" to the development of Tianjin and "fully recognised" the achievement of local cadres. However, unlike his Chongqing counterpart Bo Xilai, who took a high-profile approach showcasing the development of Chongqing and attracted negative attention in the process, Zhang said there was no such thing as a "Tianjin model" that other cities should follow. "The development of Tianjin cannot be named as a model, and it is not appropriate to promote such a kind of model. We are just doing concrete work in accordance with the scientific development outlook," he said. The remarks were seen as an attempt to avoid Tianjin overshadowing the central authorities. And about a month after the dismissal of Bo, Zhang said party cadres should stick to the party central committee line.

Zhang faced a crisis when a fire swept through a five-storey commercial mall in Jixian county on June 30, 2012. Authorities put the death toll at 10, but some internet users estimated 300 people were killed. But analysts said the incident was unlikely to harm Zhang's political career.

CHAPTER 5

Power Behind the Curtain

Retired Chinese leaders traditionally shun public appearances and making headlines. Not so octogenarian Jiang Zemin, who stepped down from his last leadership post in 2004 but subsequently became the most active retired leader in this dynastic-style, communist-ruled nation.

by **Cary Huang and Shi Jiangtao**

The presence and role of former president Jiang Zemin were clearly apparent before and during the 18th party congress. In the shadowy power game, analysts believed that Jiang wielded considerable influence in the selection of the new generation of leaders — and in doing so he outmanoeuvred the man who succeeded him as party and state boss, Hu Jintao.

Jiang Zemin

"One thing is obvious, Jiang has played a big role and his faction seems to have dominated this process," said Liu Kang, director of US-based Duke University's China Research Center. Hu, who stood down as Communist Party secretary general at the congress, failed to install his own allies in several key positions, particularly membership of the party's innermost Politburo Standing Committee. "By and large, we can see a line-up dominated by Jiang's men," said Liu.

Johnny Lau Yui-siu, a veteran China watcher, said: "Of these seven people [appointed to the Standing Committee], it's really six versus one

because only [Premier] Li Keqiang is seen as Hu's man, coming from the Communist Youth League." The League, Hu's power base, is traditionally seen as a training ground for China's future leaders.

Most China watchers agreed the single most important factor in the selection of the Standing Committee and the wider 25-member Politburo was "patron-client ties". Cheng Li, director of research at the John Thornton China Center at the Brookings Institution in Washington, characterised the leadership as "one party, two coalitions". One coalition, the so-called Shanghai faction that included the "princeling" offspring of revolutionary leaders, was led by Jiang's protégés. The other coalition consisted primarily of former officials from the Communist Youth League and was led by Hu.

Gu Su, a political affairs analyst at Nanjing University, said: "The latest line-up of the Politburo Standing Committee means Jiang was a clear winner. I have always thought there would be at least one more man from the Communist Youth League in the Standing Committee. Li Keqiang will be fighting a very lonely battle from now on."

Analysts viewed the failure to promote party organisation head Li Yuanchao and then-Guangdong province party boss Wang Yang as signs of Hu's loss of influence. Of the 25 Politburo members, nine are from the Communist Youth League. Analysts said Hu also failed to get Hunan province party chief Zhou Qiang and his former chief of staff, Ling Jihua, promoted to the Politburo. Chen Shiju, Hu's personal aide, failed to win promotion to the 205-strong Central Committee or become one of its 171 alternate members.

Outgoing premier Wen Jiabao also appeared to have lost in the battle to promote his protégés. A glaring example was Ma Wen, who surprisingly did not retain her spot on the Central Commission for Discipline Inspection, the party's anti-graft watchdog. However, analysts said Hu's protégés were well positioned to become leading candidates for the Politburo Standing Committee in 2017 when, as Lau pointed out, five of its seven members — all Jiang allies — reach retirement age. New party general secretary Xi Jinping and Li Keqiang are the only Standing Committee members expected to be the core of the new leadership for the next 10 years.

"We can expect Hu's allies to outclass Jiang's on the Politburo Standing Committee at the 19th party congress," Lau said. Analysts also said Hu protégés Sun Zhengcai, appointed party chief in scandal-plagued Chongqing municipality, and Hu Chunhua, Guangdong province party boss, were both from the Communist Youth League. At 49, they were the youngest Politburo members and among leaders expected to reach the pinnacle of power in a decade after the 18th party congress.

Jiang, who turned 86 shortly before the party congress began, was also believed to have played a key role in Beijing's decision to bring the hammer down on disgraced Politburo member Bo Xilai, who was removed as Chongqing party chief in March 2012, stripped of his party leadership roles and then ousted from the party altogether and subjected to criminal prosecution.

Analysts said Jiang provided crucial support to breaking the months-long impasse over how harshly to punish Bo, whose downfall plunged the country into its worst political turmoil in decades. Jiang's backing helped Hu and his successor Xi — who is believed to be a Jiang protégé — to broker a critical deal on how to handle Bo, whose wife is serving a life sentence for her role in the murder of British businessman Neil Heywood in a Chongqing hotel room in 2011.

Despite differences between Hu and Xi on a wide range of personnel and policy issues, it was understood that they were in full agreement on the need to oust Bo, whose crusade against organised crime and Maoist-tinged populism struck some in Beijing as a public challenge to their leadership.

But their plan to punish Bo to the fullest extent of the law met much resistance, due to Bo's pedigree as the princeling son of a revolutionary elder and his popularity among hard-core leftists at all levels of society. Although Jiang was considered part of that same hard-line faction, he was also a supporter of Xi, whom the former president and his allies tipped to succeed Hu at the previous party congress in 2007. Jiang's move at that congress upset Hu's own succession plan which favoured Li Keqiang.

"Jiang gave his endorsement to Hu and Xi because Bo's controversial manoeuvring effectively offended Jiang and challenged the transition scheme he proposed [in 2007]," said China watcher Lau. Bo's high-profile campaigns after becoming Chongqing party secretary were seen as an attempt to demonstrate his discontent with Xi, a fellow princeling, and prove that he was the country's most capable leader, Lau said.

Professor Zhang Ming, a political analyst with Beijing-based Renmin University, also believed Jiang threw his weight behind cracking down hard on Bo. "It appears that mainland authorities wanted to protect Bo from harsh punishment when Gu stood trial in August because his name was not mentioned at all throughout the trial," Zhang said. "But things changed eventually."

Speculation that Jiang was finally set to withdraw from China's political stage came in late January 2013 at a funeral for veteran revolutionary General Yang Baibing, 92. For the first time, Xinhua news agency ranked Jiang behind Politburo Standing Committee members. Until a week earlier Jiang ranked third in state media reports.

While the latest ranking at the funeral suggested that Jiang would finally retire from politics, some analysts remained unconvinced. Beijing-based analyst Chen Ziming said: "Jiang can still exert his power, even if he has no ranking in the top leadership." China watcher Lau agreed that the ranking did not necessarily mean that Jiang would play no role in Chinese politics from then on. "On the contrary, I think that his political influence will extend for quite a while at least."

Bo Xilai
Slide from Fame to Shame

It was political drama of the highest order, even by China's standards. High-flyer Bo Xilai, once destined for the highest ranks that the Communist Party can offer, crashed spectacularly in disgrace amid lurid headlines. His hard-driving lawyer wife was subsequently convicted of murdering a British businessman, and his police chief ally was jailed after attempting to defect at a US consulate. The crisis threatened to upset the intense jockeying in the run-up to the 18th Communist Party Congress called to usher in the so-called fifth generation of leaders. *South China Morning Post* reporters distinguished themselves in providing comprehensive blow-by-blow coverage of this worst scandal to rock China in decades and its repercussions in the febrile atmosphere of Beijing's corridors of power.

by *South China Morning Post Reporters*

In his heyday Bo Xilai, a good-looking charismatic figure, easily stood out from his peers in China's upper leadership ranks, boasting pedigree credentials, a sizeable track record and media-savvy charm. But in 2012 he was successively ousted as party boss of China's most populous municipality Chongqing, stripped of his membership of the Politburo and the Central Committee, and months later deprived of his Communist Party membership as well as being told he faced

Bo Xilai

criminal prosecution. Bo was the highest-ranking party official to be sacked and investigated in more than a decade and his downfall signalled a major setback for the rising leftist forces within the party, for whom he was regarded as the poster boy.

However, in early March 2012, just days before his downfall, Bo was still basking in the media limelight, enjoying near-celebrity status during the otherwise dull and ritualistic annual session of the National People's Congress, China's legislature. The former Red Guard and Cultural Revolution prisoner, who rose to become commerce minister and Liaoning provincial governor before becoming Chongqing party boss, seemed to have almost everything he needed to match his ambition for a seat at the top leadership table. His qualifications included being the son of one of the party "immortals", Bo Yibo, and hence a member of the elite circle known as *taizidang*, or princelings.

But the younger Bo had played a high-stakes political gamble that clearly carried political risks. His much-publicised crusade against organised crime gangs in Chongqing was unsurprisingly popular among locals, who detested the city's lawlessness, and it even prompted calls for similar action elsewhere in China. But critics accused him of employing "gangster tactics" against triad gangs and of riding rough-shod over the rule of law. And many questioned the timing of the crackdown, launched shortly before a gathering of the Communist Party's top echelon — the Central Committee — saying it was Bo's calculated move to seek as much media exposure as possible amid intense political horse-trading before the crucial 18th party congress. Bo was clearly aware of such criticism. Asked if he had a personal agenda behind his crackdown, he looked annoyed and refused to give a direct response. And as writer Dai Qing, who questioned the anti-triad drive, said: "He may have snared many corrupt officials, but he has failed to eradicate the political basis for deep-rooted corruption."

Bo also campaigned vigorously in Chongqing to promote traditional communist ideology. He mobilised bureaucrats to work alongside farmers in the countryside and kicked off a campaign that sent quotations from Mao Zedong to millions of mobile phone users. A 100,000-strong rally was organised to sing revolutionary songs to celebrate the party's 90th anniversary in 2011. This flamboyant populist style ruffled feathers within the party, especially among his rivals who saw it as career-climbing, over-the-top showmanship. His promotion of the "Chongqing model" as a pattern for the rest of the country to follow was seen in similar critical light.

Indeed, his use of the populist card was rare in the context of the Communist Party's more than 90-year history. Professor Steve Tsang, director of the China Policy Institute at the University of Nottingham, said at the time: "Bo's style of politics is not the norm and is not well liked by his colleagues, who cannot and will not compete against him on Bo's chosen ground. He is among the exceptions." Professor Roderick MacFarquhar, a China specialist at Harvard University, said: "Populist politics goes against the grain of the Communist Party tradition. Besides, it could be dangerous for the regime if leading politicians rivalled each other in appealing to the public."

Professor Kerry Brown, of the University of Sydney, said charismatic politics was poisoned by the Mao years, despite the powers of Bo's personality, and "China is still recovering from the deep historic stain".

While it was believed that Bo's princeling status helped him craft his showmanship and boost his career, Bo knew too well that it could become a curse, too. When his father was purged during the Cultural Revolution, Bo, a Red Guard then, also suffered. The 17-year-old was put in jail for five years and his mother hanged herself during his incarceration. "I never denied that I have benefited from my father. Thanks to my father, I was also sent to prison when I was still a high-school student," he later recalled in a *People's Daily* article.

Privileged upbringings, career backgrounds and family connections usually put princelings in good positions to gain promotion, but their Achilles' heel is also glaring. Due to public antipathy, princelings often have difficulties gaining wide acceptance within the party, without which they are unable to garner enough support or at least neutralise opposition, according to Tsang. Brown added that the ascent of princelings seemed to have given rise to a popular perception that "the party is becoming more and more a self-interested, self-serving clique, where power is literally handed from generation to generation".

Like many other princelings, Bo spent his childhood in the capital. He was born in Shanxi province shortly before the founding of the People's Republic of China in 1949. His much-acclaimed media savvy may be attributed to his graduation in the early 1980s from the journalism department of the Postgraduate Institute of the Chinese Academy of Social Sciences, the cradle of professional journalists. But instead of becoming a journalist, he was sent to oversee a poor county in the city of Dalian, in the rustbelt province of Liaoning, in 1984 under an arrangement made by his father.

Bo did not join the party until he turned 31, a rather advanced age compared with most Communist leaders who did so in their early 20s. Bo's career began to pick up when in 1992 he was made mayor of Dalian, a booming port city, and its party secretary in 1999. He became Liaoning governor in 2001. Bo's ambition to turn Dalian into "the Hong Kong of North China" was well received by locals, which bolstered his popularity. During his time in Dalian, the city recorded phenomenal economic growth and launched a series of public infrastructure projects, including the building of China's first expressway, linking Shenyang and Dalian.

But Bo's rather swift success attracted immediate resentment from critics, many alleging nepotism. They argued that his bold decision-making, an unattractive trait widely shared among princelings, often left little room for discussion and was perceived as arrogance. Bo's grandiose face-lift scheme to revitalise the old industrial city was also labelled a vanity project for his own political future.

Although the party hopeful managed to emerge unscathed from a flurry of corruption cases involving senior provincial leaders that occurred during his reign, his image as a reformer was inevitably tainted. Bo gained notoriety over the persecution of a reporter who accused him of covering up corruption. The reporter, Jiang Weiping, was sentenced to eight years in prison in 2001 on charges of supplying state secrets and inciting subversion.

Known for his close ties with domestic and overseas media, Bo was largely spared the often negative press plaguing other princelings over corruption and abuse of their family connections. But as one of the best known princelings, Bo still paid a dear price in 1997 when he failed to enlist enough votes to gain access to the 15th party congress. He later failed to be elevated to the Central Committee that year, despite his father's lobbying, dashing his hopes for a vice-premiership the following year.

When he was appointed commerce minister in 2004, he quickly soared to international fame with shrewd negotiation skills and a charm offensive both at home and abroad. His skilful handling of numerous trade disputes with the United States and Europe won him plaudits from international media. In the same year that he became a Politburo member, he was on the move again, but this time to the country's most populous municipality, Chongqing.

After the hammer blows fell on Bo and following his ousting from the party leadership and then his removal in September 2012 from the Communist Party, it was announced that he would face criminal prosecution over bribery and other corruption charges. At the same time the date for the start of the 18th party congress, November 8, was announced, showing that the top leadership had set aside differences and put the leadership transition back on track.

Bo, by then 63, was accused of a laundry list of serious crimes and violations of party discipline including covering up for his wife, Gu Kailai, in the murder of British businessman Neil Heywood, receiving "huge" bribes and "maintaining improper sexual relationships with a number of women", Xinhua said. "Bo Xilai's actions created grave repercussions and did massive harm to the reputation of the party and state, producing an extremely malign effect at home and abroad," Xinhua said, citing a Politburo statement.

While Bo became the third Politburo member to stand trial in the previous two decades — following former Beijing party boss Chen Xitong in 1998 and Shanghai party chief Chen Liangyu in 2008 — he was expected to face a harsher sentence, according to legal and political analysts. They said that unlike Chen Liangyu, who was sentenced to 18 years' jail, and Chen Xitong, who got 16 years, Bo could even face the death penalty. "Given the ... allegation that he took huge amounts in bribes, Bo is likely to face life imprisonment or even a death sentence, although it is rare to sentence senior party leaders to death," Beijing-based lawyer Liu Xiaoyuan said.

Zhang Ming, a political analyst at Beijing-based Renmin University, said: "[Former NPC vice-chairman] Cheng Kejie was sentenced to death for receiving bribes alone, and there are other accusations facing Bo." Another lawyer, Mo Shaoping, also said Bo was likely to face capital punishment on bribery charges because China's criminal law said that it could be applied in cases involving the taking of more than 100,000 yuan in bribes.

In an unusual step to further incriminate Bo, Xinhua said: "Investigations found that Bo seriously violated party discipline while heading the city of Dalian and the Ministry of Commerce as well as serving as a member of the CPC Central Committee, Political Bureau and party chief of Chongqing."

According to sources, the official line held that Bo was ruined by his wife who was portrayed as "powerful and greedy" and took all the bribes. It said it was also Gu's idea to promote Wang Lijun to become Chongqing's police chief. Wang later fell out with Gu after Gu's murder of Heywood in November 2012. Wang then made his dramatic trip to the US consulate in Chengdu.

As the political scandal swirling around Bo, his wife and his police chief Wang subsided, a joke circulating among Beijing's elite suggested that party chief Xi Jinping, who took power at the party congress, owed much thanks to an infamous face slap that changed history. As the crisis unfolded early in 2012, Bo raised his hand to Wang after the latter confronted Bo with allegations that his wife was involved in the killing of Heywood. Subsequent developments saw Wang flee to the US consulate in Chengdu with incriminating evidence against Bo and his wife, and the scandal exploded.

Before the Bo-Wang confrontation, Bo, flag-bearer of China's leftist movement, was an odds-on favourite to join the elite Politburo Standing Committee. Just imagine if Bo had reacted differently to Wang, and if the murder scandal involving his wife didn't come to light until after the congress. Bo would most likely have been in power as a Standing Committee member.

Never has a member of the Standing Committee been sacked or arrested for a non-political reason. Many Chinese also subscribed to the conventional belief that those in the political elite were above the law. And given Bo's ambitious and ruthless nature, he would have surely been a wolf among sheep on the committee, meaning that history would likely have been on a much different course. That would have been a scary thought for Xi and the other incoming leaders. So it was no wonder that, according to a report by a quasi-official Chinese news agency based in Hong Kong, then president Hu Jintao and Xi joined hands in calling for Bo to be punished harshly.

An even scarier thought was that Chinese leaders were reportedly divided on how to deal with Bo after the scandals broke. This led to months of political uncertainty about the party's plan to install a new generation of leaders, including Xi and Premier Li Keqiang.

Some within the party reportedly sought leniency for Bo, suggesting he be disciplined internally rather than face criminal charges. But then Bo was out of the game, and the leadership trumpeted his expulsion and the prospect he would face criminal charges, calling the moves unmistakable signs of the fight against corruption and vowing "no mercy for corrupt officials, no matter who is involved or how great his or her power is".

In fact, there were deeper reasons for Bo's harsh punishment. As a charismatic leader, Bo's populist policies and open embrace of Mao Zedong's egalitarian era had won him strong support among the country's leftists, who were unhappy about official corruption and the nation's rising income gap between the rich and the poor. Harsh punishment of Bo served also to help curb his support group, particularly after waves of anti-Japan demonstrations saw some protesters holding up pictures of Mao — an action seen by many as a show of support for Bo.

China's top leaders may have thought they had gone for the jugular against Bo, but this could also backfire, as it was likely to enrage the public and embolden people to raise questions about the party's anti-corruption efforts and the extent of corruption within it. More importantly, it would lead to questions over one-party rule and result in more calls for political reform.

Indeed, if Bo was corrupt for 20 years, why was he not stopped earlier? The detailed allegations involving Bo, his wife and his police chief showed that they held little regard for the law. If Bo lived above the law, what about the party chiefs of other provinces and municipalities, and those leaders in the central government? The more that Chinese demand answers to those questions, the more scared Chinese leaders should feel.

Diary of a Downfall

2007
November: Bo Xilai is appointed Communist Party chief of Chongqing municipality after 15 years as an official in Liaoning province.

2008
June: Wang Lijun, Bo's close ally, is made director of public security in Chongqing.
July: The Chongqing municipal government begins its "red culture" movement, releasing a list of communist revolutionary songs which it encourages locals to learn.

2009
July: A "red text messages" campaign sees Bo send out quotes from Mao Zedong's *Little Red Book* to Chongqing's 13 million mobile phone users. The city also launches its anti-mafia campaign targeting government officials and police officers suspected of working with local gangsters. High-level officials, including Wen Qiang, former director of the Chongqing Municipal Judicial Bureau, are arrested.

2011
May: Wang Lijun becomes vice-mayor of Chongqing.
November: British businessman Neil Heywood is murdered in a Chongqing hotel room.

2012
February 6: Wang takes refuge in the US consulate in Chengdu for a day in an apparent attempt to defect. On leaving the consulate, he is whisked away by government officials.
February 8: The Chongqing information office says on its weibo account that Wang is receiving "vacation-style treatment".

February 9: The Ministry of Foreign Affairs acknowledges Wang's visit to the US consulate, saying the matter is "under investigation".

March 5: A Chongqing government spokesman says Wang left the US consulate only after "earnest and patient persuasion" from three of Chongqing's top officials and a degree of central government intervention. Huang Qifan, Chongqing's mayor, says Wang is being investigated by the Ministry of State Security.

March 8: Bo is absent from the second plenary session of the National People's Congress.

March 9: Bo makes his first comments on Wang's case in a question-and-answer session on the sidelines of the NPC meeting, saying he had picked the wrong man for the job.

March 14: Premier Wen Jiabao comments on Wang in his annual news conference at the closing of the NPC session, saying Chongqing authorities should seriously reflect upon and learn from the incident, and that Beijing took the matter "very seriously".

March 15: Bo sacked as Chongqing party boss.

September 28: Bo expelled from Communist Party, Beijing announces November 8 as start of 18th party congress.

Fall of "the Jackie Kennedy of China"

The accepted behaviour for wives of China's leaders is that they should be seen rarely and heard even less. Long gone are the days when Jiang Qing, the wife of Mao Zedong, stirred up chaos within the party through her vociferous bids for power, only to end up jailed for life. In the following decades, few in China could name the wives of most leaders. That marked Gu Kailai, a high-profile lawyer, the

Gu Kailai

daughter of a revolutionary hero and the wife of fallen Chongqing party boss Bo Xilai, as a woman apart.

Gu probably dreamed of a grand and glittering destiny for herself when she married the "princeling" Bo in 1986. But the former high-flying lawyer now languishes in jail, convicted over the murder of a British businessman, Neil Heywood, 41. It was a spectacular plunge from grace for a woman who achieved notable success in her legal career and married Bo, heir apparent to membership of the Politburo Standing Committee.

The drama burst into the open in February 2012 when Wang Lijun, a former Chongqing police chief and a key Bo ally, sought refuge in the US consulate in Chengdu. Wang had angered Bo by claiming that Gu was involved in the death of Heywood, who was close to the couple's son Bo Guagua and helped him to enrol at private schools in Britain. He also allegedly helped Gu smuggle family money out of the country to invest overseas.

China's most sensational criminal trial in decades heard that Gu murdered Heywood by pouring poison into his mouth. According to Xinhua, Gu and her son at first enjoyed good relations with the British businessman but these soured as commercial conflicts arose. Heywood's body was cremated before an autopsy could be performed. Gu and fellow defendant, family aide Zhang Xiaojun, did not contest the murder charges.

The trial on August 9, 2012, lasting just six hours, attracted widespread international interest. About 200 mainland Chinese and overseas reporters flocked to the courtroom in Hefei, capital of Anhui province, even though the hearing was open only to selected state media.

"On the evening of November 13, 2011, Bogu Kailai went to Heywood when he was staying in Room 1605 at Building No. 16 of the Nanshan Lijing Holiday Hotel and drank alcoholic drinks and tea with him," Tang Yigan, vice-president of the Hefei Intermediate People's

Court, told reporters. "After Heywood became drunk, vomited and asked for a drink of water, she poured a poison into his mouth that had been prepared beforehand and that she had given to Zhang Xiaojun to bring along, causing Heywood's death."

The prosecution told the court that Gu believed Heywood posed a threat to the safety of her son after a financial dispute with the Briton and she decided to kill him. She arranged for Chongqing municipal officials and Zhang to invite Heywood to fly from Beijing to Chongqing.

Two government-appointed lawyers for Gu argued that her "ability to control [her] behaviour" was weaker than a normal person when committing the crime, and that the victim, Heywood, bore "responsibility" in the initiation of the case. They also said Gu had significantly made up for her wrongdoing by "reporting crimes committed by others" and merited consideration when the court deliberated on her sentence.

When Gu was in the dock she maintained her composure. The images from her trial shown on state-run television depicted a well-groomed woman, with a hint of a smile. Gu was given a suspended death sentence, which was widely anticipated and likely to be commuted to life imprisonment. "The verdict is just and reflects a special respect towards the law, reality and life," she said. Gu's accomplice, Zhang Xiaojun, was jailed for nine years.

There were many odd aspects surrounding the trial, predictably giving rise to rumour and speculation, including Xinhua's reference to Gu as "Bogu Kailai", a combination of her and her husband's family names. Some observers suggested that Xinhua's use of an outdated practice, which is now used only by Chinese living outside the mainland, implied she had foreign residency rights. Under party rules, senior leaders and their families are not allowed to hold foreign citizenship.

Gu's name — which shares the same character of "lai" with Bo's name — had already been a topic of discussion. In 2007, Gu told magazine *Vista* that her "lai" was a different character to Bo's "lai", adding that Bo had asked her to change it to his.

Less strange was the decision to hear the case against Gu more than 1,000 kilometres from Chongqing, which was in keeping with Beijing's preference to try senior officials far from their power base. "The practice is aimed at preventing officials from using their personal connections to tamper with legal proceedings," said Wang Yukai, a professor with the Chinese Academy of Governance.

The scandal also roped in French architect Patrick Devillers, who lived in China during the 1990s and was once married to a Chinese woman. Devillers was believed to have been a friend of the couple at one point, and had business dealings with them. Some reports said he had an intimate personal relationship with Gu and that he shared an address with her between 2000 and 2003.

Devillers, living in Cambodia, was arrested in Phnom Penh in June 2012 at the request of Chinese authorities who wanted to question him about Gu and Bo's financial dealings. After several weeks of negotiations between Cambodia, China and France, Devillers boarded a plane for Shanghai to take part in the investigation.

Like her husband, Gu came from a revolutionary family. She was the youngest daughter of Gu Jingsheng, a communist veteran and the former deputy secretary of the Xinjiang party committee. After graduating from secondary school, Gu worked in a butcher's shop during the Cultural Revolution. Chinese media reported she could "slice meat with a great skill".

In 1978, and despite failing her mathematics exams, Gu enrolled at Peking University, one of the country's most prestigious institutions, where she studied law and international politics.

Bo also enrolled there some years earlier, as a student of history. But the pair first met in 1984 when she went on a research trip near Dalian, Liaoning province, where Bo had taken a post as county party secretary. "He was very much like my father, who was an extremely idealistic person," Gu told the media. She became Bo's second wife two years later and Bo Guagua was born the following year. Like his celebrity parents, Bo Guagua earned a reputation for a love of high living and preference for luxury sports cars. Gu accompanied him in 1998 on his move to Britain, where he attended a private preparatory school, and later the elite Harrow School. Bo Guagua went on to Balliol College, Oxford. He graduated from Harvard's Kennedy School of Government after his parents' detention.

When Bo became mayor of Dalian, Gu went there too, moving into a small apartment in which they lived until 1996. Gu pursued her own legal career after the marriage, running a law practice in Dalian and setting up the Kailai Law Firm in Beijing in 1995. She soon became one of China's most successful lawyers, particularly after she helped several Chinese companies in Dalian win a legal battle in the US in February 1997. A court-appointed bankruptcy trustee in Mobile, Alabama, had successfully sued the Chinese companies for US$1 million after accusing them of attempting to steal trade secrets and of defrauding an American company. Gu succeeded in having the judgment set aside.

Gu shared the experiences in a book entitled *Uphold Justice in America*, which was made into a popular television series. In it, she said the Dalian justice bureau asked her firm to take the case even though her husband was the mayor. She said in an interview with *China Reading Weekly* in 1998 that she did not charge for the case, but was simply "looking for justice".

The Wall Street Journal quoted Denver lawyer Ed Byrne — who was hired by Gu to represent the Chinese companies in the lawsuit — as saying: "I was very impressed with her. She was very sharp, and fortunately her English was very good." He said she seemed like "the Jackie Kennedy of China". This line was picked up and republished worldwide, with pictures of her looking slender and vigorous.

Before his downfall Bo told the media that his wife's law firm had closed and that she had been a stay-at-home mother for a long time. But well-substantiated reports showed the firm's operations continued as her husband ascended to greater prominence in Chongqing, a region 80 times the size of Hong Kong, which he oversaw as party secretary.

Gu was portrayed in many ways after her disgrace: as an astute but ruthless businesswoman, an unhappy wife, a terminal cancer patient. But if her book is anything to go by, Gu was an idealistic lawyer who believed in the spirit of the law and aspired to raise her country's legal standards. The book is laden with patriotic sentiment and describes the US judgment as unfair and ignorant of Chinese culture. Gu also cited the O.J. Simpson case to argue that a litigation system that allows a murderer to be let off on a technicality is "an illustration that American law is reaching its end".

Elsewhere in the book, however, she complimented the US court system on its fairness. "In China, litigation is about networking. Many clients expect lawyers to invite judges to dinner, and if lawyers don't do it, they say you are useless," Gu lamented. "Very fortunately, this practice has not spread to this southern city in the United States. Very fortunately, none of us here could see the judge when he was not in his robes."

Some were unimpressed by the book. Commentator Michael Anti said: "It's all boasting, turning a simple case in the US into a big drama," while journalist Jiang Weiping, who was jailed during Bo's tenure in Dalian, said Gu wrote the book to "wow and fool the public".

In her book, Gu wrote: "Courage is more important than wisdom." As she settled into her new life in prison, she had time to reflect on the importance of both qualities.

CHAPTER 7

Beijing's Big Reshuffle

New faces installed on the 25-member Politburo at the 18th party congress included several figures who were promptly appointed to posts likely to provide a tough challenge to their leadership and management capabilities and also serve — depending on how well they acquitted themselves — as a springboard to higher things. We profile the Politburo members, plus one high flyer whose fortunes were abruptly curtailed by scandal.

Next Generation Steps Up

Among the new arrivals on the Politburo were at least two politicians widely tipped as likely candidates for top posts when Xi Jinping's generation leaves office in 2022. They were **Hu Chunhua** and **Sun Zhengcai**, both members of the so-called sixth generation of leadership prospects.

Hu, formerly Inner Mongolia party secretary, and Sun, who had been Jilin province party chief, were, at 49, the youngest members of the new Politburo, and both were appointed to weighty posts. Hu was named to steer the economic powerhouse of Guangdong province, while Sun headed southwest to lead Chongqing municipality, which was still recovering from the crisis surrounding disgraced Politburo member Bo Xilai. Analysts said the tasks would test their mettle and provide them with valuable experience to pad their political resumes.

It is a tradition among Communist Party leaders to groom their successors across a generation. For example Hu Jintao, who stepped down as party chief at the 18th party congress, was handpicked by the late paramount leader Deng Xiaoping. This was why Hu Chunhua — dubbed

"Little Hu" because his political rise followed a similar path to that of the senior Hu — stood out among the new Politburo members. Hu Jintao would be 75 at the next party congress in 2017, holding a better chance of picking his protégés to the supreme Politburo Standing Committee than his predecessor, Jiang Zemin, who would be 92.

Dr Peng Peng, a researcher with the Guangzhou Academy of Social Sciences, said Hu Chunhua's priority in Guangdong would be avoiding economic stagnation and continuing the reform work praised by Xi Jinping when the new party chief visited the province following the party congress. However Hu's first urgent task was to step in to calm a storm that broke out at the outspoken Guangzhou newspaper *Southern Weekly*, where journalists threatened a rare strike after accusing propaganda authorities of censoring one of the newspaper's editorials. Hu's personal intervention appeared to be successful and the strike threat was withdrawn.

Speaking at a provincial party committee meeting soon after arriving in Guangzhou, Hu pledged continuity and consistency in policies. "Do not think that a new party secretary will necessarily yield new vision." He also stressed the need to continue "emptying the cage and letting the right birds in", referring to an initiative to transfer low-tech, labour-intensive and highly polluting industries out of the Pearl River Delta region.

Like Hu, Sun was considered a contender for a top leadership post in the next 10 years. Analysts said that running the huge Chongqing municipality had become an eye-catching role and a touchstone for judging the performance of potential top leaders. "It is so important. If Sun can handle the new job well, it could clear the way for a higher position in the future," said Hu Xingdou, a political commentator at the Beijing Institute of Technology.

Other appointees among the new crop of Politburo members included **Zhao Leji** who replaced Li Yuanchao as head of the party's powerful Organisation Department. Li lost his bid for a seat on the party's Politburo Standing Committee, the apex of power. But instead he became vice-president and one of the top officials to oversee Hong Kong and Macau affairs.

In another expected announcement, **Meng Jianzhu**, as well as joining the Politburo, became the country's new security czar, taking over from the former Politburo Standing Committee member Zhou Yongkang. Analysts said Zhou's replacement by newcomer Meng effectively signalled the downgrading of the party's Political and Legal Affairs Commission, which oversees China's judiciary, prosecutors and police and had become extremely powerful under Zhou.

Echoing widely held public opinion in China, analysts welcomed the leadership's move to slash the power of the party's law and order body, which had been criticised for its crackdowns on rights activists, lawyers and petitioners in the name of maintaining stability. Professor Kerry Brown, executive director of the China Studies Centre at the University of Sydney, said: "In any case, this sort of line-up is at the very least a very big rebuke to Zhou, who has truly been a disaster for 1.3 billion Chinese people."

New Politburo member **Han Zheng** succeeded Yu Zhengsheng as Shanghai's party chief. **Ma Kai**, also newly elected to the Politburo and with strong experience in managing the economy, became a vice-premier.

Other new Politburo arrivals included former Beijing mayor **Guo Jinlong**, a shrewd political survivor and widely perceived as a staunch supporter of former party chief Hu Jintao. **Liu Qibao**, who won praise for his achievements in the recovery efforts following the devastating earthquake in Sichuan province in 2008, not only won election to the Politburo, but he was put in charge of the country's publicity machine as head of the party's propaganda department.

Sun Chunlan, former head of the All-China Federation of Trade Unions and one of two women on the new Politburo, was appointed party secretary of the port city of Tianjin, succeeding new Politburo Standing Committee member Zhang Gaoli. Sun was previously party chief of Fujian and a Central Committee member.

The People's Liberation Army had two new representatives on the Politburo, namely generals **Fan Changlong** and **Xu Qiliang**. They were appointed as the two military vice-chairmen of the Central Military Commission (CMC), which is headed by Xi Jinping. Fan distinguished himself for his vigorous role in relief efforts following the earthquake in Sichuan province in 2008. Xu made his name in the air force and enjoyed close ties with former CMC chairman and party chief Jiang Zemin.

As the new post-congress appointments were made, Bo Zhiye, a China watcher at the National University of Singapore, commented that at the 18th party congress the next generation of China's leaders had taken one step forward. "They've started the so-called grooming period."

*   *   *

Profiles

Han Zheng

*by **Louise Ho***

Unlike most stars in the Chinese Communist Party's firmament, Han Zheng did not cut his teeth on a rotation through backwater postings followed by a stint at a second-tier city. He has spent his entire career in Shanghai and is part of the Shanghai clique, drawing power and possibly protection from former leader Jiang Zemin. Han Zheng was 48 when first named mayor of Shanghai in 2003, the youngest person to hold the post in 50 years.

His lack of experience in roles elsewhere in China appeared to limit his upward mobility, according to the party's own rules. But Han was allowed to sidestep that obstacle and was ushered into the Politburo at the 18th party congress and appointed Shanghai party chief, replacing Yu Zhengsheng, who ascended to the Politburo Standing Committee.

As mayor of Shanghai his tenure was punctuated by impressive successes — the city's hosting of the World Expo in 2010, its rise as the world's busiest container port that same year and the strides it made towards becoming the top renminbi trading centre by 2015.

His master's degree in economics from Shanghai's East China Normal University served him well. But there were scandals that unfolded on Han's Shanghai watch — the most notorious, perhaps, being the jailing of his predecessor Chen Liangyu. Chen was sentenced to 18 years' imprisonment for his role in a city pension fund corruption case in which up to 3 billion yuan in pension assets were diverted to improper investments.

Han started his career as a warehouse keeper, joining the Communist Party in 1979 and becoming head of the party's Youth League committee at a petrochemical factory, a position he held for three years. After being appointed party secretary of the Dazhonghua plastics factory in 1988 and party secretary of the Youth League committee in Shanghai in 1990, he gained experience in managing state-owned firms and grew familiar with Shanghai cadres.

A career highlight was attracting Hong Kong property developers to help with the renovation of several Shanghai landmarks, such as Huaihai Road and Xintiandi, when Han was party chief of Luwan district from 1992 to 1995, analysts said. "After the makeover, Huaihai Road was like little Hong Kong," said Yao Xinbao, a professor of journalism at Shanghai's Jiao Tong University. "You could see places similar to [Hong Kong's] Times Square and Central Plaza."

After his spell as chief of Luwan, Han became a member of the party's Standing Committee in Shanghai in 1997 and mayor in 2003. Yao said: "After years of running Shanghai, Han has developed a good understanding of how the party operates in the city from top to bottom." But his reputation took its share of knocks. A fire on Jiaozhou Road on November 15, 2010, which killed 58 people exposed problems with fire prevention measures in Shanghai. And when a partially built 13-storey building collapsed in a residential area in Minhang district on June 27, 2009, the spotlight centred on official corruption.

Media reports claimed that many of the property developer's shareholders worked in local government. But such incidents, and his lack of experience outside Shanghai, did not hinder Han's ambitions. He was close to officially taking up the Shanghai party chief post in 2006 when then Shanghai party chief Chen stepped down for misappropriating social security funds. Han was appointed acting party secretary on September 25, 2006. "The central government's decision to let Han Zheng become acting Shanghai party secretary shows [our] trust in Han," said senior party official He Guoqiang.

Han resumed the post of mayor in March 2007 when Xi Jinping, then the party chief of Zhejiang province, went to Shanghai. "Han didn't have enough qualifications to be head of the party in Shanghai at the time," said Johnny Lau Yui-siu, a Hong Kong-based political analyst. There was speculation Han might have been linked in some way with Chen's case. Joseph Cheng Yu-shek, who teaches Chinese politics at Hong Kong's City University, said: "The public felt Han was certainly implicated. He was able to retain his position because ... he knew Shanghai well and would be helpful in keeping up the morale of officials." There were reports Han was not punished because of his connections to former leader Jiang or then-president

Hu Jintao. Furthermore, Han worked in the Youth League committee in 1990, so he could be categorised as a member of the Youth League faction, a power base for Hu and his political allies.

But Yao, of Jiao Tong University, said it was far-fetched to conclude Han was protected by Jiang or Hu. "It was most likely that at that time, the top leaders gave him a vote of confidence in his ability to lead Shanghai during a transition period."

* * *

Li Yuanchao

by *Cary Huang*

Three decades prior to the 18th party congress, Li Yuanchao, one of Beijing's top officials in charge of Hong Kong and Macau affairs, seemed destined for a life in the classroom, not the intrigue-filled corridors of power in Beijing. Li, who was appointed vice-president at the National People's Congress meeting in March 2013, was among the first students to enter the prestigious Fudan University in Shanghai after the upheavals of the 1966–76 Cultural Revolution. The university, under the leadership of the famous "first geometer of the Orient", Su Buqing, was developing into the cradle of China's burgeoning mathematics community.

Like most students in his classes, Li seemed wholly devoted to his studies and showed little interest in politics. He had taught secondary school mathematics before entering university, and many expected him to have a long career in teaching after his studies were complete. One former classmate, Wu Zongmin, a mathematics professor at Fudan, told *Southern Metropolis Weekly*: "His only prospect in life was to learn mathematics and continue his career as a secondary school teacher after graduation."

Those who know Li said his humble, flexible and easy-going manner was already well established during that modest period of his life. Analysts believed such characteristics would serve him well in his role looking after Hong Kong and Macau affairs. Friends, classmates and colleagues described him as a reform-minded leader open to new ideas and initiatives, provided they met a careful cost-benefit analysis. That could possibly include controversial political reform proposals for China and Hong Kong.

A former subordinate of Li's said: "He is flexible in policy and thus he would adopt a more tolerant approach in regard to Hong Kong affairs as it is under the 'one country, two systems' formula. However, he is not radical. While he is bold in accepting new things, he is also cautious in trying experiments."

Li was born in 1950 in Liangshui, Jiangsu province. His father Li Gancheng was a vice-mayor of Shanghai in the 1960s, making him a member of the Communist Party elite. But that status, which made Li a "princeling", did little to protect him in Mao Zedong's purges during the Cultural Revolution. Like many of the children of revolutionaries, he was "sent down" to the country to work as a labourer.

He was among the first wave of students to enrol in universities when entrance exams resumed in the two years after Mao's death in 1976, the so-called 77th and 78th classes. Those students now make up much of the country's ruling elite. Chen Zhimin, a professor at Fudan's School of International Relations and Public Affairs, said: "The 77th and 78th students have played major roles in sowing new thinking, reforming the old system and guarding the new in the past three decades."

At university, Li established a reputation for being both accommodating and assertive. His classmate Wu recalled how Li accepted a less desirable bed near a door so that a classmate could have a better one near a window. On another occasion, Li, acting as student representative, asked Su to push back the dormitory's scheduled lights-out time to 11 pm from 10.30 pm so students could continue reading without having to go into the lobby.

Although he joined the party in 1978, Li did not seem to pay much mind to politics. Many expected him to pursue a career in academia, like large numbers of his classmates who scattered across the renowned universities of the world. "Like most students of sciences, who are usually indifferent to politics, Li showed no particular interest in controversial political issues at that time," the former colleague said.

His shift towards politics came after graduation, when Li became an assistant professor at Fudan's School of Management and agreed to serve as the school's secretary for the Communist Youth League. In 1983 an early patron of Li's, Shanghai party chief Chen Pixian, recommended the young professor to then general secretary Hu Yaobang to serve as Youth League secretary for the entire university. It was a major break. The Youth League was becoming a key power base for Hu Jintao and Li rose quickly through the ranks of what is known as the *tuanpai* or the Youth League faction of the party.

By the end of his first year as a Full-time League leader, Li had become secretary of the Shanghai League. He later moved up to the same post in Beijing, where colleagues remembered him as intelligent and personable, with a ready smile. "He is poised, but without an official air," a former colleague said. "He is cautious, but not indecisive; he is flexible, but not unprincipled; and he is pragmatic, but not without ideals." He attended Peking University and the Central Party School, earning bachelor's, master's and doctoral degrees. In 2002, he completed a five-week training programme at Harvard University's Kennedy School of Government.

Li was later appointed to top party posts in Nanjing and Jiangsu province before being promoted to the Politburo and placed in charge of the Central Committee's Organisation Department in 2007. In that powerful role, he oversaw the personnel assignments for the entire 80 million-member party.

With such a background, Li was often seen as an exemplar of the new generation of party leaders: well educated, with a good administrative track record and exposure to the outside world. Professor Steve Tsang of the University of Nottingham's China Policy Institute, said: "While all the third- and fourth-generation leaders received an education in Soviet-style planned economics, the new leaders are generally younger, better educated and, to some degree, less ideological, as many received an education increasingly influenced by Western ideas in economics, law and politics."

Because of his background and ties to Hu Jintao, many expected that Li would ascend to the Politburo's Standing Committee at the 18th party congress. That did not come to pass, if only because the Standing Committee was reduced from nine to seven members. In the reshuffle following the congress, Li was replaced as head of the party's organisation department by rising star Zhao Leji.

Political affairs analyst Chen Ziming said the vice-presidency could be seen as a consolation prize for Li following his surprise failure to secure a seat on the Politburo Standing Committee. "Li will at least have plenty of chances to meet foreign visitors in that prestigious, if powerless, position from time to time."

Analysts added that Li remained a figure to watch and young enough to be promoted after the next party congress in 2017.

*   *   *

Liu Yandong

by *Zhuang Pinghui*

The women politicians who have shaped modern China form one of world's tiniest elite clubs. Hopes that Liu Yandong would rise to become the first woman to join the all-powerful Politburo Standing Committee were dashed at the 18th party congress, but she still stands out from the dour technocrats and grim generals who traditionally make up the ruling bodies. Liu was named one of the four vice-premiers under incoming Premier Li Keqiang.

Unlike many of the central leadership's top members, Liu, one of two women members of the 25-strong Politburo, displayed an easy charm, having a knack for photo opportunities — holding hands with scientists at the South Pole or visiting athletes Yao Ming and Liu Xiang while they were injured.

When Yi Siling won the 2012 London Olympics' first gold medal in the women's 10-metre air rifle event, Liu sent a congratulatory message. She sent a congratulatory telegram almost immediately after tennis player Li Na won the French Open in 2012. She also made headlines kissing the arm of teacher Zhang Lili who lost her legs after saving children from oncoming traffic in Harbin, telling her: "You may call me big sister now."

Liu had ties to former president Hu Jintao going back to when they both served in his power base, the Communist Youth League. She rose to prominence through the influential United Front Work Department, which builds alliances with key groups and people who are not members of the Communist Party. At the 17th party congress in 2007, she was made a Politburo member, in charge of health, education, science and sports, and appointed a state councillor, one rank above other cabinet members, the following year.

Pu Xingzu, a professor at Fudan University's School of International Affairs and Public Relations, said elevating Liu to the Politburo Standing Committee would have sent a strong message that China's political sphere was evolving. "For a country that stresses equality of the sexes, having a woman state leader would be an affirmation of the saying that women hold up half the sky. Liu Yandong has always appeared very elegant and she exudes charm ... China's politics needs that gentler image.

"She has years of experience working at the central level, so that is a big advantage in allowing her to see the big picture involved with policy decisions. But at the same time, she has never been in charge of a province or municipality. That could be an obstacle to her promotion."

Liu, who was born in 1945 in Nantong in Jiangsu province, joined the party at age 19 and enrolled in Tsinghua University to study chemical engineering. She was one of the few women in the department, she told fellow politicians decades later. Her driving ambition at the time, she said, was to win a Nobel Prize. After graduating, Liu took a job working in a chemical plant in Tangshan in Hebei province. In 1972, after the dust from the Cultural Revolution had settled somewhat, she was transferred to the capital in Beijing, where she spent the ensuing decade engaged in low-level party work, but was widely considered a member showing strong promise.

In 1982, along with Hu, Liu was elected secretary of the central committee of the Youth League. Other political heavyweights, such as then vice-premier Li Keqiang and Central Committee Organisation Department head Li Yuanchao, were elected to the League the following year.

Not only is Liu one of Hu's protégés, she is also a member of the "princeling" class, being a child of party veteran Liu Ruilong, who was vice-minister of agriculture. She has strong connections with other princelings, and is known to have recommended Liu Hu, her former classmate and son of late party general secretary Hu Yaobang, as a member of the party. Jiang Shangqing, the stepfather of former president Jiang Zemin, was a neighbour of Liu's father and one of his good friends.

Serving as the head of the United Front Work Department from 2002 allowed her to forge more connections with elites drawn from across the spectrum of Chinese society. In 2007, the department recognised the presence of a rising "new social class" — composed mainly of businessmen and academics working in the private sector — pledging to unite them to consolidate the party's foundation and help bolster the nation's economic development. "The department has made at least 50 million new friends for the communist party over the past five years," said the department review, which praised Liu's leadership.

Liu also has a reputation for reaching out to people who hold views different from her own. Although party members are supposed to be atheists, Liu has made connections with religious people. During a visit to Sanqing Mountain in Jiangxi province, which is well known for its Taoist temples, she insisted on climbing a steep peak "reaching into the clouds" to visit monks and to carry financial aid to them. The monks, who had never before been visited by such a high-ranking official, said they were deeply moved.

But Liu's career was not without controversy. After a string of accidents involving crowded school buses and vans, Liu remarked that the central government could not afford school buses. The comment was widely criticised as insensitive in light of government spending on banquets and overseas trips.

In the course of her work, Liu was responsible for reaching out to key members of the community in Hong Kong, Macau, Taiwan and overseas to help exert the party's influence. Her first official visit to Hong Kong as the United Front Work Department chief in 2004 showed her changing into four stylish outfits in one day — a stark contrast to the dour image projected by most Chinese officials. Local media reported at the time that she had changed clothes for different occasions, which showed respect for Hong Kong people and demonstrated a diplomatic savvy with social etiquette.

Liu's ties with the city proved not only professional but personal. In April 2009, her only daughter gave birth to a girl in Hong Kong and Liu reportedly stopped by the city after a visit to the US. During her stay of less than a day, Liu took time out to attend a home banquet hosted by then chief executive Donald Tsang Yam-kuen and brought her daughter Yang Fan along.

Professor Steve Tsang, of the China Policy Institute at the University of Nottingham, said Liu's job had been to manage Hong Kong and make sure that nothing went wrong in Hong Kong that ended up getting the attention of the central government. "In that regard she has been very successful from Beijing's perspective."

* * *

Ma Kai

by Jane Cai

Ma Kai, who was elected to the Communist Party's Politburo at the 18th party congress, built up a rich store of experience in managing the economy over the years. So it was no surprise when he was named one of four vice-premiers to assist Premier Li Keqiang in the new government appointed in March 2013.

Ma was appointed one of five state councillors — one rank above ordinary cabinet ministers — in 2008. He was also secretary general of the State Council, dean of the Chinese Academy of Governance and head of the cabinet's west China development office. His résumé included a spell as head of the National Development and Reform Commission (NDRC).

The well-educated Ma was born in 1946 into the family of a senior military cadre in Shanghai. The family moved to Beijing when he was nine and he studied at the prestigious Beijing No. 4 Middle School, a cradle for China's elite. After graduation, he became a teacher at the school and joined the Communist Party.

As an intellectual, he was persecuted during the Cultural Revolution and forced to work as a labourer in Beijing's suburbs for two years from 1971. However, he then landed a position teaching philosophy and politics at the party's school in Beijing's Xicheng district.

In 1979, at the age of 33, he enrolled at Renmin University in Beijing, going on to earn a master's degree in economics. From 1982 to 1988, Ma took up various positions in Beijing's city government, focusing on economic affairs. In 1993, he was transferred to the State Commission for Economic Restructuring and Reform, becoming its deputy director.

Premier Zhu Rongji appointed him deputy secretary general of the State Council in 1998, where he helped the top leadership handle a wide variety of issues from economic planning to finance, agriculture, land resources, urban construction and environmental protection. Ma later told state media that the State Council job broadened his vision a great deal. In 2003 he became head of the NDRC and director of the energy leadership office. During his five years in charge of the NDRC it became one of China's most powerful government bodies, adjusting macroeconomic policy by issuing industry policies and approving big investment projects.

Tsinghua University economist Wei Jie, who studied with Ma at Renmin University, said Ma had a challenging job at the NDRC because he had to balance various interests in its more than 70 departments and divisions and find a balance between the needs of reform and development. Yuan Gangming, a researcher at the Chinese Academy of Social Sciences, said the NDRC made a "serious mistake" under Ma in

2004 when it overreacted to robust economic development and forced the closure of many steel plants, most of them privately owned.

"The NDRC's judgment that the economy was overheated was wrong," Yuan said. "Closing private steel companies was also a flawed move which discriminated against the private economy." In 2003, fixed-asset investment in the iron and steel industry surged nearly 97 per cent to 142.7 billion yuan, while the economy grew by 9.1 per cent, the most in seven years. In the first quarter of 2004, completed investment in the iron and steel sector was up 107 per cent year on year, prompting concerns about overcapacity.

In 2004, the NDRC ordered Tieben Iron and Steel to stop building a 10.6 billion yuan steel plant in Changzhou, Jiangsu province, after government officials were found to have played a role in the misappropriation of land for the project, which had been approved by the local government but was out of line with Beijing's industry policy. The NDRC later organised state-owned steel groups, including Nanjing Iron and Steel, to take over the half-finished plant. However, the plan failed to work out and the plant was auctioned to a Jiangsu steel company in 2009.

"It is a Chinese characteristic that macroeconomic policy is adjusted by the NDRC's intervention in the investment and production of industries and even companies, instead of by market," Yuan said. "This is problematic."

Ma's role, working under Premier Li Keqiang, was to oversee the development of China's finance sector. Yuan said he was not optimistic that "an official with a deep planning mark" could help achieve breakthroughs in much-needed financial reforms. China had taken initial steps towards liberalising interest rates and exchange rates, fostering the under-developed bond market and cleaning up the scandal-stricken securities sector, but more progress was keenly anticipated.

* * *

Sun Zhengcai

by *Li Jing*

Sun Zhengcai, who at 49 was one of the Politburo's two youngest members when he was admitted to the powerful body at the 18th party congress, was recognised as a powerful contender for a future top leadership post. Sun's high-flyer status was confirmed immediately after the congress when he was appointed party chief of Chongqing municipality, epicentre of the 2012 scandal that led to the ignominious downfall of flamboyant politician Bo Xilai.

Sun, born in 1963, became party secretary of Jilin province in 2009. Jilin joined "the trillionaire GDP club" in 2011 when its economic output hit 1.04 trillion yuan, a 14 per cent rise on the previous year. By comparison, the nation's average growth rate was 9.2 per cent.

The achievement was highlighted in special coverage of the province carried by the *People's Daily*, the Communist Party's mouthpiece, as part of a propaganda warm-up for the leadership transition at the 18th party congress. The province's fiscal income in 2011 was 2.5 times higher than in 2006, while the per-person disposable income of urban and rural residents increased 1.8 and 2.1 times, respectively, during the five years, the newspaper said.

In a political system where rosy economic indicators still count in evaluations of government officials' performance, such top marks could only help Sun's standing with the party elite. The newspaper's eight-page report, which included a lengthy interview with Sun on Jilin's growth strategy, was interpreted by some analysts as an endorsement by the central government. Sun told the *People's Daily* he adhered to the central government's strategy of emphasising economic restructuring and improving social welfare.

Industrial strongholds like Jilin must ensure their economic base allowed for flexibility to guard against unsustainable development, Sun said in the interview. He emphasised the importance of boosting agricultural output and eliminating the widening wealth gap between urban and rural people.

Tenure as Jilin's party boss prepared Sun for promotion to the top of the party, according to Dr Bo Zhiyue, a senior researcher at the National University of Singapore. Before Sun was put in charge of Jilin, he was party secretary of Shunyi district outside Beijing. "To govern a vast country like China, a national leader must have both local and central experience. The front runners are then recruited to the Politburo and positioned to take over from the preceding generation," Bo wrote in *East Asian Policy* in 2010.

"Most significantly, Sun is a strong candidate for the premiership after Li Keqiang," he said. Sun was appointed minister of agriculture in 2006 following a long career in the sector. According to reports, he keeps a copy of a debit note written in 1934 by the Chinese Red Army for grain borrowed from peasants. It serves as a reminder of "the farmers' contribution to the country".

Sun was born in Wulongzui in Shandong province in 1963 and obtained his bachelor's degree from Laiyang Agricultural Institute in 1984. He earned a master's degree from the Beijing Academy of Agriculture and Forestry Sciences three years later. He is said to have been a top student, who would give up holidays to remain on campus to study.

Zhao Jiuran, a classmate of Sun's at the academy, described him as a troubleshooter, extremely diligent and meticulous. "His academic training gave him the ability to identify and solve problems, no matter how complicated they might be," Zhao told *Global People*, a magazine under the *People's Daily*, in a 2009 interview.

Sun devoted time to studying English, according to Zhao, allowing him to study in Britain for one year. In his hometown, Sun is remembered as one of the hardest-working students in his high school. He was always polite, said several elderly residents of Wulongzui village, who were quoted in Chinese media. "People didn't have much money back in the 1970s," said one of his high school classmates, surnamed Qiu. "We had to bring our own basic meals to school ... and so did Sun. We used to go home together on weekends, but Sun was always the first to go back to school for studying."

At 1.8 metres in height, Sun played basketball at college, but he gave it up to spend more time studying, according to Zhao. After graduation, Sun worked at the Beijing academy for 10 years, becoming vice-president and deputy secretary. He also obtained a doctorate at the China Agriculture University in 1997. That same year, Sun was transferred to Beijing's Shunyi district as deputy director, marking the start of his political career. The suburban district is known for its agricultural sector, allowing Sun to hone his expertise. He was promoted to district party chief in February 2002 and three months later elected as a standing member of Beijing's party committee.

From there, he appeared to be fast-tracked for promotion. He was appointed general secretary of Beijing's municipal party committee in November, 2002. Four years later, he became minister of agriculture. A major test of Sun's crisis-management ability came with the nationwide scandal over melamine-adulterated milk. At least six babies died and more than 300,000 developed kidney problems in 2008 when the industrial chemical melamine was found to have been added to dairy products to fake protein content.

The Ministry of Agriculture, though not directly in charge of quality supervision, had responsibilities to ensure the overall safety of agricultural products. But it also had to protect the interests of more than two million dairy farmers, who were hard hit when dairy firms stopped buying from them. Sun's ministry, along with others, authored a series of policies to support farmers across 12 provinces. Public confidence in the dairy industry has wavered since, however.

*   *   *

Li Jianguo

by *Choi Chi-yuk*

To the surprise of many domestic analysts and foreign China watchers, Li Jianguo secured a place in the Communist Party's 25-member Politburo at the 18th party congress.

Li was a dark horse despite his seniority qualifications and long experience in the Communist Party. He became an alternate member of the Central Committee as early as 1992 and a full member at the 15th party congress five years later.

A native of Shandong province, Li studied Chinese literature at Shandong University and spent nearly three decades in nearby Tianjin municipality, the power base of party veteran Li Ruihuan. Li Jianguo was generally seen as the elder Li's protégé.

After serving as a Central Committee member and Shaanxi provincial party secretary for two terms of about 10 years, Li Jianguo was experienced enough to fight for Politburo membership as early as the party's 17th party congress in 2007. However he failed to win that coveted rank and instead became one of several vice chairmen of the National People's Congress legislature in early 2008.

Few people thought Li had any hope of playing a bigger role on China's political stage, but his tenacity finally paid off with elevation to the Politburo.

Some pundits suggested that Li Ruihuan may have played a key role in his protégé's belated advancement. "As the leader of the Tianjin gang, a second-tier political clique, Li Ruihuan still boasted enough power and influence to send Li Jianguo into the Politburo to safeguard his interests," one veteran Chinese political analyst said. "Particularly as the red-hot power struggle between key factions such as the Shanghai gang and the Communist Youth League camp may have made more room for others seeking to rally their own support."

After becoming National People's Congress vice chairman in 2008, Li Jianguo served as the legislature's point man on Hong Kong affairs, making regular visit to the Special Administrative Region. Hong Kong City University political scientist Dr James Sung Lap-kung said Li's elevation to the Politburo indicated he was likely to play an important role in cross-border affairs in the years to come.

However roughly a month after Li's promotion to the Politburo a renowned Chinese internet activist, Han Chongguang, openly accused Li of nepotism for promoting his alleged nephew, Zhang Hui, from a deputy county-level rank to a plum job as a deputy prefectural-level official within a period of eight months when Li was Shandong party secretary. The activist's challenge against Li could not be confirmed independently. Han said a senior official on the Shandong provincial party committee had told him the story on condition of anonymity, adding that he had reported the case to the party's anti-corruption watchdog.

It is extremely rare and risky for anybody to point a finger publicly at an incumbent high-ranking official over alleged wrongdoings. Political commentator James Sung said: "An old Chinese saying suggests that 'Wind does not come from an empty cave'. I am convinced that the informant's charges against Li may not be totally groundless, especially when he takes on a political heavyweight who is still in power as Li."

Sung said that, judging by the way Li's case was handled, the Central Committee leaders might have dropped the case against him since the alleged crime was not sufficiently severe, even if the charge was proved. However, Li would have to be cautious in the years head to ward off potential attacks against him.

In April 2013, as North Korea ratcheted up tensions on the Korean peninsula, *The New York Times* reported that Li Jianguo had led a small Chinese delegation to North Korea in November 2012. He carried a letter from China's new leader Xi Jinping to Pyongyang's young leader,

Kim Jong-un, urging him not to launch a ballistic missile. But to no avail. Twelve days later, Kim went ahead and did just that.

* * *

Zhao Leji

by *Choi Chi-yuk*

Zhao Leji's dedicated service in remote areas of China and his lack of factional affiliation stood him in good stead to be the Communist Party's personnel chief as well becoming a Politburo member at the 18th party congress.

So there were few surprises when his appointment to the post, as head of the party's powerful Organisation Department, was announced after the congress. And given his relative youth — he was born in 1957 — that put him in a prime position for membership of the party's Politburo Standing Committee in the next national congress in 2017.

Zhao was born into an intellectual family in Xining, the capital of northwestern Qinghai province, but his ancestral home is Xian in Shaanxi province. He spent more than three decades scaling the political ladder in Qinghai after graduating from the philosophy department at Peking University in 1980. He was among the first batch of students to graduate after the 1966–76 Cultural Revolution.

In 2000, at the age of 42, he became governor of Qinghai and the youngest provincial-level star. That early start made him one of the most senior and experienced regional leaders, but it did not help him win a Politburo seat at the party's 17th party congress in 2007. Zhao's failure to secure promotion at that congress could have been due to his lack of a committed factional affiliation. But that was not a hindrance at the 18th party congress.

Beijing-based political analyst Chen Ziming said that Zhao's relatively independent political background was in fact in his favour. "Unlike past practice, if you take a look at the recent power reshuffles among military officers and regional officials, you will see that those with weak or no associations with a particular political faction have obviously got their rewards this time," he said.

Chen said Zhao's long service in the remote, arduous and underdeveloped northwest also stood him in good stead. "Cadres with experience in backwaters such as Xinjiang, Tibet and Qinghai have been considered a strong suit for advancement since President Hu Jintao [a former Tibet party secretary] took the helm in 2002."

However, Zhao did not win much favour with journalists. In stark contrast to some of his more eloquent regional counterparts, the poker-faced Zhao remained largely silent in a group discussion on the sidelines of the meeting of the National People's Congress in March 2012. "As a so-called rising political star, Zhao's lethargy not only made the meeting boring but also spoiled his chance to show off his talents, if any, in front of domestic and foreign media," said a Hong Kong-based reporter at the session.

A Xian-based media source said Zhao's first meeting with the media as Shaanxi party secretary was also a disappointment. "When he arrived in his new capacity as Shaanxi provincial party secretary and had his debut meeting with reporters in early 2007, everybody was earnestly looking forward to his remarks," the source said. "But he failed to make his inaugural speech before their deadlines expired." He said the anti-climax stunned most of the reporters and left editors with a lot of space and airtime to fill at the last minute.

"After keeping a close eye on Zhao for more than five-and-a-half years, I dare say that he has never delivered anything remarkable and cannot, at any rate, be regarded as a liberal-minded official," the source said. But a local official in Shaanxi who declined to be named said Zhao had spared no effort in improving the livelihood of residents and advancing the Xixian

New Area development zone. He had also handled well the eviction of tens of thousands of residents of other areas in recent years.

Xixian, named after its location between the cities of Xian and Xianyang, is the country's fourth new district, following Pudong in Shanghai, Binhai in Tianjin and Liangjiang in Chongqing. It enjoys a number of development incentives for foreign and domestic investors, including relatively low taxes, good land supply and easy access to financing.

*   *   *

Guo Jinlong

by **Shi Jiangtao**

Guo Jinlong, a shrewd political survivor and former athlete, found himself literally in the eye of a storm within days of his appointment as Beijing party chief in early July 2011.

Widely perceived as a loyal henchman of then Communist Party general secretary Hu Jintao, Guo was promoted to party boss of the capital on July 3 after less than five years as the capital's mayor. His emergence as a surprise early winner of the behind-the-scenes horse trading added intrigue in the lead-up to the 2012 once-a-decade leadership transition.

But before he could savour the limelight, he was embroiled in a major crisis — and one of the toughest tests of his political career — over a deadly rainstorm. The heaviest downpour to hit the capital in almost six decades battered Beijing just 18 days after he became party secretary, flooding large swathes of the metropolis, triggering landslides on its mountainous outskirts and leaving at least 79 people dead.

Although the authorities claimed it was a natural disaster of unprecedented scale, the unusually heavy toll in a city that hosted the Olympics just four years earlier and often boasts of its modern infrastructure sparked a nationwide outcry. Breaking with form, the usually tame state-run media questioned the human errors that had exacerbated the disaster, including the authorities' failure to fix the city's outdated drainage system. Personally, Guo faced scathing criticism over his government's inept response to the rainstorm, despite an accurate weather forecast a day earlier, and the clumsy handling of its aftermath under a blanket of secrecy.

The authorities were accused of under-reporting the human cost of the deadliest disaster to hit the capital in more than 30 years after the death toll was pointedly not updated for nearly a week. Their response to the rain might have been sluggish, but the authorities were lightning fast in banning public displays of mourning, scaling down media coverage and removing online discussions from popular microblog sites. Appeals for serious soul-searching about the city's reckless expansion and inadequate infrastructure were flatly rejected.

The few daring online voices questioning Guo's leadership and scattered calls for his resignation were quickly censored. But the clampdown on public opinion backfired into a full-blown crisis. Not only was Guo's carefully crafted image as a populist shaken, but the credibility of his political patron, then party general secretary Hu Jintao, was at stake.

In a counter-assault, Guo was seen on local television working late at flood control headquarters, eating instant noodles at emergency meetings the night the disaster hit and visiting storm-struck villages in the following days. Still, public distrust remained high. Crumbling confidence in the municipal government was obvious when an official appeal for donations to help with disaster relief was met with boycotts. "We want to help, but can we trust the government this time given its lack of accountability and transparency and reports of widespread mis-use of donations and public funding?" asked one microblogger in a posting that was soon deleted.

The central government was entangled in the crisis, too, as questions emerged over where top leaders had been as the disaster unfolded and local authorities struggled to cope. State leaders kept resolutely tight-lipped about the disaster that occurred right under their noses. None stepped outside the secluded city centre leadership compounds to visit disaster-stricken suburbs.

Yet Guo appeared to escape unscathed. Analysts said his political loyalty and willingness to shoulder the bulk of the blame would not go unrewarded.

For Professor Hu Xingdou, a Beijing-based political observer, it was another case of the much-touted official accountability amounting to empty promises. "Although losing in the court of public opinion, Guo will not be affected because his loyalty to Hu has paid off. In mainland politics, loyalty is always valued over competence," he said.

Despite Guo hitting the supposedly mandatory retirement age of 65 in July 2012, his promotion extended his political life by at least five years and won him a seat on the Politburo. His elevation to the capital's top party post was also seen as a calculated move by Hu to wield influence through his allies after his retirement and to cement his legacy.

While Guo's new job will frequently put him in the international spotlight, it is not always an enviable position. But as an aficionado of the traditional Chinese board game Go, which emphasises complex strategy and great patience, this is a politician who certainly knows when to talk in clichés, which lofty promises to renew and, crucially, how to toe the party line. In a speech after his promotion to Beijing party chief, Guo said: "We are keenly aware of our difficult task and grave responsibility. We must strive to deliver satisfactory results for all the people of Beijing."

A native of Nanjing, Jiangsu province, Guo graduated from the University of Nanjing in 1969, majoring in physics. He was then sent to a mountain town in the heart of the Yangtze River Three Gorges during the height of the 1966–76 Cultural Revolution, and spent the next 16 years rising through the party ranks. He started as a technician with an electricity bureau in Zhong county, then part of Sichuan province and now under the administration of Chongqing. Guo, who used to play volleyball for his alma mater, was also chosen to become the county's first coach of the sport in 1973.

While little information is available about the four years he served as volleyball coach, several Chinese media outlets cited this period as a proof of his athleticism, rarely seen among Chinese bureaucrats. Then in 1983 major promotion called. Guo was appointed Zhong county chief. Former county party chief Huang Dengyin later recalled Guo as a "well-educated and capable" cadre who was good at resolving disputes among officials and departments, the *Southern People Weekly* reported. He left Zhong county in 1985 and became party chief of Leshan, Sichuan, in 1990.

In 1993, a year after he was elected to the provincial party committee in Sichuan, Guo was transferred to Tibet as deputy party secretary. He became the autonomous region's party boss seven years later. It is believed that his unusually long 11-year stint in the restive Himalayan region and his performance there were Guo's calling card with Hu — he had spent four years as Tibet party secretary between 1988 and 1992.

But unlike Hu, and most other Han Chinese cadres who advocated a hardline approach on such issues as religious freedom for Tibetans and worship of the Dalai Lama, Guo was known as being more pragmatic, shifting his focus from political sticks to economic carrots. It was under his watch that Tibet began to see massive inflows of state subsidies, including the building of the Qinghai–Tibet rail link, which started in 2001, and a growing financial reliance on Beijing under the central government's economic integration policies.

The improvements in material prosperity were far from enough to win the hearts and minds of Tibetans, but Guo's time as the region's top official between 2000 and 2004 was viewed as relatively calm in comparison with those of his predecessors and successors, including Hu, which were marred by conflicts and riots.

At the end of 2004, he was appointed party secretary of Anhui, Hu's home province, before moving on to the capital in November 2007, first as an acting mayor. Two months later he formally took over from Wang Qishan as Beijing stepped up final preparations for the Olympics. The move, again orchestrated by Hu, was later described by many as stealing the fruits of the Olympic preparations from Wang, who had run Beijing since 2003 and was later elevated to vice-premier.

* * *

Hu Chunhua

by Teddy Ng

Hu Chunhua raised the eyebrows of many political observers with how quickly he rose from a staff position with the Communist Youth League in Tibet to become party chief of Inner Mongolia. His further ascent to the Politburo came after surviving two major scandals that would have cost many top politicians their jobs.

Appointed party chief of Guangdong province following the 18th party congress, Hu had to act rapidly to deal with a crisis not of his own making: a rare and inflammatory confrontation pitting workers at the outspoken *Southern Weekly* newspaper against propaganda authorities accused of interfering in editorial operations. Following Hu's personal intervention, newspaper workers ended their strike, and protest demonstrations outside the newspaper's offices in Guangzhou faded away.

Born in 1963, Hu shares a similar background with former president Hu Jintao, earning him the nickname of "Little Hu". The two spent long stints in Tibet and had a shared base in the Youth League.

The older Hu was Tibet's party chief from 1988 to 1992, while Hu Chunhua worked in the region on and off for nearly 20 years after 1983, becoming its first deputy party secretary in 2006. The mutual rapport was so strong that the older Hu was reported to have manoeuvred to promote his star protégé into the party's top decision-making body, the Politburo Standing Committee. However, other senior party figures opposed the idea.

Upon graduating from prestigious Peking University with a degree in Chinese language in 1983, Hu decided against remaining in the capital. He turned down job offers in Beijing and chose to work in Tibet. "The areas where minority people reside are the places where we can develop our skills to the fullest," he said at a meeting at the Great Hall of the People in 1983 before leaving for Tibet. "China is a country of many ethnic groups. The modernisation of the Han nationality does not equal the modernisation of all ethnic groups, neither does it mean that the whole of China is modernised."

Hu began his career as a cadre in the organisation department of the regional Youth League, and then rose to deputy secretary in 1987 at 24, making him the youngest deputy director in the country. He returned to Beijing in 1997 to serve in the secretariat of the Youth League and as a vice chairman of the All-China Youth Federation. In 2001, Hu left again for Tibet for five years, taking up the post of deputy party secretary and executive vice-chairman and head of the region's party school.

His time in Tibet earned him praise by state media, which often described him as a person who could "eat bitterness". State media reports said Hu played a significant role in developing the Tibetan economy, curbing the separatist movement and developing infrastructure.

The "bitterness" cited by state media was in reference to Hu's tough work ethic. He rarely took vacations to visit his home in Hubei province. Even when he did in 1991, his holiday was cut short because of an emergency. State media celebrated Hu's ability to speak Tibetan fluently and mingle with the Tibetan populations with ease. Hu's tenure in the region appears to have earned him the attention of the older Hu.

"His experience with ethnic minorities has really helped the younger Hu further advance his career. Having work experience in ethnic-minority regions is still considered special among mainland politicians," said political commentator Zhang Lifan.

In 2006, Hu was appointed head of the national Youth League. He was 43 at the time, making him one of the youngest senior officials at the ministerial level. Two years later, Hu was made governor of Hebei, the youngest provincial governor in the country.

Hu built up a reputation for working around the clock, visiting Hebei's 11 prefecture-level cities within a few months. His crisis-management abilities were tested when a milk scandal erupted in 2008. At least six infants died and 300,000 victims were left ill because of widespread melamine contamination in baby milk formula. The chemical was added to make the products' protein content appear higher than it actually was.

Hu's political career survived, with public anger directed mostly at dairy-product firms and government departments. "Hu was not targeted. The manufacturers bore most of the responsibility, and Hu managed to stay clear of the whole saga. It is probably because he has built good protection for himself, and he is shielded by the Youth League faction or someone from higher up," Zhang said.

About one year after the scandal, Hu was transferred to Inner Mongolia, where he was made the regional people's congress chairman in January 2010. Hu said the region would no longer strive to be ranked first in gross domestic product growth, but would instead focus on sustainable development, amid concerns rapid growth widened the wealth gap between rich and poor. Tensions between Han people and Mongolians simmered, with some of the latter complaining they had not benefited equally from the economic boom.

In May 2011, Mongolian students protested following the hit-and-run killing of a herder by a Han truck driver. It was the first major protest reported in the region in more than 20 years. Hu was untarnished by the incident and launched a policy of appeasement combined with force, making a visit to Xilinhot where the herder was killed and tightening security across the region. "Please be assured, teachers and students, the suspects will be punished severely," he said.

Zhang said: "Hu handled the protests in a moderate manner, and demonstrated he can properly manage crises." Despite the successes, Hu maintained a low profile. An article by Xinhua in 2006 described Hu as unknown to most people. He seldom made public appearances to advance his political agenda. He answered only four of 20 questions posed to him in a press conference held on the sidelines of the National People's Congress in March 2012, refusing to comment on his personal ambitions or whether he had an account with the Weibo microblog site.

However, following the dismissal of rising star Bo Xilai as Chongqing party chief in 2012, Hu immediately toed the party line and showed his loyalty to Hu Jintao by stressing that party members should be resolute in following the decisions of the party authorities.

* * *

Li Zhanshu
by Choi Chi-yuk

Li Zhanshu became probably the most powerful chief of staff to a Communist Party leader since China embarked on its policy of reform and opening up to the world in 1978.

Li assumed the post of director of the General Office of the party's Central Committee in September 2012 before becoming a member of its Politburo, and one of the seven secretaries of the Central Committee's Secretariat, at the 18th party congress. Li got the job after the promising political career of his predecessor, Ling Jihua, was derailed after a scandal over a crash of a Ferrari that killed his son, who was driving, and injured two female passengers.

Although the major task for the General Office is to deal with affairs with the Central Committee on a daily basis, its chief, with no exception, has to be deeply trusted and heavily relied upon by his immediate boss, the party's general secretary. Li was the first General Office director to concurrently hold such a senior political status within the party since Wang Dongxing, a loyal protégé of Mao Zedong. None of Li's predecessors in the General Office enjoyed such a party status as high as Li's Politburo membership, although a number of them became prominent political figures after heading the influential department.

Li should have had ideal political prospects for further promotion if his relatively advanced age was not against him. Aside from leapfrogging from being an alternate member of the Central Committee to a full member of the Politburo, rarely seen in recent years, Li was also exceptional for being the only director of the General Office who was older than his boss, the party head. Li is three years older than Xi Jinping.

In 1983, Li served as the magistrate of Wuji county in his home province of Hebei at the age of 33 while Xi was in charge of nearby Zhengding county. It was generally believed that Li and Xi stayed in touch over the years even thought their career paths varied hugely. Still, some suggested it was Xi who handpicked Li as his right-hand man when he was about to take the reins of the party. Meanwhile, Li should also be acceptable to former party chief Hu Jintao as Li worked as the Communist Youth League's Hebei provincial secretary between 1986 and 1990. The Youth League was a power base of Hu.

However, a Beijing-based source close to Xi's family said Li had kept good relations with Xi's family for decades, and that Jia Qinglin, the former chairman of the Chinese People's Political Consultative Conference advisory body, had given Li a push before he landed his crucial position. "When most people at home and abroad are convinced that Li is either Xi's or Hu's man, they seldom realise that it is Jia who recommended Li to Xi for the post at the party's General Office at the very beginning," said the source.

In 2011, Jia paid a visit to impoverished backwaters in mountainous Guizhou province and lavishly praised the remarkable economic and social development under the leadership of Li, who had become provincial party secretary in August 2010.

With Jia being a close ally of former party chief Jiang Zemin, the head of the so-called Shanghai Gang, Li could be regarded as the ultimate personification of the balance of power and compromise among three of the party's main cliques — "the princelings" faction headed by Xi, Hu's *tuanpai* camp and Jiang's Shanghai Gang.

Apart from his extensive political connections, Li amassed plenty of regional management experience by serving as a top official in four provinces over two decades. Li was appointed a vice-ministerial-level standing member of the Hebei provincial party committee in 1993 before being transferred to become a standing member of Shaanxi's provincial party committee five years later.

He was promoted to deputy party secretary of Shaanxi in 2002, serving as party head of its capital Xian at the same time, before being named deputy party chief of the northeastern province of Heilongjiang the following year. Li became Heilongjiang's governor in 2008, before being promoted to become Guizhou province party secretary in 2010.

On the eve of his rise to becoming a key official in Guizhou, Li called on leading figures in the province to be honest and upright before making these qualities their overriding priority in performing their duties. Li also on occasion highlighted the importance of serving the people, a call that harks back to the days of Mao Zedong.

* * *

Liu Qibao

by Zhuang Pinghui

Just six months into his job as party chief of western Sichuan province, Liu Qibao had to co-ordinate recovery from one of the country's most devastating natural disasters in 60 years — the magnitude-8 earthquake in 2008 that killed more than 86,000 people.

Liu can boast of his achievements in the recovery effort: reconstruction work was completed in 2011 — a year earlier than expected — and Sichuan's annual economic output has doubled. Liu's successes in Sichuan had analysts tipping him as a rising star, and he was duly promoted to the Politburo at the 18th party congress and put in charge of the country's publicity machine as head of the party's propaganda department.

He was well-experienced for the latter role having spent seven years in charge of propaganda for various agencies and served as deputy chief editor of the party mouthpiece the *People's Daily*.

Professor Ding Lin, a political scientist at Sichuan Agricultural University, said Liu was the most skilful writer among the crop of provincial party secretaries. "He writes a lot in the *Economic Daily* and

Seeking Truth," he said. "His words are simple but very insightful and show a profound grasp of theory."

The media-savvy Liu is also one of the few party officials to use new media to reach out to people. He once told his subordinates to prepare for the changes brought about by the internet and ordered government agencies to respond to internet users' comments on a regular basis.

Liu was born in 1953 and graduated from Anhui Normal University in 1974 with a history degree. He obtained a master's degree in economics in 1993. His first job was in the theory study office of the propaganda department of Anhui's provincial party committee. He later became a secretary in the provincial party committee's general office, working for reformist party secretary Wan Li.

Wan, whose liberal yet practical attitude was believed to have had an influence on Liu, pushed through a contract responsibility system that allowed farmers to divide communal land and work it individually. They were allowed to sell surplus produce independently and the practice later spread across the country.

In 1980, Liu was put in charge of propaganda at the Anhui committee of the Communist Youth League, and three years later, aged just 30, he became the committee's secretary. In 1985, he was promoted to secretary of the Youth League's central committee working alongside current Premier Li Keqiang before joining the *People's Daily* as deputy chief editor for a year in August 1993. He then spent six years as the State Council's deputy secretary-general. Liu has said his 13 years in the Youth League boosted his career. "Working in the Youth League ... made us understand the common people better," he said.

Liu's political career took an important turn in 2000 when he was appointed deputy party secretary of Guangxi Autonomous Region. When he became the region's party chief six years later, he promoted co-operation with Taiwan, Hong Kong, Macau and

Southeast Asian nations in a bid to boost the backwater's economy. He also worked on improving government efficiency and the urban environment.

At the end of 2007 when then Sichuan party secretary Du Qinglin was made head of the party's United Front Work Department, Liu was named his successor. Unlike most newly appointed party secretaries who typically take at least half a year to come up with a development blueprint, Liu produced one for Sichuan within a month, said Yi Peng, a researcher with the National Development and Reform Commission. It focused on building up the province's industrial capacity and modernising agricultural production.

The massive quake that rocked Sichuan on May 12, 2008, gave Liu the chance to shine, Yi said. "The earthquake brought enormous pain to Sichuan, but as the wound healed, the economic ... rebound has been quite extraordinary," he said. The quake made Sichuan an early benefactor of what became known as China's 4 trillion yuan stimulus package — a response to the global financial crisis. In 2010, just two years after the disaster, the province's economic output surpassed that of Shanghai, ranking eighth in China.

*   *   *

Meng Jianzhu

by *Minnie Chan and Cary Huang*

Meng Jianzhu, appointed as expected to succeed iron-fisted Zhou Yongkang as China's new security czar at the 18th party congress, lost little time in making his mark in his elevated post, making headlines around the world in January 2013 by announcing that the notorious Mao Zedong-era labour camp system would be halted, a step long demanded by reformists.

Meng earned sufficient political capital to replace Zhou as secretary of the party's powerful Central Politics and Legal Affairs Committee through his actions to reinforce security ahead of the 2008 Beijing Olympic Games and celebrations of the 60th anniversary of the People's Republic, according to Professor Mao Shoulong of Renmin University's school of public administration and policy.

Less expected was the move to halt the *laojiao* forced labour system which was established in the 1950s to contain "class enemies" but which evolved into a convenient means of silencing government critics, drawing international condemnation. The extensive system developed into some 350 camps where about 160,000 inmates toiled in prison factories and on farms for up to three years without trial.

But this development was just the first step. Meng also said the government would proceed with reform in three other key areas during the year: the petitions system; the use of judicial power; and the *hukou* household registration system. Analysts said Meng's announcements represented a litmus test of new leader Xi Jinping's oft-repeated commitment to transparency and the rule of law.

Meng also criticised excessive interference by officials in court proceedings — a practice so rampant that judges frequently received notes, usually passed by members of lower-level politics and legal affairs committees, telling them how to rule.

Meng was born in Suzhou, Jiangsu province, in July 1947. In 1968, as a 21-year-old rusticated youth during the Cultural Revolution's Down to the Countryside Movement, Meng joined the Qianwei Collective Farm on Changxing Island in Shanghai and began his climb up the political ladder.

He spent 16 years on the island farm, set up as the municipality's main food production base in 1958, and became a party member after working there for three years. In the first decade he worked as a seaman, dispatcher, secretary of the farm's Youth League branch and publicity head of the local party branch's political department, before becoming the farm's deputy party head in 1977, at the age of 30.

A rising star in 1984, he was sent to the municipality's party school for two years of management training. After completing the course, he became party head of Shanghai's Chuansha county. In the early 1990s he became one of two Shanghai deputy mayors in charge of rural work and was appointed the municipality's deputy party head in 1996.

Professor Zhu Lijia, from the Chinese Academy of Governance where Meng studied in 1993, said he was "honest, studious and hardworking", adding: "He is a rare respectable minister in today's ministerial leadership."

Zhu became a close friend of Meng while he was studying at the academy and said that as a vice-mayor he never put on airs when dealing with scholars and subordinates. "He is also a workaholic," Zhu said. "I know he's slept just four to six hours a day since he was very young."

Zhu added that Meng was a scholarly leader, keen on discussing political opinions with academics, but had never lost touch with the grass roots because of his agricultural background. He said he once called Meng, urging Shanghai to offer aid to herdsmen on the Hulunbuir grasslands in Inner Mongolia. Meng personally led a team from Shanghai's Bright Dairy to the grasslands and it ended up establishing a production base there.

In 2001, Meng left Shanghai and became party chief of the southeastern province of Jiangxi, a post he held for six years. The party magazine *Xiaokang Fortnightly* said he inspected all 99 cities and counties in the province in his first three years there and talked to grassroots farmers to learn about their struggles. The magazine said, however, that the usually amiable Meng adopted a tough approach to official misconduct while in Jiangxi, punishing many officials who neglected their duties.

He also encouraged local officials in the traditionally conservative province to be more innovative, inviting them to attend speeches by open-minded senior officials from other provinces, as well as by heads of multinational companies and other specialists.

He helped the province to double its economic output during his first three years in Jiangxi, the *China Economic Times* reported, and was a popular leader, with one song featuring the line: "If Jiangxi wants to acquire wealth, let's keep Meng Jianzhu."

Meng kept a low public profile in Shanghai, shying away from the media, but that stance changed in Jiangxi, where he often gave interviews. He was transferred to Beijing to head the Ministry of Public Security in 2007, replacing Zhou, who became a member of the Politburo Standing Committee that year.

In May 2012, overseas media said Zhou had been forced to hand over operational control of China's security apparatus to Meng after being asked to confess his errors in front of party leaders following the ousting of disgraced Chongqing party boss Bo Xilai.

Zhou was criticised for his heavy-handed tactics in overseeing the judiciary and public security, and Renmin University's Professor Mao said Meng was likely to adopt a different style. "Some leaders who oversee security and legal affairs want to turn our police and legal agencies into political tools, but others want to see them become more professional," Mao said. "I think Meng will adjust some things Zhou leaves behind and he might concentrate on the internationalisation and professionalisation of China's police and legal systems."

But Mao added: "Meng still needs to stick to the party's basic line. Some reforms he might introduce would just be aimed at preventing senior police officers from following the fates of [former Chongqing deputy police chief] Wen Qiang, Wang Lijun and other Chongqing police officers."

Wen was executed in 2010 for corruption uncovered in an anti-triad crackdown spearheaded by Wang, Bo's right-hand man and former police chief. But Wang fell out with Bo and went to the US consulate in Chengdu with evidence against Bo and Bo's wife Gu Kailai, triggering a huge political scandal. He was jailed for 15 years.

Mao said the downfall of Wen and Wang had damaged the morale of China's police officers, and Meng might seek to restore it and also retain talent by improving the promotion system.

* * *

Sun Chunlan

by Zhuang Pinghui

Sun Chunlan, former head of the All-China Federation of Trade Unions, and one of two women in the new Politburo, was promptly appointed after the 18th party congress to be party secretary of the port city of Tianjin. She succeeded new Politburo Standing Committee member Zhang Gaoli.

Starting out as an ordinary worker in a clock factory in Anshan, Liaoning, in 1969, Sun spent the following 40 years in the northeastern province, working in its women's federation and trade union and rising all the way to deputy party chief of the province.

She was appointed party secretary of Fujian in 2009 after four years as deputy chairwoman of the All-China Federation of Trade Unions. Hu Xingdou, a political analyst at the Beijing Institute of Technology, said Sun, the second highest-ranked woman in the party hierarchy behind Vice-Premier Liu Yandong, should be well suited to her new role given her trade union background and experience in overseeing two provinces, Fujian and Liaoning.

"Although Tianjin is a place of great importance, it's smaller and easier to oversee in terms of population and size," he said. "Besides that, she should be a clear-minded person who will not wallow in the mire with others, considering the history between her and Bo Xilai."

Sun was reportedly a long-time foe of Bo, the disgraced former Chongqing party boss. After taking over from Bo as party chief of Dalian in 2001 when Bo was appointed governor of Liaoning, she removed nearly all Bo's trusted subordinates in the city. Bo is also rumoured to have laughed at Sun because she used to be a worker in a clock factory.

When Sun was appointed party secretary of Fujian province in 2009 — only the third woman to hold a provincial-level party secretary position — observers hailed the decision as an affirmation that more women would receive promotions in the near future.

Local officials and academics said Sun proved herself more than qualified for the job thanks to her extensive connections, solid knowledge about Taiwanese enterprises investing in Fujian and rich background in commerce that brought investment opportunities to the province. "She is very well connected and on good terms with enterprises and Beijing," said Lin Qing, professor of economics at Fujian Normal University. "She doesn't talk empty rhetoric and is very down-to-earth during meetings."

Another source in the provincial government said Fujian had not been developed to its full potential in the previous decades because it was geographically close to Taiwan. If war broke out with Taiwan, Fujian would turn into a battleground.

The province was heavily dependent on donations and investment from overseas Chinese with roots in Fujian, and the official said Beijing expected Sun, with her connections with state-owned enterprises, to attract more investment from such companies. "And Sun has lived up to those expectations." The official said Sun was friendly, charismatic and popular among residents.

Born in 1950, the Hebei province native began as a worker at the Anshan Clock and Watch Factory in Liaoning province in 1974 after graduating from a vocational school. After a spell in Anshan city administration in charge of textiles, Sun spent 14 years as a senior official in another textile company in Anshan. She was later appointed head of the city's women's federation, and then head of the province's women's federation and trade union.

Sun became deputy party secretary of the province in 1997 and four years later was appointed party secretary of Dalian. In 2005 Sun was moved to Beijing to become deputy chief of the All-China Federation of Trade Unions. During her time in office, Sun was recognised for advancing the work of establishing trade unions in foreign-, Hong Kong- or Taiwan-invested companies to solve disputes between employees and employers.

In 2008 Foxconn, the biggest Taiwanese-invested company in Shenzhen, established a workers' union and the next year 12 Taiwanese workers, for the first time in 30 years of Taiwan investment in the mainland, joined China's workers' union.

When Li Jianhua, then deputy of the Communist Party's organisation department, made the announcement of Sun's appointment as Fujian party secretary, he spoke highly of her. Sun's political stance was firm and she had a good command of policy theories, he said. "A visionary with rich experience in leadership and brave in exploiting frontiers, Sun has strong leadership skills and the ability to control the overall situation. She is practical and decisive and is highly capable of handling complicated and tough challenges. She is also decent and fair, sticking to principles."

Local media reported that Sun went to the cities of Xiamen and Fuzhou on the third day of taking office in Fujian, visiting Taiwanese-invested businesses in the province and charming Taiwanese businessmen.

Sun pledged that provincial GDP per capita and total fiscal income would double by 2016, with regional GDP per capita surpassing the average level of eastern China.

* * *

Wang Huning

by *Cary Huang*

At first glance, Wang Huning was the biggest loser in the government reshuffle announced at the National People's Congress legislature session in March 2013, being the only party Politburo member without a senior job in government. But the former academic remained an influential figure as director of the Central Policy Research Office, a think tank he had already headed for more than a decade.

In the previous 18 years, since he joined the office as head of its politics team, Wang helped develop many policies for former presidents Jiang Zemin and Hu Jintao. He also played a major role in crafting China's diplomatic strategy and foreign policy. Some analysts said Wang had played multiple roles, equivalent to a combination of national security adviser, White House chief speech writer and other key advisory roles in the United States.

"He will continue to play such multiple roles from behind the scenes, with his deep academic background in political science and deep understanding of US- and Western-style politics," said Jin Canrong, Wang's former classmate and associate dean of Beijing's Renmin University's school of international relations.

In domestic politics, Wang played an important role in crafting Jiang's "theory of the three represents" as well as Hu's "scientific theory of development", both of which were written into the party's constitution. Wang was seen as a trusted aide of Jiang and a member of Jiang's "Shanghai Gang" faction. But when Jiang ceded leadership to Hu, Wang managed to become a driving force behind Hu's policies as well — a miraculous political feat given the competition for power between the two leaders. Jin said Wang would help new President Xi Jinping craft major policies and write his speeches.

Wang travelled extensively with Jiang and was with Hu on nearly all his trips abroad. Immediately following the 18th party congress, he played a similar role for Xi, appearing at his side on almost all domestic trips. In the foreign affairs area, Wang was serving as top adviser to Xi and the whole leadership team, ranking above the two-tier foreign affairs establishment led by State Councillor Yang Jiechi and Foreign Minister Wang Yi.

As a specialist in international politics, Wang visited the US in the 1980s and captured what he saw in a 1991 book *America against America*.

China had not had a Politburo-level official in charge of foreign policy for a decade, meaning that following the leadership transition Wang could act in that role as the only foreign affairs expert with a seat on the party's decision-making body.

Born in Shanghai in 1956, Wang enrolled in the department of international politics at Shanghai's Fudan University in 1978. He became a professor after graduation and spent time as a visiting professor at the University of California, Berkeley, in the late 1980s. He was appointed dean of the international politics department at Fudan University in 1989.

* * *

Wang Yang

by *Mimi Lau*

Few benefited more than Wang Yang when the murder of British businessman Neil Heywood in a Chongqing hotel room late in 2011 triggered a chain of events that ultimately ended the political career of the city's party chief, Bo Xilai.

As the father of the "Chongqing model", Bo was seen as the standard bearer for a hardline brand of Communist Party leadership that focused on robust economic growth driven by state-run companies, severe crackdowns on crime and corruption, with a dose of Mao-era nostalgia.

Then, there was Wang, whose relatively liberal, high-toned approach in his job as Guangdong province party chief was dubbed the "Guangdong model". Rather than central planning, Wang stressed personal responsibility, innovation and compromise. Rather than emphasising party pride, Wang told citizens that only they could make themselves happy.

Both men — and thereby both models — were viewed as top contenders for the Politburo's Standing Committee at the 18th party congress. Their ascension to the party's uppermost echelons would set up a battle royal between the two visions for the nation's future.

Wang was believed to have the support of departing president Hu Jintao; Bo was thought to have backing from Hu's predecessor, the still influential kingmaker Jiang Zemin.

Then suddenly Bo was disgraced and gone. Wang had seemingly won the fight, without having to throw a punch. Many China watchers then saw him as one of two or three contenders competing for the last seat on the Politburo Standing Committee.

However he failed to make the cut, appearing to lose out in the intense horse trading among various factions. His chances of entering the top body were damaged, at least in part, by the downsizing of the elite body from nine members to seven, as well by Jiang's continuing influence in the choice of the final line-up.

Also working against Wang was his relatively young age. At 57, If he had been appointed to the Standing Committee, he could theoretically stay on until 2027 — an unusually long period at the height of power. In December 2012 he left the post of Guangdong party chief and was named one of four vice-premiers in the incoming government of Premier Li Keqiang.

In the run-up to the 18th party congress, Wang had launched a frenzied campaign to polish his image as a more sensitive brand of leader — promoting Cantonese culture during a trip to Beijing, for instance — while simultaneously burnishing his credentials as a true communist. He even visited the revolutionary cradle of Yanan in Shaanxi province to pay homage to the statue of Mao Zedong, a move that appeared designed to counter the concerns of some party hardliners who see him as too liberal. It was as if Wang was telling them: "It's safe to pick me."

It was a lucky coincidence for Wang that Bo's downfall coincided with an event that earned the Guangdong party boss international recognition as an advocate of reform: the rural elections in the village of Wukan.

In September 2011, villagers furious over government land grabs rose up against local leaders in the coastal Guangdong community. Rather than violently suppressing the protests, as is common practice, Wang removed the despised village officials and negotiated democratic elections. A leading activist was appointed village party boss.

After taking office in 2007, Wang led a massive crackdown on corruption resulting in several high-profile convictions, including those of Guangdong political adviser Chen Shaoji and Shenzhen mayor Xu Zongheng. The government says the campaign netted more than 10,000 wayward cadres in 2012.

Wang also oversaw a rise in government transparency, making the provincial capital of Guangzhou China's first city to publish its budget. At times, his reformist rhetoric took on an almost Western tone — he appeared to paraphrase the US Declaration of Independence at the provincial party congress in May 2012. "It is the people's right to pursue happiness and it is the responsibility of the party and government to do good for the people," Wang said. "We should eradicate the idea that happiness is a benevolent gift from the party and the government."

Interestingly, Wang's approach won praise from party organs such as the *People's Daily*, which called his Wukan fix an act of "political courage". His actions also earned him an unusual amount of attention from foreign media, academics and diplomats, who saw in him hope for a kinder, gentler form of communist rule. *Time* magazine cited the Wukan vote in its decision to rank Wang at 74th — 11 spots behind leader-in-waiting Xi Jinping — on its "100 most influential" people list. German Chancellor Angela Merkel, Australian Prime Minister Julia Gillard and Canadian Prime Minister Stephen Harper paid him visits.

A 2008 US diplomatic cable released by the anti-secrecy website WikiLeaks suggests Wang caught the eye of Washington as well. In it, Robert Goldberg, then-US consul general in Guangzhou, described Wang as "relaxed, confident and very much on top of his brief" during a meeting with top diplomats. "Sounding like someone with his eye on the prize — [that is] leadership at the national level in 2013 — Wang called on consuls general to work closely and co-operatively with his office and promised to work directly with foreign governments," he said.

But some observers cited other moves during Wang's tenure that undercut his reformist image, such as a reported crackdown on the province's relatively free media in the run-up to the 18th party congress.

In June 2012, an investigations editor resigned from the *Southern Metropolis News* after being suspended for inadvertently posting online comments deemed critical of the government. The previous month, a top official of the provincial propaganda department was installed at the helm of the Nanfang Media Group. Nanfang Media reporters said they were then on a tighter leash when it came to meeting foreigners, including diplomats and journalists.

They said more stories were being spiked, including one about a woman who leapt to her death to protest against the forced demolition of her home. The potentially embarrassing suicide happened to coincide with Wang's "happiness" speech to the party.

"Wang has always presented himself as liberal," said Cheng Yizhong, the founder and former editor of the *Southern Metropolis News* and *Beijing News*. "How did he fail to maintain the outspoken tradition of Guangdong media?"

While Wang might be one China's leading voices for reform, analysts noted that he was first and foremost a party loyalist. A look at his career shows someone who, though outspoken, has worked well within the system.

Hailing from one of the country's poorest provinces, Anhui, Wang lacked the revolutionary pedigree of the so-called "princeling" party leaders. Born in 1955, he quit school at 17 to work in a food-processing plant. He joined the Communist Party and became a teacher at a re-education camp for intellectuals.

He enrolled in the Central Party School in 1979, just as paramount leader Deng Xiaoping was launching his historic economic reforms. After graduation, he returned to Anhui to teach at a local party school and joined the Communist Youth League, soon to come under the leadership of Hu Jintao. Wang rose quickly through the ranks of government, becoming mayor of Tongling in 1989. At 38, he was appointed vice-governor of Anhui, the youngest at the time. Even then, Wang was gaining a reputation for being outspoken and was quoted at least once urging Beijing to loosen its grip on the economy.

In 1999, he got a chance to participate directly in economic planning when he was made deputy minister of the National Development and Reform Commission under Wen Jiabao, who would soon become the country's premier. Wang was made deputy secretary general of the State Council in 2003.

But Wang did not really start making waves until 2005, when he began a two-year stint as Chongqing party secretary. There, he helped put the western city of 30 million residents on the map for international investors and received praise for helping bring a high-profile stand-off over a demolition site to a tidy end.

Directives ordering the media to focus on the actions of top officials were replaced with an emphasis on common citizens, a change welcomed by reformers.

From there he moved to Guangdong, where Wang made headlines by urging the province to move heavily polluting factories away from urban centres and shift its focus towards hi-tech and service-sector jobs. He also promoted smaller government, presiding over the consolidation of dozens of departments and agencies in cities like Shenzhen and Foshan. He encouraged civic organisations to pick up the slack, removing party-supervision requirements and bans on private fundraising and hiring foreigners.

"The government should surrender the responsibilities and powers that should not belong to it to society and the market, and concentrate on doing well those things that belong to the government," Wang has said. "[We] should implement a division between government and society."

Although such actions made him stand out among his peers, analysts contended that Wang's policies were carefully crafted to fit within Hu's doctrines of "scientific development" and "social harmony". Analysts said Wang walked a fine line without crossing his mentor. "He is someone who likes to test the water and he won't challenge the central leadership if he comes across any pressure," said Dr Joseph Cheng Yu-shek, a political science professor at Hong Kong's City University. "Wang is a trusted ally of Hu and his policy programme closely follows Hu's vision. He's a reformist, certainly, but there are serious constraints."

Wang's tenure was not without its problems as the province's export-dependent economy was battered by the global financial crisis, the European debt crisis and stagnation in the United States. Guangdong's gross domestic product grew 47 per cent to 5.3 trillion yuan during Wang's first four years in office. While still impressive, it was less than half the growth that his predecessor Zhang Dejiang witnessed over a similar period. Wang argued that GDP was the wrong measure of success. His advocacy for a development model that placed more emphasis on political reform and personal well-being than economic growth was a central argument in his debate against Bo.

"Wang Yang looks and feels like he is going in the right direction, though he had been no friend of a free press," said Professor Kerry Brown, of the University of Sydney's China Studies Centre. "In the end, we have nothing solid to say whether Wang is going to be a big reformer in the social-political arena."

*   *   *

Xu Qiliang

by Choi Chi-yuk

As widely predicted, People's Liberation Army air force General Xu Qiliang became one of the two military vice-chairmen of the Central Military Commission (CMC) after the 18th party congress, thanks to his military talent and close ties with a former CMC chairman, Jiang Zemin.

Like his fellow CMC vice-chairman, General Fan Changlong, General Xu enjoyed a double promotion, having also entered the Politburo.

For many years "princelings" — the children of communist veterans — have dominated high-ranking positions in the PLA and there had long been rumours that Xu was one of them, owing his rise to being the son of late lieutenant general Xu Lefu, a former deputy political commissar of the air force. But the politically savvy Xu said he came from a peasant family and distanced himself from the princeling group following the spectacular downfall in 2012 of Chongqing party secretary Bo Xilai.

A Beijing-based military source said that Xu Qiliang was born into an ordinary family in Shandong province in 1950. He was a Jiang Zemin protégé from the 1980s, when Jiang was Shanghai mayor and then the municipality's party secretary. Xu was a senior air force officer in Shanghai at the time. Jiang still wielded huge influence in the party leadership transition, even though he retired from his last formal post as CMC chairman in September 2004.

Xu was first identified as a rising military star in 1992, when he became an alternate member of the party's Central Committee at the 14th party congress at the age of 42. Two years later, he was named air force chief of staff.

Xu then became air force commander of the northeastern Shenyang military area command in 1999 and a deputy chief of general staff five years later. He became air force chief and a member of the CMC in 2007.

In recent years Xu appeared to have had a chequered relationship with then president and CMC chairman Hu Jintao. One incident in 2011, which sparked widespread discussion at home and abroad, saw US defence secretary Robert Gates remark that Hu appeared to have been in the dark when Gates raised a question about the first test flight of China's J-20 stealth fighter that took place just hours before a meeting in Beijing.

That led to intense speculation about possible discord between the PLA's civilian leaders and their military subordinates. Antony Wong Dong, a PLA-watcher based in Macau, said: "This tiny clue has revealed a lot of hidden and underlying conflicts between Hu and Xu, even though the official Chinese media later tried to clarify that Gates had misread Hu's response."

Hu also appeared to snub a ceremony in Beijing in November 2009 to mark the 60th anniversary of the founding of the PLA air force, instead choosing to pay a visit to Malaysia and Singapore. That contrasted with his attendance at a naval review in April that year to celebrate the 60th anniversary of the founding of the PLA navy.

"Taking these two cases into account, I wonder how come Hu shows such little respect to the air force," Wong said, adding that this proved ties between Hu and Xu were strained.

Although low-profile outside the military, Xu appeared to be not averse to befriending or serving retired senior officials. During an opening ceremony at one of the biennial Zhuhai air shows, Xu bustled between former premier Li Peng and CMC vice-chairman General Guo Boxiong on the podium. He whispered to Li and Guo every now and then, even though their seats were separated by those of other dignitaries.

Xu, who joined the air force as a trainee pilot in 1966 and went on to become an outstanding aviator, had long been a keen proponent of air force modernisation. In remarks at a ceremony to mark the signing of a deal to set up a pilot training programme in September 2011, Xu said: "As we turn a new page in the new century, we need a quality air force to better safeguard national security and interests, while the general public also expects sound air power as well."

Wong said Xu was a professional military leader with the vision to advance the air force's development. He said that under Xu's leadership, the air force had made remarkable progress in research and the development of a range of jet fighters. "Xu has worked hard on the upgrading of military equipment and the quality of personnel training, aside from his insights on the need to build up a modern air force which strikes the correct offensive and defensive balance," Wong said. He added that unlike the navy, the air force was able to match up against that of Japan, with almost twice as many jet fighters as the Japanese and a closing of a gap in pilot quality thanks to improvements in training.

* * *

Fan Changlong

by *Choi Chi-yuk*

For General Fan Changlong, commander of the Jinan Military Area Command, the 18th party congress marked a double promotion: as well as entering the Politburo he became one of the two military vice-chairmen of the powerful Central Military Commission (CMC).

Prior to the congress General Fan was seen by some observers as something of a dark horse for the CMC post, partly because of his relatively advanced age — 65. However, having risen right through the ranks of the People's Liberation Army, he was more experienced than the commanders of China's six other military regions. The CMC is chaired by party chief and President Xi Jinping, while Fan's co-vice-chairman is air force commander General Xu Qiliang.

Fan, born in 1947 in Donggang, Liaoning province, joined the PLA as a rank-and-file soldier with the 16th Army Corps in the Shenyang Military Area Command in January 1969. Fellow fresh recruits spoke warmly of Fan's resolve and devotion to the army. One quoted Fan as saying: "From the moment you put pen to the recruitment form, you have actually struck a deal with the mother country and compatriots that you have surrendered the right to control and use your own life."

Fan became commander of the 16th Army Corps in 1995 and five years later became chief of staff of the Shenyang Military Area Command. He left the northeastern military region three years later, when he became an assistant to then chief of general staff General Liang Guanglie.

Fan became commander of the Jinan Military Area Command in 2004, after serving at the General Staff Headquarters in Beijing for less than a year. One of the main tasks of the Jinan Military Area Command, thanks to its ability to mobilise quickly and deploy airborne troops, was to serve as a supporting force for military or emergency missions. That ability saw Fan play a key role in the emergency relief efforts launched after a huge earthquake struck Sichuan province in 2008.

Troops from the Jinan Military Area Command who parachuted into the quake zone led the relief effort in many remote villages cut off from the outside world and running low on food and water. General Chen Bingde, chief of general staff, revealed in a memoir published in 2010 how he bypassed routine procedures and called Fan at 9.34 pm, seven hours after the quake struck, ordering two army corps from the Jinan Military Area Command to prepare immediately for a relief mission in the quake zone and "await orders to set out at any time".

More than 20,000 soldiers from Jinan military region were sent to the area, with most going to Beichuan county, one of the worst affected areas. Fan himself went to the disaster's front line, one of only a few high-ranking military officers who rushed to the scene and served as on-the-spot commanders of relief work.

Having spent three decades in the Shenyang Military Area Command, Fan was regarded as a prominent member of the so-called "northeast army" — a powerful PLA faction in the PLA. Conversely, the Lanzhou Military Area Command had long been seen as the power base of the "northwest army" faction. Pundits said that making Fan a

CMC vice-chairman instead of a general from the Lanzhou Command would strike a better balance between the different factions.

* * *

Zhang Chunxian

by *Choi Chi-yuk*

Since Zhang Chunxian took the helm in April 2010 as party boss in the vast and restive Xinjiang Autonomous Region, his government wielded a fearsome iron fist in suppressing unrest among Uygur ethnic communities, showing little hesitation in using force at the first hint of separatist violence.

"We cannot be benevolent to the terrorists," Zhang said at a news conference in 2012. "They are brutal to innocent people, including the elderly and even boys and girls." In several cases, police have simply shot dead suspects without making arrests. In this regard, Zhang's approach did not depart substantially from that of his predecessor, Wang Lequan. Wang's heavy-handed tactics spurred a massive riot in Urumqi on July 5, 2009, in which at least 197 were killed and hundreds injured. His failure to regain control after the riot ultimately led to his removal.

Zhang, however, relied on his keen understanding of public relations to soften the government's image and avoid the sort of problems that plagued Wang. During Wang's rocky 16-year tenure, journalists' calls to publicity officers were routinely ignored when violence broke out. In contrast, Zhang's publicity chief made himself seemingly available around the clock to answer all kinds of queries from both domestic and foreign media.

Zhang also bolstered his image as a forward-looking leader by showing a greater interest in China's influential social media scene than many of his peers, putting out daily updates on his official Tencent microblog account. "He is someone who is eager and capable of doing something big," said Professor Wen Yuankai, a respected Chinese economist who has kept a close eye on Xinjiang's development.

For years, Zhang's news conferences on the sidelines of the National People's Congress were one of the most popular events among journalists covering the otherwise highly scripted legislative affair. In contrast to his fellow provincial party bosses — or just about anyone in the party leadership, for that matter — Zhang was known to host free-wheeling press events in which he encouraged reporters to ask any questions they liked.

It probably did not hurt Zhang's accessible image that he married Li Xiuping, one of the most popular evening news anchors on Chinese state broadcaster CCTV. Dubbed the "face of the country", Li met Zhang, then transport minister and a rising political star, in Beijing in 2004, and married him the following year. It was the second marriage for both. "Some say Li ... has helped him a lot in this respect," said Chen Ziming, an independent political analyst based in Beijing. "But I do think that the open-minded and media-savvy image can be largely attributed to Zhang himself."

When assessing Zhang's capacity for higher office, analysts noted that he had been a member of the party's Central Committee since 2002 and as Xinjiang party secretary he had what was widely regarded as one of the country's toughest and most important jobs. In addition, few potential candidates had résumés as substantial as Zhang's, who served three terms in provincial-level leadership posts involving vastly different portfolios.

Born in 1953 in Yuzhou, Henan province, Zhang spent five years in the People's Liberation Army and holds a master's degree in management from Harbin Institute of Technology. He rose to prominence in the Ministry of Transport, being appointed deputy minister in 1998 and minister in 2002.

In 2005, he was made party boss of Hunan province. There, he established a reputation for showing concern about the poor and gained notoriety for remarks that suggested he favoured faster political reform. In particular, Zhang raised eyebrows with a televised speech in August 2008 in which he appeared to advocate more democracy while expounding on then president Hu Jintao's plan to build on the two phases of "thought liberation" begun by late paramount leader Deng Xiaoping.

While the first two rounds aimed at raising prosperity, Zhang said, there would be a third stage focusing on democratic development and fine tuning the market economy. Beijing-based analyst Chen said Zhang's speech seemed bolder than any given by the Guangdong province party secretary Wang Yang, who was widely seen as the leading voice for the party's liberal wing. "Zhang appears to be a reform-minded official," Chen said.

In Xinjiang, Zhang was credited with reducing the province's seemingly endless demands for money and support from Beijing and for kick-starting its long-lagging economic development. "The situation has totally changed since Zhang took the top job," said Professor Wen, who cited, among other changes, Zhang's efforts to encourage public share offerings by local companies.

But while Xinjiang's economy showed signs of improvement under Zhang, ethnic tensions continued to plague the region, where the predominately Muslim Uygur community makes up about 45 per cent of the population.

In July 2011, a group of Uygurs armed with knives, axes and home-made petrol bombs stormed a police station in the region's southern city of Hotan, killing four, including an armed policeman. Police killed 14 of the attackers during a half-hour stand-off. In December that year, police in a remote mountainous area near Hotan shot dead seven Uygur men whom they said were en route to a jihadi training centre. In 2012, just days ahead of the anniversary of the July 5, 2009 riot, police arrested six Uygurs whom they accused of plotting to hijack an Urumqi-bound airliner in the region's southwestern city of Kashgar.

Some Uygurs and human-rights groups blamed the incidents on suppressive religious policies enacted by the Han-dominated government, such as banning some traditional Islamic dress and preventing Uygurs under the age of 18 from praying in mosques. But Zhang's government said the continued threat of violence prevented it from relaxing such religious restrictions.

Similarly, it said that taking a hard line against episodes of violence remained the best way to ensure that fewer incidents occurred in future. Professor Wen argued that Zhang was left little choice but to follow the path he had chosen because the central government made social stability its overriding priority.

*   *   *

Ling Jihua

by Keith Zhai

> *Rated a favourite to join the Politburo, Ling Jihua tripped up over a scandal just months before the 18th party congress opened.*

Around midnight, an observer privileged enough to gain access to the secretive General Office of the Communist Party's Central Committee in Beijing would often find the lights on in the office recreation room.

Inside, one of the country's most powerful but least-known men would likely be engaged in something of a ritual: playing table tennis. After a long day, Ling Jihua liked to release some stress with a late-night match — and Ling had his share of stress. As chief of the General Office and then-president Hu Jintao's personal secretary, Ling oversaw many of the affairs of Beijing's highest leaders, from their paperwork and their doctor's appointments to, perhaps most importantly, their security. That is until September 1, 2012, when Ling was abruptly reshuffled to lead the party's United Front Work Department, a less powerful post, after a scandal over a crash of a Ferrari in Beijing that killed his son, who was driving, and seriously injured two female passengers. (The worst of the political crisis for Ling may have passed in March 2013 when he was named one of 23 vice-chairmen of China's top political advisory body, the Chinese People's Political Consultative Conference, albeit with the lowest number of votes, with 90 of the 2,191 delegates voting against him.)

At first, Ling's subordinates found his nightly ping-pong sessions endearing, something that humanised his demanding work ethic. That was, until they realised that he usually intended to return to his desk after match point. "Ling never gets rest," one of his subordinates said. "He always works until midnight and plays table tennis for about half an hour. In the beginning, we thought: 'That's the end of a long day'. But then he comes back to the office and works for another few hours."

Despite his powerful position, relatively little was known about the intense, driven man who sat at the right hand of the president. Although he often accompanied Hu on official trips, photographs of Ling were rarely published. But those who watched him rise from a tiny village in rural Shanxi province to a key place in the influential Communist Youth League by his early 20s would not have been surprised by his ascension to the inner reaches of power in Beijing.

Neighbours and family friends described Ling, 55 at the time of his demotion, as someone who even as a boy displayed an unusual passion for study and a determination to succeed. The fourth son of a revolutionary father, he always appeared eager to please and showed a flare for executing any task exactly as expected. A retired official remembered

Ling as an ever-smiling young cadre in his native Pinglu county. "Ling was a pleasant, dapper little man. He knew how to please the leaders and could always fulfil their needs."

Indeed, one could say it was Ling's destiny to become the president's taskmaster, the man who made sure every event and trip went exactly as expected. His given name translates roughly to "planning". Ling's father was a doctor named Linghu Ye, who joined the Communist Party while at its base of Yanan in the late 1930s. Filled with party zeal, he named each of his children after pillars of its philosophy. Ling's three brothers were named Luxian, "direction"; Zhengce, "policy", and Wancheng, "completion". His elder sister was Fangzhen, "guideline".

Linghu was also close friends with fellow Shanxi native Bo Yibo, the revolutionary father of ousted Chongqing party boss Bo Xilai. The pair were so close that, according to family friends, the elder Bo once tried to convince Linghu to let him adopt one of his children. Linghu politely declined.

Linghu divorced his first wife, a midwife with whom he had fathered a daughter, and married the woman who would become Ling's mother. In the early 1960s, he moved the family back to his hometown of Gezhao village. During the 1960s, Linghu gained a reputation in Gezhao for being a demanding father and an aloof neighbour. At some point, Linghu changed his family's name to the more common Ling, probably in an effort to appear more modest.

His father's lessons appeared to resonate with Ling. A high school classmate described the younger Ling as an especially diligent student with a natural interest in political science. "He worked so hard. I remember once looking at Ling's textbook and being surprised at the amount of highlighted text, and how many footnotes there were."

After graduating from high school in 1973, Ling served in a local printing factory and soon had more responsibilities in county government. The retired official who worked with Ling recalled the young man being so driven that he refused to turn on the heat in winter. "He told us the chill in the air kept him sober, so that he could absorb more knowledge."

By 1975, Ling had been admitted into the Communist Youth League committee for Pinglu county. Within four years, at the age of 23, Ling had secured a position in the propaganda department of the Youth League's Central Committee. It was a fateful promotion, as the Youth League would soon come under the leadership of an up-and-coming cadre named Hu Jintao. The League and its young officials would form a key base of support for the future president and general secretary.

The first clue that Ling was destined for the upper echelons of power came in December 1995, when Hu — then serving as head of the Central Secretariat — tapped him to serve as his personal assistant. Officially, Ling was appointed head of the General Office's research office, which prepared reports and speeches for members of the all-powerful Standing Committee. Hu kept Ling close. Hu, like many party officials of his generation, is an avid table-tennis player and Ling was reportedly one of his favourite partners.

In 1999, after Hu's ascension to vice-president, he took Ling with him to lead his office. Later that year, Ling was appointed to be the youngest deputy chief of the General Office, the powerful agency that he led until his demotion.

Back in Ling's hometown of Gezhao, some complained that Ling had forgotten about them since becoming powerful. One of the villagers interviewed said Ling returned only once after his appointment to lead the General Office. However, the retired county official said the village's native son would always be welcome. To make his point, he pointed out a modern highway being built over what for generations had been a dirt road. "This is dedicated to Ling. If he wants to return home with honour after becoming a member of the Politburo, he is always welcome."

CHAPTER 8

Jangling Global Nerves

As the 18th party congress convened, China's military development was generating more international heat and controversy than at any time in recent years, with fears mounting over China's increased assertiveness and the growing strength and reach of the People's Liberation Army (PLA). This chapter assesses the PLA's strengths and frailties and reviews how new leader Xi Jinping smoothly asserted his authority over the military. We also dig behind the misleading headline figures for China's defence budget, and look at how a lack of trust and understanding clouds the diplomatic strategies of the big three players in East Asia — China, Japan and the United States.

Quick March — To Catch Up

by *Minnie Chan*

Beijing's growing military muscle, with rapid advances being made by the PLA in key areas in military technology and combat capabilities, has long rung alarm bells in its Asian neighbours.

But in the years leading up to the 18th party congress, the ripples of concern spread across the Pacific to the United States, which indicated it would focus more on the Asia Pacific — the so-called "Pivot to Asia", a move under which it shifted forces back to the western Pacific from the Middle East and was criticised by China.

At the time of the congress, China's territorial quarrels included a rancorous dispute with Japan over rocky islets in the East China Sea called Diaoyu in China and Senkaku in Japan. China was also sparring with nervous neighbours such as Vietnam and the Philippines over China's longstanding territorial claims in the South China Sea, potentially energy-rich and a vital trade route. Furthermore, Beijing had never dropped its threat to use force against Taiwan if that island ever sought to become independent.

In its annual training directive issued in January 2013, which could not have calmed concerns in the region, the PLA said it aimed to beef up its troops' combat readiness and prepare for actual war situations. "In 2013, the goal set for the entire army and the People's Armed Police force is to bolster their capabilities to fight and their ability to win a war … to be well-prepared for a war by subjecting the army to hard and rigorous training on an actual combat basis," the training blueprint said. The directive came in contrast to its 2012 predecessor, which placed more emphasis on joint military training and co-ordination among different PLA services. In the new statement, the phrase "fighting wars", or *dazhang*, was used as many as 10 times in the article, whereas the phrase did not appear in the 2012 directive.

Military observers agreed that the decade prior to the 18th party congress had been a golden era for PLA's modernisation, with Beijing busily harvesting the fruits of weapons research and development made possible by three decades of rapid economic growth.

Beijing had stressed the need to upgrade its military capacity since the early 1990s, with double-digit annual increases in defence spending. It speeded up the development of new weapons projects including China's first stealth fighter jet, the Jian-20, its first aircraft carrier, a carrier-killing ballistic missile, the DF-21D, and a third-generation, nuclear-armed, solid-fuel intercontinental ballistic missile, the DF-41. In February 2013, China also announced that its navy had taken delivery of a stealth frigate, designed to be harder to spot on radar.

Shortly after the close of the party congress, China announced that it had landed a jet fighter for the first time on its first operational aircraft carrier, an abandoned Soviet warship converted by the Chinese and called the Liaoning. A Pentagon report said that another carrier, this one made with Chinese components, might already be under construction and ready to sail in 2015. However, "it will take several additional years for China to achieve a minimal level of combat level for its aircraft carriers".

But China has been known to surprise the world before with its advances in aerospace technology. One shock came in January 2007 when China succeeded in shooting down a weather satellite 850 kilometres above the Earth, sparking fears that it could become engaged in a secret "star wars" battle with the United States. But back at sea level, the PLA Navy set new benchmarks for international co-operation and blue-water missions, playing a key role in the international anti-piracy effort off the coast of Somalia from late 2009.

Tai Ming Cheung, an associate professor and director of the Institute on Global Conflict and Co-operation at the University of California, said the PLA had taken advantage of 10 years of growing prosperity, continued peace and rising technological sophistication to make important progress in its defence modernisation, narrowing the gap with leading global powers and becoming more professional. "There is certainly a greater sense of pride and prestige in the PLA's progress and accomplishments from within the ranks," Cheung said. But, he added, the PLA's fighting capability still lagged that of Western forces. "[The PLA] still can't operate jointly, it lacks combat experience, its defence modernisation has been concentrated in limited pockets, and personnel quality is still mixed. So rather than giving the PLA a gold for achievement, its performance was a silver or bronze."

Antony Wong Dong, president of the International Military Association in Macau, said China's achievements in military modernisation could be attributed to the efforts of China's former leaders. Hu Jintao and Wen Jiabao, the immediate predecessors of President Xi Jinping and Premier Li Keqiang, were the lucky ones who reaped the rewards.

"Hu and Wen's contributions were that they did not interfere in the PLA's modernisation in their era because they do not understand military affairs," Wong said. He added that Hu, as chairman of the powerful Central Military Commission, had been only a "so-so" military chief because many of the top leaders in the PLA were promoted by his predecessor, Jiang Zemin, which meant he was living under Jiang's shadow.

Some military experts warned that Hu and Wen's failure to introduce political reforms to counter corruption and unfairness in both the military and civilian sectors could lead China into a new period of crisis. Ni Lexiong, director of a defence policy research centre at Shanghai University of Political Science and Law, said a modern army should be built on the base of a modernised country, but Beijing had to spend more than 700 billion yuan in 2012 on maintaining social stability. That was nearly 5 per cent more than the country's defence budget.

Spending on internal security — "building a harmonious society" — had exceeded the defence budget since 2009, much of it directed at cracking down on mass protests and preventing individuals from petitioning higher levels of government.

Ni warned that papering over those cracks could weaken the army's fighting ability. "The army is an important part of our society," Ni said. "Everything that happens in our community will have an impact on their morale. PLA soldiers enjoy high salaries, the best equipment and other benefits in the army ... but it is a fact that their parents, brothers, sisters and friends are not living well because of the expanding gap between rich and poor and other social problems in our country, which Hu and Wen have failed to solve."

Wong said the PLA's modernisation stood at odds with its poor transparency and conservative image. "The PLA's current transparency is much lower than in the 1980s," Wong said, saying the exact number of army personnel was a secret. "In 1982, the State Statistics Bureau announced that the PLA had 4,238,210 servicemen. Now, even the number of troops in the Hong Kong garrison is unclear."

Cheung said China's reluctance to increase transparency in the military had hindered efforts to build international confidence and trust. "The paucity of detailed information about China's defence budget is at the centre of international concerns, as is the limited amount of detailed information contained in its defence white paper. The PLA is making steady efforts to improve its transparency with press conferences, the establishment of a defence ministry spokesman's office and a willingness to disclose more defence-related information online ... but the push for defence transparency should come from domestic sources, through popular demand via the media and the political system, and not be driven by foreign requests."

Ni, citing the examples of China's disastrous Beiyang Fleet and the New Army in the late Qing dynasty (1644–1911), warned that a powerful army risked being annihilated by outside forces or becoming a tool to trigger a civil war if it was not part of a society that underwent social and political reform.

In 1888, the Qing dynasty ordered 12 warships from Germany and Britain to establish Asia's finest navy — the Beiyang Fleet — which was sunk by the Japanese during the 1894–95 Sino-Japanese War. The New Army was a modern military force, trained along Western lines, that was raised during the Qing government's military modernisation project in 1907. But this powerful force mutinied and played a key role in the 1911 Revolution that ended more than 2,000 years of imperial rule in China.

"The key reasons for the defeat of the Beiyang Fleet and the uprising of the New Army was not their weakness — they were well-funded and powerful — but ignorance of the need for political and social modernisation. I hope the new leadership will carefully learn the historical lesson of the Qing government about the need to introduce comprehensive social and political reform, otherwise it will be a disaster for the Communist Party," Ni said.

* * *

Xi Stamps Authority on PLA with Ease

by *Minnie Chan*

New party chief Xi Jinping surprised many with how quickly he established his authority over the People's Liberation Army.

Just one week after taking over as chairman of the party's Central Military Commission — a post some believed departing president Hu Jintao might attempt to keep for two more years — Xi Jinping demonstrated his grip on power by appointing his first PLA general. In a Xinhua photo of the ceremony to install Wei Fenghe as commander of the country's strategic missile force, Xi looked confident, wearing a relaxed smile and a ceremonial suit. He was the only civilian among the 11 members.

Analysts credited Xi's ability to quickly settle into the position to his diverse background, including military service and his status as the "princeling" son of a revolutionary leader. Such experiences made him better prepared than predecessors Hu or Jiang Zemin, who both struggled to solidify their control. "Xi will likely be a stronger military leader than his predecessors because of his political capital, as well as his character and personality," said Lin Chong-pin, a former deputy defence minister of Taiwan.

Having a strong commander-in-chief was of growing importance to China as it entered a new era of increased territorial disputes with its neighbours and their anxiety over the country's rise in military power. Xi's biggest challenge might be recovering amicable relations in the Asia-Pacific region, a task that was arguably easier for his predecessors such as Mao Zedong and Deng Xiaoping, who were in power when the country was still recovering from decades of war and internal turmoil.

"Xi is facing the most knotty military-diplomatic problem that his predecessors Mao, Deng, Jiang and Hu never had to face," said Antony Wong Dong, president of the International Military Association in Macau. "But today, the PLA is trying to narrow its gap with Western countries, especially the US."

The drive to modernise the PLA became a subject of increased scrutiny in the region as China took increasingly assertive steps to enforce territorial claims. "China's assertiveness when dealing with territory disputes in the South and East China seas is telling the world that the world's biggest army is not merely a defensive army, but proceeding in an aggressive way now," Wong said.

At the age of 59, Xi was the youngest leader to take command of the country's 2.3 million troops since Mao's chosen successor, Hua Guofeng, took the helm in 1976. Hua was 56 at the time. Xi not only served in the PLA, but had an opportunity to see military diplomacy up close. When he was a 27-year-old junior officer, Xi accompanied then defence minister Geng Biao on a trip to the Pentagon, which included a visit to a US aircraft carrier. He later spent 17 years in Fujian province, where, due to its close proximity to Taiwan, he would have frequently encountered the delicate issues of cross-strait relations. "Indeed, Xi is a rare top Beijing leader, one who has military-diplomatic experience," Lin said.

The ease with which he appeared to take to the job might also stem from personal experiences outside the military. He is the second son of the late vice-premier Xi Zhongxun, who was purged during the Cultural Revolution and was later close to reformist leaders Hu Yaobang and Zhao Ziyang. "I think Xi inherited some of his father's beliefs, although he probably has been very careful and more skilful because he knew the political risks," Lin said. "But that does not mean he does not have beliefs."

Moreover, Xi is the first modern leader whose ascension was not hampered by some form of overt factionalism. Neither Hu nor Jiang enjoyed such support at the beginning. Jiang had to wait more than four months for Deng Xiaoping to give him control of the CMC after becoming party chief following the Tiananmen crackdown on pro-democracy protestors in 1989. Similarly, Jiang remained CMC chairman for two years after handing the party chief's post to Hu in 2002.

Xi needed that political support if he was going to move ahead with efforts to weed out corruption and institute reform in the military. His speech after the 18th party congress showed his determination to do so, said Xu Guangyu, of the China Arms Control and Disarmament Association in Beijing. "Xi's anti-corruption campaign will not face any obstacles because he is the top leader of our party, which the army should absolutely obey, according to the PLA's core principle. Xi's early military experience in both army and local government will help him to make smart political decisions, with tackling corruption being the most efficient way to win public support and save our party's regime," Xu said.

* * *

Behind the Budget Smokescreen

by *Tom Holland*

The numbers that China issues for the amount it spends on its armed forces are routinely believed not to tell the full story about its military expenditure. The defence budget for 2013 was no exception.

China said it would jack up defence spending by 10.7 per cent in 2013 to 720 billion yuan. And with tensions in both the East China Sea and South China Sea running high, another double-digit increase in Beijing's military budget was bound to make China's neighbours nervous. Yet although the increase sounded like a big jump, by itself the headline figure was pretty meaningless.

On the surface, it looked as if Beijing's increase in defence spending outpaced even the growth of China's gross domestic product, which the government targeted at 7.5 per cent for 2013. But the GDP target was real growth, which adjusted for inflation, while the defence increase was nominal, which did not. Factor in inflation at the government's target rate of 3.5 per cent, and the increase in China's military spending fell into line with GDP growth.

That was unlikely to reassure China's neighbours, who could legitimately point out that Beijing's military expenditure was already the second-highest in the world, after the United States. What's more, there were widespread suspicions that the official defence budget deeply understated Beijing's actual spending on China's armed forces. For example, the cost of arms imports — largely high-technology weaponry from Russia — did not show up in the defence budget, while analysts said that China's own weapons research and development was funded by a separate budget under the Ministry of Science and Technology.

In addition, it was unclear how much of China's defence costs — financing local garrisons for example — was carried by provincial governments on their own budgets. Attempting to factor in this hidden spending, the London-based International Institute for Strategic Studies estimated in 2012 that China's true defence budget could be some 40 per cent bigger than the official figure.

Even then, however, China's defence spending did not look excessive. Assuming the institute's estimate was accurate, Beijing's total military spending in 2013 would still be less than 2 per cent of GDP, little changed in relative terms over the previous 10 years. That was also relatively modest in international terms. It was roughly what Australia spent, and far less than the US defence budget, although twice as much as Japan's military expenditure.

Again, however, it was Beijing's absolute spending, rather than its spending relative to GDP, that concerned China's neighbours. Here as well the 2013 headline figure of 720 billion yuan was uninformative. In US dollar terms, 720 billion yuan equalled US$116 billion, which was small compared to the Pentagon's US$614 billion budget.

But the two figures could not be compared. Although the prices of standardised commodities can be assessed using market exchange rates, armaments are not freely traded and prices vary widely from country to country. Spend US$1 billion on a radar system, and you get a lot more for your money in China than in the US.

That means we have to adjust national defence budgets for differences in local purchasing power. Unfortunately, there are no reliable price indices for military spending. But if we use the economy-wide purchasing power parity, or PPP, exchange rates calculated by the International Monetary Fund, the value of China's 2013 defence budget jumped by almost 50 per cent. Factor in Beijing's hidden expenditure, and the real value of China's defence budget climbed to double the announced headline figure.

Even then, however, it still amounted to less than 40 per cent of the US military's budget for that year.

*   *   *

Chinese Maritime Plan "a Threat"

by *Julian Ryall*

China's decision to place all its maritime law enforcement agencies under unified control was likely to dramatically enhance Beijing's naval capabilities and pose a significant threat to Japanese interests, analysts in Japan said.

Beijing announced at the National People's Congress meeting in March 2013 that it intended to bring up to 17 organisations — the largest being the Public Security Ministry's coastguard operations, the Agriculture Ministry's fisheries patrols and the anti-smuggling operations of the General Administration of Customs — under one umbrella led by the National Oceanic Administration. The restructuring was in part a response to territorial tensions with neighbouring states Japan, Vietnam and the Philippines.

"This will give the new organisation greater authority and co-ordination capabilities at a higher level in the Chinese government, while at a functional level it will give these naval assets more partnerships in exercises, for example, when it comes to disputed territories," Masayuki Masuda, a China analyst at the National Institute of Defence Studies, said. With a unified command structure, the new entity would be able to co-ordinate its maritime forces and "pose a very serious challenge" to Japanese forces in waters close to the disputed Senkaku archipelago, which China calls the Diaoyus, he said.

"This suggests that China feels uncomfortable with the Senkaku situation and that they are aware they need to step up their patrols in the region to show Chinese sovereignty over the islands," Masuda said. "China wants complete control of the situation and this poses the danger of an unexpected escalation of one of the territorial disputes, with Japan or any of the other nations."

Go Ito, a professor of international relations at Tokyo's Meiji University, agreed that Beijing's proposal was "very significant for its impact on Japan's efforts to protect its maritime interests". Ito said physical ownership of the islands was not China's priority because the barren and inhospitable isles offered little to its residents. More important, he believed, was the ability to use sovereignty over the territory to extend China's exclusive economic zone (EEZ) farther away from its shoreline and to simultaneously limit other countries' access to the waters of the East China Sea.

"China's concept of an EEZ is different to how other states understand the concept and how the United Nations recognises such territory," he said. "Beijing is also making intentional obstacles to the freedom of navigation of ships in the South China Sea. In order for China to protect its interests and claim these zones are under its control, it needs to strengthen the coercive capabilities of its maritime forces, so this proposal is very important."

Enhancing naval capabilities to claim territory was being done in tandem with other measures, Ito said, such as the introduction of the Spratly and Paracel islands on maps of Chinese territory printed in Chinese passports. And while China officially claimed that the addition to its nationals' travel documents was merely a declaration of its hope that one day the islands might be recognised as Chinese territory, Ito expected the argument to come full circle in "a few decades" when Beijing could claim that because the islands had been on Chinese passports for many years, they must be Chinese territory.

"Strengthening its naval forces is very important for China, but at the same time it severely damages Japan's interests. The size of Japan's maritime territory is larger than that of China at present, but Beijing expanding the areas that it claims — this is truly a case of 'gunboat diplomacy' — will inevitably bring the two nations into further confrontation."

*   *   *

Could the Unthinkable Happen Again?

by *Chow Chung-yan*

> *As tensions between China and Japan rise, it would be perilous to ignore the terrible lessons of history.*

The world watched in bewilderment as two of its largest economies inched ever closer to war. It was all the more puzzling given that the countries had become close trading partners and the arguments between them seemed trivial. Their economies were so interdependent that any confrontation — let alone a full-scale war — would surely bring ruin to all.

The scene described is Europe 100 years ago. It may be an exaggeration to compare the 21st century's Sino-Japanese tension to Europe on the eve of the first world war, yet there is a danger of history being repeated. Bitter nationalistic rivalries in Europe — including between France and Germany — helped light the fuse that sparked the first world war, one of the greatest catastrophes in history. Viewed from today's perspective, the tragedy appears unavoidable and for many Europeans of the time, the conflict seemed unthinkable. But the unthinkable could happen again if the lessons of history are ignored. Listening to retired generals and government advisers at the third Sino-US Colloquium in Hong Kong held shortly after the 18th party congress, it was hard to shake off a sense of déjà vu.

Xiang Lanxin, of the Graduate Institute of International Studies in Geneva, said the root of the problem, as it was 100 years ago, was the lack of trust and understanding between the major players. The three key players in East Asia — China, Japan and the US — are all undergoing tremendous transformation at home and are introspective in their thinking. None of them has formulated a clear diplomatic strategy that others can trust and understand — even though to their leaders, their plan seems to be clear and focused. "The problem here is the difficulty of reading others' minds," Xiang said. Without a clear understanding of others' strategic intentions, any move can be interpreted in the wrong way.

China, praised by British historian Professor Paul Kennedy 20 years ago for having the most coherent and forward-looking plan among major powers, seems to have lost its clear purpose. For more than a decade, Beijing faithfully followed the famous *taoguang yanghui* principle set down by late paramount leader Deng Xiaoping. An imperfect translation of the phrase is "to keep a low profile and nurture your strength".

The main thrust of the concept is that China needs a long period of peace to develop and time is on its side. If China can modernise its economy, the external problems will melt away. The best move is not to take any unnecessary initiatives. With some patience, the sheer momentum that this growth creates will bring to China what reckless adventures cannot achieve.

Many argue that this position has, however, become increasingly difficult to maintain. In many ways, China is a victim of its own success. Its economy has surpassed Japan as the second-largest economy and is projected to overtake the US soon. Lying low is almost impossible.

While *taoguang yanghui* has never officially been ditched, Beijing is starting to seek a replacement. Under departed president Hu Jintao, China temporarily toyed with the idea of "the peaceful rise of China". The emphasis on "peaceful" was an attempt to persuade the world — particularly the dominant power, the United States — that China did not seek to revise the status quo as it grew stronger. But the term was deemed problematic from the start. "It is a most misleading and ideology-motivated concept. It suggests that this is something new, which is historically incorrect," Xiang said, pointing out that the country had always been the world's leading economy, at least until the 1820s.

China's new leadership, under Xi Jinping, prefers the catchphrase "national restoration", Xiang says. It implies that Beijing does not seek a new world order — it just wants to revert to the millennia-old tradition. That tradition, however, is vague and hard to define. Before the arrival of Western powers, China exercised undisputed sway over East Asia. Its "foreign policy" was non-interventionist by nature, focusing on a subtle influence and prestige over acquiring territorial gains. It exercised authority through an elaborate system of tributes.

While that is clearly impossible in modern times, many still believe China's tradition of benign power projection is the answer to defining the country's new role. Observers note China's more assertive stance towards rival claims in the South China Sea, and in the East China Sea with Japan over the Diaoyu/Senkaku islands, but Beijing stresses it did not make the first move in these disputes. Chinese leaders still prefer to delay territorial settlements, but they have to act tough when the country's prestige is at stake. A large part of the reason for this is the need to keep internal pressures under control. Beijing's primary concern for the future is still its domestic situation, Xiang said.

"As the world is talking about a China threat, the Chinese government is talking about internal revolution. The leadership today is reading
[French Revolution scholar Alexis de] Tocqueville, while countries
like Japan worry about China's intention to take over their territories,"
Xiang said.

"This is absurd. The Chinese leaders realise the condition in China
today is more like pre-revolutionary France in 1789 [rather than
Germany in 1913]. There is a dangerous trend of [the party] resorting
to nationalistic sentiment to consolidate its position. This is like riding
a tiger — it's easy to get on its back but hard to get down."

Chinese leaders, in their own way, have gone to painstaking lengths
not to appear assertive to their neighbours. They have gone as far as to
refrain from using the phrase "great power" in official text or speech for
fear that it may lead others to see China as developing hegemony.
Instead, they use the phrase *xinxing daguo*. "They hesitate even in how
to translate it. Sometimes they use the term 'big country' — referring to
the physical size, which is absurd," Xiang said.

With Beijing struggling even to find the right word to describe its
strategy, it's no wonder that its neighbours have misgivings and difficulty working out China's true intentions. In comparison, the American
outlook seems much clearer. In 2010, President Barack Obama
announced that the US was to return to Asia-Pacific, pivoting away
from other parts of the world towards East Asia. He pledged to be the
first "Pacific president" of the US. The pivot calls for a concentration of
American resources to strengthen its presence in the region on all
fronts — economic, diplomatic and security. The core of it is to
strengthen its alliances and also its military presence.

"We will not downsize our presence in the Asia-Pacific even as we
have to scale back the overall military spending," said Walter Sharp,
retired four-star general and former commander of US Forces Korea.
Sharp stressed that the US presence was the key to peace in the region
and respect for international rules.

William Fallon, retired four-star admiral and former commander of US Pacific Command, said the "pivot to Asia" was in line with America's long-term demographic and economic shift towards its Western regions. "This is not a panic reaction [to the rise of China]."

Still, to many Chinese officials and observers, America's new stand is flawed. America's alliance system in Asia-Pacific, forged during the Cold War, was built with a clear objective: to counter and contain the Soviet Union. The containment strategy, as diplomat George Kennan explained in his famous "Long Telegram" in 1947, is based on the premise that the Soviet Union did not see a chance of long-term peaceful coexistence with the capitalist world. It was an expansionist power by nature and needed to be countered. The best approach was not through direct military confrontation, but to unite the Western world and wait for the internal weakness of the Soviet system to undo itself.

Pan Zhenqiang, a retired PLA major-general, said in order to revive the old alliance system, Washington needed a new enemy. It could not be a mere rogue state like North Korea, but must be comparable to the old Soviet Union. "In our view, the US strategy is contradictory. It has left behind unanswered a critical question: what kind of role should China play in this security structure? For all the benefits to contain China, the US is also keenly aware that China has become an indispensable partner to its own prosperity and sustained security."

By not clearly spelling out the role of China in this new structure, Washington will keep Beijing guessing on its real intention and send confusing signals to countries in the region. In the long run, these confusing signals may create unnecessary tension, Pan argued.

With its revolving-door leadership, it's hard for Japan to have a consistent regional strategy. The dominant sentiment of the day is centred on regaining the status of a "normal country" within the international community and responding to China's growing influence and assertion. While the majority of Japanese believe it's time for the country to put its wartime past behind it and return to the international community as a fully-fledged member, the question for them is what kind of "normal country" should it be?

Tokyo could simply be more willing to speak out and act over its national interests, without changing its peaceful constitution or weaning off its one-dimensional reliance on the US for defence protection. A more radical approach, as advocated by the likes of former Tokyo Governor Shintaro Ishihara, is for Japan to become a fully-fledged great power, restoring its right to keep a powerful army and pursue an independent foreign policy. Japan would not only be responsible for its own defence, but would become a linchpin for East Asia's peace and security.

As Japanese themselves can't agree on the extent of the "normalcy" the country should return to, its neighbours are also divided. Some Southeast Asian countries would welcome the second scenario as they hope a more assertive Japan could counter China's influence.

For countries in East Asia — China, South Korea, North Korea and even Russia — the reaction is far more negative. While many Japanese people think they have put the past behind them and rightly point out that Japan has undergone tremendous change since the second world war and made significant contribution to the world's peace and prosperity, its neighbours are not convinced. Today's Japan may be very different from the militant Japan of 70 years ago, but the country has never really cleansed its wartime past like Germany did in Europe. "The dominant value in Japan is postmodernism, not nationalism," said Professor Soeya Yoshihide of Keio University. He said any concern that Japan might return to its militant and nationalistic tradition was far-fetched, since the country has evolved so much.

But the Chinese participants disagreed. "Unfortunately, we don't feel Japan is willing to address the issue [its wartime past] and China is not alone in this. South Korea — which is also a key US ally — also repeatedly asked Japan to reflect on its past. Nobody can accuse South Korea of acting to advance China's agenda," Pan said.

Ultimately, Beijing knows that despite Tokyo's tough posture, Japan lacks the political will and consensus required for a major showdown. At the same time as China engaged in a war of words with Prime Minister Shinzo Abe's government, Beijing invited former Japanese prime minister Yukio Hatoyama for a high-profile visit. It knows that Japan's internal friction and the lack of a unified strategy will force it back to the negotiating table.

CHAPTER 9

Reform
Easier Said Than Done

Is Xi Jinping a mould-breaking reformist? That was the million-dollar question investors and analysts asked about China's new leader when he came to power as head of the Communist Party at the 18th party congress. We examine the prospects for reform in general, and focus on specific areas of civil liberties where reformist pressure for change has been hotly debated and on the renewed battle against corruption. We also have eloquent and moving reminders of how elderly Chinese activists have spent a lifetime waiting for reform. Did they wait in vain?

Good Start but Drastic Reforms Unlikely

by *Wang Xiangwei*

According to a popular Chinese saying, "new leaders should burn three fires" to establish their authority and demonstrate they are getting off to a new start. It is a much more colourful idiom than its Western equivalent that "a new broom sweeps clean".

China's new leader Xi Jinping has certainly lit up enough "fires" to generate exciting chatter at home and abroad about himself, his new administration and the future direction of the Chinese economy since he officially took over the reins of the Communist Party on November 15, 2012. And judging from reactions at home and abroad to his early months in power, Xi got off to a good start.

Through his public speeches and meetings, Xi sought to mould himself as a reformist to carry the baton of the late paramount leader

Deng Xiaoping as someone who was willing to crack down on corruption and official excess while also coming across as a down-to-earth person who could relate easily with ordinary Chinese.

Xi lit his first fire on the day he became party chief by promising to fight corruption. In subsequent speeches and meetings, he adopted an unusually tough tone on the urgency of fighting graft, saying that the Chinese leadership would deal with the corrupt "tigers and flies" at the same time.

This greatly spurred China's internet users to use social media to expose scandalous behaviour by corrupt officials, ranging from extramarital affairs caught on videos to uncovering hard evidence of apparatchiks owning dozens of properties. Such online sleuthery led to the sackings and arrests of a number of mostly junior-ranked officials.

Xi also launched a campaign against official pomp and excess, which again produced initial results. According to the Ministry of Commerce, high-end restaurants in Beijing and Shanghai where officials frittered away taxpayers' money on wining and dining reported 30 to 40 per cent falls in revenues during the Chinese New Year holidays.

Xi's second fire was aimed at burnishing his credentials as a reformist. On his first official trip outside Beijing, he flew to Guangdong where he retraced the footsteps of Deng in his 1992 "southern tour" to call for bolder economic reforms. He also raised hopes that China would step up efforts to push for rule of law by signalling his new leadership planned to scrap the controversial 56-year-old re-education-through-labour system that had enabled police to lock up people for three years without trial.

Xi and the other new leaders also showed more willingness to embrace social media than the earlier generation of leaders as a number of microblogs have been allowed to report on their movements and post their family photos.

It went without saying that Xi's fires ignited hopes at home and abroad that he would undertake not only drastic economic reforms but also political restructuring very soon. But that is unlikely. While Xi might have indicated that he intended to be a reformer, his first priority had to be to consolidate his power so that he was confident of tackling the more difficult reforms.

Second, the leadership's obsession with maintaining social stability also meant that new reforms were unlikely to be drastic. The fact that central bank governor Zhou Xiaochuan had his decade-long stint in charge of the bank extended despite reaching the mandatory retirement age showed that the new leaders placed great emphasis on policy stability and continuity as long as economic uncertainties persisted in China and overseas.

Even Xi's tough stance on corruption carried a caveat. Just as his tough words raised hopes among analysts and state media of more reforms, including a long-delayed measure to compel officials to declare their family assets, Wang Qishan, the country's top anti-graft official, tried to play down expectations. He said that his agency would pursue the policy of treating the symptoms first by investigating and punishing the corrupt officials.

As for finding a permanent cure by introducing effective anti-corruption measures, that would have to wait.

Xi could also ride the momentum by abolishing the petitioning system, and instead allowing petitioners to take their grievances to the law courts rather than various government offices. Under the existing system, many petitioners ended up in jails as inmates of the system of re-education through labour.

* * *

Heeding Lessons of Old Regime

by *Cary Huang*

A treatise on the 1789 French Revolution has found a new readership in today's China.

"What they read might reflect what they think," a middle-aged man said as he picked up a book recommended by Wang Qishan, appointed head of the Communist Party discipline watchdog following the 18th party congress. "I am really keen to learn what Wang Qishan is thinking and what he wants officials to learn from the book," the man, a civil servant, said at the Wangfujing Bookstore in Beijing.

The book is Alexis de Tocqueville's *The Old Regime and the Revolution*, the French historian's treatise on the French revolution that started in 1789. A saleswoman at the shop said it had become unusually popular following reports that Wang had recommended that officials read a Chinese translation published in 1994.

"Wang Qishan's recommendation reflects the Chinese leadership's sense of crisis, as the book provides a realistic way of thinking to analyse the current situation in China, though it might not necessarily help in finding [a] solution to its problems," said Gu Su, an expert on Tocqueville at Nanjing University.

Wang began recommending that officials read the book in 2012 at the height of the scandal engulfing politician Bo Xilai, the former party chief in Chongqing municipality and disgraced along with his wife, Gu Kailai, who was sentenced to life imprisonment for murdering British business associate Neil Heywood. Wang made the book a must-read for party officials after he became secretary of the Communist Party's Central Commission for Discipline Inspection.

Tocqueville (1805–1859) wrote his book in 1856, six decades after the French revolution. More than 150 years later, China's communist leaders are trying to make sense of his observations. Tocqueville analyses the causes of the French revolution by examining social conditions under the "old regime". He wrote that when the revolution erupted, the "old regime" of Louis XVI was at its most prosperous, but that prosperity had fuelled social disparity, leading to the revolution. He offered an explanation as to why prosperity did not prevent a major revolution but, on the contrary, fomented one.

Although China has become the second-largest economy in the world, with its people enjoying unprecedented wealth, polarisation has also reached an all-time high. At about the time of the party congress the country's Gini coefficient, which measures income disparity, was 0.61 — way above the internationally recognised danger threshold of 0.4. On the scale, 0 means perfect equality and 1 maximal inequality.

Tocqueville also believed that not all the revolution's legacies were positive, even though it overthrew the old regime and took France into a new era of equality and democracy. After overthrowing the autocratic monarchy by violent means, social ills reappeared after undergoing a makeover.

Economist Hua Sheng, president of Yanjing Overseas Chinese University, recalled on his blog a comment that Wang made about the book when advising Hua to read the book. "For a country like China, with substantial weight in the world, historical and contemporary experience shows that its transformation towards modernity will not be smooth. The Chinese themselves have not paid a sufficient price yet."

Analysts said Wang's remark reflected the fear among leaders that a revolution — the price to pay for modernisation — was looming in the world's last major communist-ruled nation. The factors that contributed to the French revolution and the waves of revolution that reverberated through North Africa and the Middle East early this decade could be seen in China. These included widespread discontent caused by despotism, corruption, social inequality, social injustice, unemployment and inflation, along with the rise of the middle class. Public protests in China, officially described as "mass incidents", have exceeded 100,000 a year.

"This is exactly why Wang and other senior leaders wanted officials to study the book, because what Tocqueville saw in France two centuries ago has an almost exact replica in today's China," Gu said. He added that one of Tocqueville's observations was particularly pertinent to China's leaders: that great revolutions did not occur during a time of poverty. Instead, they took place when economic development had brought about acute polarisation. At such times, conflict between social classes was easily incited, with those at the bottom of society turning their anger into the flames of war.

Another of Tocqueville's conclusions was that a regime with centralised power actually intensified tensions between social classes. The French political system had placed executive, legislative and judicial powers under centralised authority before the old regime was toppled.

China, with its system of one-party rule, has been seen by some as the modern-day equivalent. Many academics said the party's monopoly on power was the chief reason behind China's widening wealth gap, rampant corruption and abuse of power by officials — all major sources of public dissatisfaction with the government.

But the most discomforting of Tocqueville's conclusions for China's leaders was that the "most dangerous moment for a bad government is when it begins to reform".

"It is almost never when a state of things is the most detestable that it is smashed, but when, beginning to improve, it permits men to breathe, to reflect, to communicate their thoughts with each other, and to gauge by what they already have the extent of their rights and their grievances. The weight, although less heavy, seems then all the more unbearable," Tocqueville wrote.

Gu said this advice that reform could be just as dangerous as the status quo, if not more so, presented the Communist leadership with a dilemma, given the party's long-held belief that as long as it could bring prosperity to the people it could maintain its hold on power. That political dilemma had also been summed up in a famous statement by late Kuomintang leader Chiang Kai-shek when he responded to his reformist son Chiang Ching-kuo's request that he overhaul the then-corrupt ruling party during the civil war. "If we reform the Kuomintang, the party will perish; if we don't, the state will perish," the father replied.

Analysts said the new Communist Party leadership was in the grip of a "Tocqueville dilemma" because while it was eager to bring about changes, it wanted to do so in a controlled fashion. "The dilemma Tocqueville pointed out two centuries ago might be the most alarming point that attracted Wang and other leaders to explore ideas from the book," Gu said.

* * *

Media Freedom Unlikely to Bloom

*by **Shi Jiangtao***

> *For those who pinned high hopes for increased press freedom on a new generation of Communist Party leaders, disappointment came soon.*

For advocates of greater press freedom in China, the honeymoon period for the new leadership under party boss Xi Jinping seemingly came to a rapid end. Less than two months after the new leaders were installed at the 18th party congress, a nationwide outcry broke out over censorship of an editorial in an outspoken newspaper in Guangzhou, *Southern Weekly*.

Although the censorship rumpus was tempered after new Guangdong province party boss Hu Chunhua stepped in to avert a full-blown crisis, it inevitably raised doubts about whether the new leadership was ready to deliver on its commitment to change.

Analysts said the show of defiance by usually tame Chinese journalists, who briefly threatened to strike in protest at the amendment of the editorial, highlighted a worsening picture for press freedom and a dilemma as Xi and his colleagues struggled to balance change and stability.

"The row at the *Southern Weekly* has evolved into an unexpected, crucial test of the new leadership," said political analyst Chen Ziming. Rising star Hu was widely praised for his shrewd handling of the row, averting an all-out confrontation as staff threatened to strike.

The fate of the man at the centre of the row, Guangdong propaganda chief Tuo Zhen, was not immediately clear. Tuo was alleged to have played a key role in a last-minute decision to change the newspaper's front page New Year editorial calling for political reform into a tribute to one-party rule. But it was apparent officials wanted to shift the blame elsewhere. In a Singaporean newspaper, provincial propaganda authorities denied accusations that Tuo or other propaganda officials had anything to do with the changed editorial.

Southern Weekly was known for its hard-hitting investigative stories and repeated attempts to test official boundaries. But such editorial zeal came at a steep price for the paper, making it a constant target of clampdowns. In 2009, editor-in-chief Xiang Xi was rumoured to have been demoted after an exclusive interview with US President Barack Obama during his first tour of China, which ruffled feathers in Beijing.

Xiang, who later quit the *Southern Weekly*, joined a long list of veteran journalists at the newspaper who fell victim to censorship, including former editors Qian Gang, Jiang Yiping and Chang Ping. But matters went from bad to worse since Tuo moved to Guangdong in May 2012, according to an open letter from editors and journalists that claimed that "a total of 1,034 stories were censored or even scrapped ... in 2012".

The letter, like another published online on the same day that the controversial editorial was published, was issued in the name of the newspaper's editorial department. "That's the most solemn way of lodging our complaints," said a senior editor.

Both letters denounced heightened censorship during Tuo's tenure and called for an independent inquiry. "The incident was like a detonating fuse. What we have been through was the endless routine of unjustifiable censorship, the killing of stories or entire pages and complete rewrites," the letter said. The row escalated when the paper's management issued a brief statement through its weibo microblog contradicting the allegations of its staff and placing the blame for the change on an unnamed senior worker.

That drew a torrent of criticism from journalists, prompting more detailed revelations about the row. Editorial staff accused Tuo, his deputy, and chief editor Huang Can of flip-flopping on the thorough investigation into censorship they had initially agreed to.

They said that not only had propaganda officials ordered the inclusion of an introductory message in the paper's New Year package without the consent of the page editor, after he had signed off on the page and left work, but also cut by almost half a commentary calling for proper implementation of the national constitution. "We believe that what we are doing can help the new leadership foster public consensus and carry out their pro-reform policy agenda. We hope the new leadership can honour its commitment on promoting the rule of law and constitutional government and go with the tide of history. What have we done wrong?" the senior editor said.

More than a dozen journalists signed a petition to say they would not return to work until the controversy was resolved. But it seemed most staff did not back a walkout.

While most of China's newspapers stayed silent on the row — on orders from Beijing — it was closely followed on microblogs, triggering overwhelming public support for the newspaper through a series of petitions. In a rare exposé, a retired censor at the paper, Zeng Li, confirmed on his blog that the weekly had been stripped of most of its autonomy since Tuo moved to Guangdong. In addition to stories being censored during the editorial process, all story ideas had to be submitted for scrutiny by Tuo's office, he wrote. On several occasions, such as when deadly rainstorms hit Beijing in July 2012, tens of thousands of copies were destroyed as censors moved to avoid critical coverage, Zeng said.

The row intensified when hundreds of the newspaper's supporters carrying banners and flowers gathered outside the paper's headquarters in the centre of Guangzhou for the first of three days of protests. The demonstrations were largely peaceful amid a heavy police presence, with only a few scuffles reported, and a counter-protest by party loyalists.

Although the details of Hu's intervention remained unknown, *Southern Weekly* journalists confirmed that they had agreed to return to work. "We did not actually go on strike and the row did not affect our daily operations much," a Beijing-based staffer said.

Many staff privately feared for the publication's future. "I wouldn't call it a victory, basically because it didn't address any of our concerns," said another journalist. "I am still worried because authorities are unlikely to relax editorial control of our newspaper in this climate of deteriorating media freedom. Although authorities promised not to take revenge against us, I am not sure how many of us can continue working under such suffocating censorship."

Editorial staff confirmed that the row lingered on, with disputes continuing between journalists, censors and management over several op-ed pieces. Weibo messages on the subject were deleted within an hour. Other outspoken newspapers, including *Beijing News*, were also targeted by propaganda authorities. Editorial staff at *Beijing News*, led by publisher Dai Zigeng, bluntly refused an order purportedly given by the country's new propaganda chief, Liu Qibao, to reprint a *Global Times* commentary critical of *Southern Weekly*.

The commentary accused unspecified "external forces" of stirring up the dispute. Most controversially, it accused blind legal activist Chen Guangcheng, who escaped from house detention and was later allowed to move to New York in 2012, of being one of the main agitators. It believed that Beijing authorities were behind that accusation as many Chinese newspapers, most of them liberal-leaning, were instructed by Liu's office to reprint the commentary.

Beijing News' defiance proved short-lived, however, and it reprinted the article after authorities threatened to shut it down. But it did receive support from thousands of internet users. Professor Zhan Jiang, a media specialist at Beijing Foreign Studies University, even called the confrontation a "defining moment" in the history of Chinese journalism. But analysts said dreams of a freer media might prove more elusive following the rows.

Professor Zhang Ming, a political analyst at Beijing's Renmin University, said authorities might have been surprised by the outrage against censorship, and they stopped short of instigating bolder reforms. "They will find it harder to strike a balance between fostering a public image of open-mindedness and maintaining tight control over an increasingly impatient public."

Most analysts, including former journalist and popular blogger Li Chengpeng, said greater media freedom was unlikely despite growing calls. "Mainland authorities must have been shocked by the public anger over the controversy, and will have to rethink censorship policy. But whether they have the guts to take the initiative and overhaul state censorship is another question."

Professor Liu Junning, a Beijing-based analyst, said censorship was essential for an authoritarian regime like Beijing. "No inquiry into the censorship row will be allowed because it will only reveal more dirty secrets about how the system manipulates the media."

But Li Chengpeng said the significance of this rare display of media defiance should not be underestimated. "It may have the butterfly effect in the long run because many great social changes start from incremental, even trivial advances."

Early in 2013, another censorship issue reared its head in China, this time involving foreign movies. Xinhua news agency published a rare admonishment of government censors for cutting and manipulating scenes in the latest James Bond movie, *Skyfall*. The state media organ said the censorship, which almost every foreign film goes through before reaching Chinese cinemas, highlighted a problem with the nation's movie-review system — that is, that decisions about cuts and changes to films were often arbitrary. In some cases, Xinhua reported, an anonymous letter drove what content was cut.

Skyfall began showing in Chinese cinemas nearly three months after the movie's premiere in Britain. Delayed release in China of foreign films is common due to the censorship process and because preference is given to domestic productions.

However, government censors rarely, if ever, admitted that content was cut or altered. Among the *Skyfall* scenes censors deleted was one in which a French hit man kills a Chinese security guard in a Shanghai skyscraper. A scene depicting prostitution in Macau was also cut, as was a line spoken by Bond's nemesis mentioning that Chinese security agents had tortured him.

Furthermore, in a scene where Bond asks a mysterious woman whether she had been a prostitute since the age of 12 or 13, censors decided to keep the audio but alter the Chinese subtitles to indicate that Bond asked her whether she had become a triad member at that age.

* * *

Pitfalls of Party Downsizing

by *Minnie Chan*

> *Efforts to slim down and revitalise the Chinese Communist Party face enormous hurdles.*

In the wake of the 18th party congress, new party chief Xi Jinping vowed to control the size of the Communist Party — with more than 82 million members the world's biggest political party — and purge "unqualified members" in a timely manner to boost its vitality and reputation.

But easier said than done, warned leading communist academic Li Junru, former vice-president of the Central Party School and a mastermind of the scheme. "When I was vice-president [of the party school] about five years ago, we once planned to cut 10 million of the party's membership of 70 million, but we found it was not an easy job."

Li said the party had set up a pilot programme at Zhejiang University in Hangzhou to expel unqualified members. "After a series of brainstorming meetings and studies, we gave up the pilot plan because many party experts found it was very hard to decide who should be given the right to design and define the qualification criteria. We failed to reach a conclusion on whether the qualification criteria should be decided and controlled by party members themselves, the public or party branch leaders.

"If party branch leaders had the right, we were afraid it might become a means for some leaders to kick out comrades who had different opinions. And if the public had the right, some aggressive members who dared to offend people when promoting policies might be thrown out."

Despite these difficulties, the party committee in Guangdong province subsequently announced a pilot programme to expel unqualified members in eight places, with local party branches allowed to set different qualification criteria.

But political analysts said the party would be better off tackling obstacles and inherent risks that had lain hidden in the party for decades. Professor Ding Li, director of the Guangdong Academy of Social Sciences' regional competition centre, suggested the pilot scheme should start at the party's upper levels. The membership criteria set for members of the party's inner-circle Central Committee should be higher than those for normal members, he said. "It's meaningless if the pilot scheme just focuses on unqualified grassroots members."

The impact of such low-level members was limited, while unqualified party leaders could ruin the party and the country. "The current key problem for the party is that many presentable party leaders do well in political shows and making fair-sounding speeches, but are actually living a decadent lifestyle. They should be the real target to be weeded out by Xi."

Professor Yuan Weishi, a political commentator at Guangzhou's Sun Yat-sen University, said the downsizing plan would not make the party purer. "The core problem of the Communist Party is the rampant corruption among senior officials, while unqualified grassroots members do not have any impact on the party's overall reputation."

But Li said: "We should encourage Guangdong party branches to try to promote the pilot programmes because local cadres may discover new measures that eluded upper-level party leaders several years ago."

* * *

Legal Reform: Promises and Hopes

by **Keith Zhai**

Legal experts chart a course heading — gradually — towards judicial independence.

Soon after the 18th party congress closed, party chief Xi Jinping promised to strengthen China's much criticised legal system under which the party had overriding powers over the courts. Hopes for reform of the legal system had risen after the congress when new security chief Meng Jianzhu promised to halt the hated re-education through labour system and to proceed with reform in three other key areas. Meng also criticised excessive interference in court proceedings by officials who routinely pass notes to judges telling them how to rule.

Weeks later, Chinese legal experts called on the new party leaders to implement reforms for judicial independence, saying such moves would be the first step towards political reform in the country. An annual report on judiciary reform, co-authored by three legal experts from the Beijing Institute of Technology and released at a legal forum organised by *Caijing Magazine,* said it should be the top priority in the political reform process as it would be the easiest related area to reach a consensus.

The report also argued that an independent judiciary should not be seen as a concept unique to capitalist countries, and a socialist country such as China should have an independent judiciary, too. "Many socialist countries have also endorsed the principle of judiciary independence," the report said. "Judiciary independence is not an issue of being capitalist or socialist, and socialism should not exclude judiciary independence."

Conceding that achieving an independent judiciary should be a gradual process, the report said authorities should at least make it a target for reform. The experts said this could start simply, by banning high-level courts from intervening in lower-court rulings, and by banning a presiding judge from intervening in case examinations by other judges. Legal expert Jiang Ping, a former president of the China University of Political Science and Law, said at the forum that the nation's judicial reform should not be a watered-down version full of "Chinese characteristics". It should be on a par with international standards. "The soul of judiciary reform should be judicial independence," he said.

The report also said that some parts of China's revised Criminal Procedure Law were actually examples of backtracking, in terms of legal reform. For example, the revision gave law enforcement agencies greater power by allowing them to detain people for up to six months if they were suspected of being involved in national security breaches.

Professor Zhang Qianfan, who teaches law at Peking University, said: "We can't talk about judicial independence if the party's political and legal affairs committees still have the power to overrule the proceedings of individual courts." Zhang drafted a petition on Christmas Day 2012 calling for authorities to uphold the constitution. It warned that public dissatisfaction would otherwise escalate to a "critical point" and the country would "fall into the turmoil and chaos of violent revolution".

* * *

Graft: The Battle Is Joined — Again

by *Keith Zhai*

It's a case of war declared, but victory understandably uncertain, in fresh calls to beat rampant corruption.

After stern warnings by Communist Party chief Xi Jinping following the 18th party congress that the party's very existence depended on whether it succeeded in curbing China's massive corruption problems, the party's disciplinary watchdog duly announced it would launch a five-year anti-corruption plan in 2013 and start spot checks on senior officials' declared personal assets. The Central Commission for Discipline Inspection also said in a communiqué after a two-day meeting that all party members should "firmly uphold the authority and seriousness of the party's constitution".

Xi had told the meeting that the party would crack down on senior and low-ranking corrupt officials and restrict officials' power by "confining them in the cage" of a regulatory system. "A disciplinary, prevention and guarantee mechanism should be set up to ensure that people do not dare to, are not able to and cannot easily commit corruption," he said.

The commission also said it would crack down on commercial bribery, as well as focusing on graft in sectors including finance, telecoms, education, medicine and land. The communiqué said government organs should accept both public and media supervision and curb spending on official functions, government buildings and official tours. It said the disciplinary body would "earnestly imple-ment" rules requiring officials to report "relevant issues related to individuals".

Rules issued in July 2010 required officials in government agencies and state-owned enterprises to report everything from personal assets to the business activities of spouses and children. But the extent of implementation was unknown, with public disclosure of such informa-tion not mandatory. Critics said corruption was too deeply ingrained to be solved by things like spot checks. "It is far from enough. The spot checks have no standard and could be a political game," said Chen Ziming, an independent scholar who closely follows politics. "People want the party officials to disclose their assets, it's that simple."

Ma Huaide, deputy director of the China University of Political Science and Law, said the notion of public disclosure of officials' assets had been around for years, but because so many party members were corrupt it was very difficult to make it happen.

Equally sceptical was Professor Zhang Ming, a political scientist at Renmin University in Beijing. "The fatal problem with the anti-graft campaign is that there are no warriors with clean hands in the party's corrupt political system."

* * *

Crooked Cadres Hide Booty in Property

by *Jane Cai*

Bricks and mortar are no longer such a safe haven for officials' ill-gotten gains.

Their titles varied and they came from all over China, but there was one thing that 10 corrupt officials reported by whistle-blowers in the weeks following the 18th party congress and the renewed calls to stamp out corruption had in common: each owned more than a dozen properties.

From local police heads to bank executives, officials who owned an unusually large number of properties — in an extreme case, one was suspected of having 192 — were reported to authorities in the wake of the new leadership's call for citizens to help in the fight against corruption.

Property, although relatively illiquid, has been a favoured investment in China because of the record high returns that it has delivered and the opportunity it provided to launder ill-gotten gains, economists said. "Property has always represented wealth, especially so after China's housing reforms in 1982, which sent property prices soaring," said Professor Hu Xingdou, a political analyst at the Beijing Institute of Technology.

Under the reforms, property became merchandise for individuals to buy instead of housing assigned by an employer. Prices were buoyant as the rich and powerful snapped up investments and ordinary people scraped savings together to buy a place to live in.

In major cities like Beijing, Shanghai and Guangzhou, prices rose more than tenfold in a decade. In Beijing, luxury housing cost as much as 300,000 yuan per square metre in 2011 before regulators pegged back prices to avoid social unrest. Urban residents' annual disposable income was 21,810 yuan per capita that year.

"In big cities there are plenty of rich people and corrupt officials, so someone owning 10 or 20 properties is hardly noticeable," Hu said. "Property is a bribe less traceable than straight cash, which leaves clues in bank accounts."

Faking a *hukou*, the household registration record that gives proof of residency, could easily make the real owner of properties less visible. Zhai Zhenfeng, a former director of the housing administration bureau in Zhengzhou in the central province of Henan, and three family members all had two *hukou* and between them owned 31 properties, it was revealed in December 2012.

Reflecting robust demand for fake *hukou*, there was a thriving business in a county in Jilin province, with a grassroots police station charging 30,000 to 50,000 yuan for an extra *hukou*, according to Xinhua.

Yuan Gangming, a researcher at the Chinese Academy of Social Sciences and Tsinghua University, said housing had the characteristic of being valuable but not high-profile. "More importantly, you cannot easily tell whether money used to buy property is clean or not, so it could facilitate laundering of illegal gains."

The transfer of ill-gotten gains into property became rampant in China because the government condoned it, Yuan added. "The central government has been relying heavily on the real estate sector to drive economic growth, and thus it tolerates the plundering of wealth by the powerful."

Experts said no official data existed for the number of vacant properties, which would be an indicator of the severity of the situation. There was also no nationwide tax on property ownership and no estate duty on inheritance. These factors made property ownership low risk and low cost.

After November, when the 18th party congress was held, a large amount of luxury housing was dumped on to the market by sellers including government officials and senior managers of state-owned enterprises, spooked by the latest round of corruption busting, a source told the *Economic Observer*. Some 714 officials fled overseas between September 30 and October 7, 2012, according to the Beijing newspaper.

* * *

Losing Patience with Democracy

by Li Jing

> *A much-vaunted blow for democracy at the grassroots level lacks the hoped-for hitting power.*

In March 2012, the tiny Guangdong provincial fishing village of Wukan made history with a democratic election to choose its local leaders. The election was the villagers' reward for months of tenacious protest against illegal land grabs by corrupt officials. The demonstrations saw them kick out their old leaders and effectively cut themselves off from the outside world. The poll was considered free and fair, and the village was held up as an example by human rights campaigners and an inspiration to other rural dwellers who had also seen land taken from them.

But a year on, villagers were losing patience with their elected leaders over the slow pace of progress to reclaim the stolen land, while the elected village committee stood accused of being too close to the authorities. Some said the committee was too focused on maintaining stability rather than fighting for the villagers' rights. Discontent was bubbling under the surface, with some speculating that another protest was possible, as villagers had waited for months for the new provincial leadership to settle down and signal a way forward on land disputes. The elected representatives, meanwhile, felt let down by the higher authorities — though some remained optimistic that the experiment in democracy would prove fruitful in the long term.

Land rights — a problem in villages across China — remained at the heart of the problem. Wu Zili, mayor of Shanwei, the prefecture-level city under which Wukan is administered, told the provincial party mouthpiece *Southern Daily* in January 2013 that Wukan had retrieved 330 of the 446 hectares of land the villagers had lost. But this claim was challenged by villagers, who listed in an open letter details of land they said was still in the hands of businessmen close to former village heads. They named Li Bingji, a delegate to the country's top legislature, the National People's Congress, as one of the businessmen.

Local people said they had won back only 233 hectares of land, with the rest feared lost forever as transactions were completed before the election. Several villagers blamed a lack of sincerity from the authorities of Lufeng county and Shanwei city for the failings. "They're just playing a delaying tactic," said Zhang Jianxing, a young activist. "If they want to solve the problems, they'll at least set a basic tone. But that is not the case now."

Chen Suzhuan, who was elected to the village committee in March 2012, said she felt betrayed by the authorities, who had pledged to give back land illegally grabbed under former village chief Xue Chang. "Now they're backtracking, saying what's been done has been done, leaving us [the village committee] in a very awkward position when challenged by villagers," she said.

Zhang said: "Some people fear they will lose the land for good if the new village committee does not keep on fighting. Without land, villagers cannot see where their future lies."

Activists showed their defiance to the inexperienced village leaders, including refusing to pay a management fee required for fishing, a step that only exacerbates a funding shortfall faced by the village committee. Government subsidies remained a key source of funding for public projects in the village, including construction of a library, roads and water networks, as the new village committee had been unable to bring in investment with land issues unresolved.

Among those who lost faith in the system was Zhuang Liehong, who was elected to the committee but quit in October 2012. He said the elected leaders should negotiate with the government to get the land back "but now they are toeing a very tight official line". For instance, the village committee had refused to release details on disputed land plots because higher levels of government did not want it to.

"This is actually a good way to engage with the villagers, explaining to them where the obstacles lie and what the plans to overcome them are," said Zhuang, who runs a teahouse. "This is the only way villagers will have faith in the leaders."

However, Lin Zuluan, the elected party chief, saw it differently. Without government support, he said, village autonomy meant next to nothing. "For a rural village, you'll need economic funding for whatever you want to do. I think a village will face tremendous difficulties in whatever endeavour without [local] government support and central consent."

Amid huge pressure from the village, the 69-year-old leader said he still believed the democratic experiment was worthwhile, but he regretted taking part as it had raised unrealistic expectations among the villagers.

The predicament of the inexperienced Wukan politicians reflected the challenges for village autonomy against a backdrop of powerful higher-level governments and entrenched interests. Officials also feared that radical moves at Wukan could lead to wider social changes they did not want to see. Although a provincial government working group was sent to the village shortly after the protests in late 2011, Zhang said it did little to solve the land disputes. "They have a lot to consider, of course: the impact on businesses, government and villagers. Also, whether nearby villages would follow Wukan's suit and whether the whole political system in China could be impacted. They have to evaluate all these issues, so they are extremely cautious in dealing with Wukan's land problems. So for them the priority is not solving the land disputes, but rather to maintain stability in the village."

In fact, the Wukan model — where protests paved the way for fair elections — had already inspired other communities. Villagers in

Shangpu, about 100 kilometres from Wukan, also requested the right to vote for their leader and on whether to approve a controversial proposal to transform rice fields into an industrial zone, amid a standoff over violent clashes with thugs linked to a local official.

But Wukan might no longer be the perfect role model. Reflecting on the election, Chen Suzhuan called democracy in Wukan "a total accident", while other villages doubted the significance of democratic rule, since it had not made a big difference in solving the land issues.

But the experiment in democracy was gradually changing the villagers, Chen said. They now dared to criticise the village leaders and had started to show more concern about political events nationally. Beijing-based political commentator Zhang Lifan said villagers had not been educated in the concepts of civil rights and responsibilities, and it would take time for them to grasp the meaning of democracy.

But Lin, the village chief, rejected the idea that Wukan's democracy had failed. "It can only be achieved through a long process, despite all the noises."

In an editorial, the *South China Morning Post* said that more time was needed for the Wukan experiment to succeed. Where once there was a widespread belief that a model had been created for communities across the nation to follow, there was disappointment. But being able to choose representatives was a significant achievement. What had been gained should not be thrown away for the sake of self-interest.

It had become clear that for some villagers the process was only about getting land back. Yet invaluable lessons were learned on shared problem solving. Villagers' agitation in 2011 prompted unprecedented concessions from Communist Party chiefs. Paramilitary troops ended a blockade, long-time officials were arrested and elections gave farmers control over their village.

But those who were elected needed time to come to grips with their new jobs, and only through perseverance and determination would

Wukan's problems be resolved. At the heart of the matter was education. Those involved had to have the skills and motivation to always work together. Individual concerns had to be put to one side so that problems could be handled with the common good in mind. Teaching and acquiring such abilities could be a drawn-out process for those unfamiliar with such concepts.

It was wrong to write off the Wukan experiment as a failure, the *Post* said. More time and effort was needed for it to take root. Those involved had to make a greater effort to nurture what was for China an important part of its development.

* * *

Feeling the Bite — China's Hospitality Industry

Xi Jinping's spartan crusade is bad news for those accustomed to garnering rich pickings from the wining and dining culture.

Xi Jinping's down-to-earth style that he exhibited soon after becoming Communist Party chief caught on well with the Chinese public, especially his crackdown on the over-the-top habits of officials, with their pomp and ceremony, waste and extravagance and lavish banquets — part of the new leadership's drive against official corruption.

The crackdown did not go down so well, however, with officials who were accustomed to wining and dining at the taxpayer's expense. They complained that the new austerity was too severe. This followed reports of Chinese New Year parties following the 18th party congress being cancelled, shifted to fast-food venues, or stripped of frills such as flowers, alcohol, gifts and prizes.

These sentiments were no doubt echoed by the hospitality industry. After the once-in-a-decade change of the top leadership, hotels and restaurants anticipated rich pickings from celebrations of the new order, to be followed by the usual New Year festivities. Instead the phones ran hot with cancellations and downsizings, with officials turning to more discreet locations like guesthouses to host entertainment.

Food and eating have also traditionally been a serious part of doing business in China. So the austerity drive ordered by Xi hit China's high-end restaurants hard. Millions of business dinners were cancelled as Xi's order was seen by many government officials and company executives as a political directive. Pessimistic restaurant owners mulled whether to close their businesses.

According to a survey by the China Cuisine Association, 60 per cent of nearly 100 restaurants saw bookings cancelled, with one Beijing-based outlet reporting an 80 per cent drop in sales. "The survey found that business owners felt pessimistic about the outlook of the industry," the association said. "They think it's necessary to readjust their business models to adapt to the new market conditions."

"Our corporate customers are seriously complying with the party's order to cut spending on meals," said Ken Xia, a restaurant owner in Shanghai. "It's not going to be a temporary business decline, and we are foreseeing further losses in the coming months if not years."

The military, too, felt the full force of Xi's spartan crusade. As chairman of the Central Military Commission he is also its commander in chief. Indeed, frugality has been catching, with private companies scaling down their parties, to the chagrin of florists, wine merchants and purveyors of party prizes such as tablets and smartphones.

That said, it was New Year as usual for the vast majority of a fifth of the world's population. They could even sleep safer in their beds, if we were to believe one report that Xi's ban on alcohol in the military had lifted officers' and men's energy levels and made more time for defence training and exercises.

* * *

Rights Treaty "Must Be Ratified"

by *Verna Yu*

Human rights are "not just Western imports", say petitioners.

In the wake of the new Chinese leadership's pledge to promote constitutional rights and the rule of law, more than 120 influential scholars, lawyers and journalists signed a petition urging the National People's Congress at the legislature's March 2013 meeting to ratify the International Covenant on Civil and Political Rights (ICCPR).

The ICCPR is part of the International Bill of Human Rights. China signed the ICCPR in 1998 but did not ratify it. The covenant commits its parties to respecting civil and political rights, including freedom of speech, religion and assembly and rights to a fair trial.

"There is still a substantial gap between the situation in China with respect to human rights and rule of law and the requirements of international human rights treaties ... but now is the best time for our country to ratify the treaty," the letter said. Signatories included scholars Qin Hui, Yu Jianrong and He Weifang, liberal Communist Party veterans He Fang and Feng Lanrui, and rights lawyers Pu Zhiqiang and Xu Zhiyong. They said they feared a society that did not value human rights or individual freedoms would plunge into "hatred and violence, division and hostility" if crises erupted.

Professor Li Gongming, a Guangzhou-based commentator who signed the petition, said it was in the spirit of a recent push for constitutional government by Communist Party chief Xi Jinping. "In light of the leadership stressing that the country should be governed under the constitution and with the rule of law, I think ratification is a reasonable step," Li said.

The petition, part of increasingly bold calls from intellectuals for political openness and government transparency, said human rights were not just Western imports but were ideals that the Communist Party itself had aspired to since its early days. The Chinese constitution says citizens enjoy freedom of the press, speech, assembly and association, and the right to demonstrate.

Professor Zhang Ming, a political scientist at Beijing's Renmin University and a signatory, said he was sceptical about whether the new leadership would be willing to implement the necessary changes to conform to the treaty's requirements. "The 'stability maintenance' regime has not ended, but then you can not call for ratification to happen."

Xu Youyu, a retired professor at the China Academy of Social Sciences who was also a signatory, said: "It's a matter of whether those in power genuinely want to safeguard human rights or not. If you want to, then you should ratify as soon as possible." Many copies of the open letter posted on Chinese websites were deleted.

* * *

Call to Legalise Same-Sex Marriage

by *Raymond Li*

Parents of Chinese gays and lesbians take up the call for equal rights for their offspring.

One of the many appeals for reform made to the annual meeting of the National People's Congress legislature in March 2013 came from more than 100 parents with children who are gay or lesbian calling for the legalisation of same-sex marriage.

"We're appealing to NPC deputies to take notice of calls from 120 million parents of gays and lesbians for a revision of the Marriage Law in order to grant our children equal rights to marriage," they said in an open letter.

Homosexuality was an offence in China until 1997, and it was only in 2001 that homosexuality was removed from the official list of mental illnesses. But homosexual relationships are not recognised under the law, which means that people involved in them face widespread discrimination in matters such as hospital care, inheritance, adoptions and home purchases.

One signatory of the letter, the mother of a 23-year-old man, said she was worried about her only son's future because legal inequality would deprive him of a decent life, having a partner, a family and the chance of adopting a child. She said she had learned to come to terms with her son's homosexuality after he came out to her four years ago and considered his well-being more important than the fact she could never be a grandmother.

Hu Zhijun, a gay rights activist from Parents, Families & Friends of Lesbians China, said the law was flawed because homosexuals in China could marry a heterosexual partner legally, although they were not in a loving relationship. This gave rise to the phenomenon of "gay wives" and "gay husbands", heterosexual women and men who unknowingly marry homosexuals seeking to use such marriages to conceal their sexuality.

Dr Lucetta Kam Yip-lo, a gender and sexuality specialist from Hong Kong Baptist University, said China might be more likely to legalise same-sex marriages than Hong Kong, where Christian beliefs exerted a strong political influence. "Most pressure on LGBT (lesbian, gay, bisexual and transgender) individuals to conform to heterosexual norms does not come from the governments but their families."

A mother from Fuzhou, Fujian province, who has a 26-year old gay son, said she was devastated when he told her about his sexuality and felt even worse when she could not turn to friends and relatives for help due to the stigma involved. But she said she had decided to take up the fight for gay marriage due to widespread hostility towards people like her son, who was forced to drop out of middle school due to bullying. "We're not asking for special treatment for my son, but wanting him to be treated equally because he is as filial and talented as anyone else," she said.

*   *   *

Veterans' Long March for Reform

by *Verna Yu*

Is this their final appeal for more freedom?

Every time one of Du Daozheng's friends passed away, he felt a growing sense of loneliness. Aged 89 at the time of the 18th party congress, the former propaganda chief was becoming increasingly isolated in his quest for political reform under the communist regime's one-party leadership. "My old friends are leaving one after another ... we are like fragile leaves falling in the winter. But this is the law of nature," said Du, publisher of China's most outspoken political magazine, *Yanhuang Chunqiu*.

As the once-a-decade leadership change in the Communist Party loomed, Du and his surviving friends — mostly retired officials in their late 80s and 90s — made what could be their final appeal for the party to introduce more freedoms and take its first steps towards democracy.

Du's relationship with the Communist Party began some 70 years ago when, as an idealistic teenager, he joined to fight against the corrupt and authoritarian Kuomintang regime. But in 2012 — almost a lifetime later — many felt frustrated they might never live to see their dream of democracy fulfilled. In the previous two years alone, several prominent figures in their circle such as Li Pu, Zhu Houze, Xie Tao and Peng Di had died. Those left still remembered times of great action. Many helped liberal leaders Hu Yaobang and Zhao Ziyang launch political reform initiatives in the 1980s.

While the former officials acknowledged changes had to be introduced gradually, they said the party had dragged its feet for too long. Political reform stalled after the Tiananmen crackdown in 1989 and had never resumed. Du wants the party to embark on bold reform measures such as allowing freedom of speech and association and "intra-party democracy" — empowering party members to elect their leaders and representatives.

A former director of the General Administration of Press and Publication, Du once believed that democratisation of China should "move forward in small steps". However, speaking shortly before the 18th congress opened, he said that would no longer suffice to cope with the social crisis it currently faced. Rapid political reform was urgently needed because the level of anger bottled up among citizens over inequality, corruption and abuse of power was reaching a dangerous stage. "The people's anger is boiling over and there are uprisings everywhere — now we need to move forward in medium-sized steps." Du was referring to social conflicts over the previous few years, including protests in Shifang, Sichuan province, in July 2012 against the construction of a copper alloy plant, and the drawn-out clashes between villagers and officials in Wukan, in 2011 over local government corruption.

Political stagnation, Du warned, was also threatening economic development — the foundation of the party's legitimacy. With unchecked government power, corruption thrived and suppressed the growth of private enterprises. But party elders said they were not placing much hope in the new leaders, even if there was optimism that they would be more in touch with the reality of citizens' lives after enduring hardship in rural China as "educated youths" during the Cultural Revolution.

They saw little evidence of a resolute figure like Mikhail Gorbachev — the last head of state under the Soviet Union — determined to dramatically overhaul the political system. New leaders Xi Jinping and Li Keqiang had particularly impressive records, but they were bland enough to be acceptable to a politically conservative bureaucracy, the elders said. "Historically speaking, crown princes cannot be too outstanding. They tend to be ordinary and obedient," Du said.

He Fang, an assistant to deputy foreign minister Zhang Wentian in the 1950s, believed the new leaders would be hesitant to overhaul the one-party system because their own privileges were at stake. Many officials had traded influence and used connections for lucrative financial gains, and their spouses, children and relatives had extensive commercial interests. "[Under a reformed system] they would just become ordinary people and lose their special privileges," 90-year-old He said.

He Fang endured almost 20 years of hard labour after being purged along with his former boss, Zhang Wentian, who criticised the radical policies of Mao Zedong that led to nationwide famine. A retired academic at the Chinese Academy of Social Sciences, He said the political reform measures the government said it was undertaking were essentially administrative tweaks. "They dare not talk about separation of party and government [powers], because [the country] is still ruled by the party."

Zhang Sizhi, 84, a prominent lawyer and veteran party member, agreed the incoming leadership would be much the same as the incumbents. "Their fundamental interest is the same, that is, to safeguard their sovereignty. It is a huge clique with vested interests and that is very difficult to change." He cited political leaders' unwillingness to declare their financial assets, despite repeated public calls, as an example.

Elders who had seen the party wheels turn for decades warned that even if individual leaders wanted to overhaul the system, the inertia of the regime was so strong it might not be possible for them to wield substantial influence. Departing premier Wen Jiabao did in the previous couple of years call for political reform and the respect for universal values, such as democracy and rule of law. But even he was unable to make his aspirations a reality. "The individuals might wield a certain level of influence, but it's hard to change an authoritarian system," He Fang said. Instead, the overriding priority for future leaders was to hold on to the Communist Party's ruling authority over the country, inherited from their fathers' generation. After all, that was the source of their legitimacy, he says.

Many top party officials set to ascend to powerful positions in the new leadership were scions of revolutionary leaders who helped fight the Kuomintang and put the Communist Party in power. "In democratic countries, political legitimacy comes from elections, but in China it's hereditary. [The last generation] fought hard to become the rulers so [this generation] has to maintain their position," he said.

Party elders agreed that any changes must be gradual and cautious, but initial steps, even if tiny ones, must be taken. "The Communist Party should first carry out an operation on itself ... then the social conflicts could be ameliorated," Du said. "Democracy is the only way; it cannot avoid embarking on this road."

But a predominant view among the conservative bureaucracy was that reforms that would limit official power, mandate transparency and empower ordinary people to have a say in how their country was run would create chaos and likely threaten the Communist Party's survival. Zhong Peizhang, the 88-year-old former head of the central propaganda bureau's information office, argued the party should not be afraid of reform — but rather what might happen in its absence. He said that without change the regime could collapse, a fate that could be averted if people saw a genuine desire from the party to serve the people. "If they rely on violence to maintain their rule that is very dangerous ... crises could break out any time. But if you speak on behalf of the people, they will support you ... Even the Kuomintang had the courage to carry out reform — why can't the Communist Party?"

The Kuomintang, which was defeated by the Communist Party, imposed martial law following its retreat to Taiwan in 1949. But Taiwanese president Chiang Ching-kuo initiated a series of political reforms in the 1980s that paved the way for multi-party elections.

Du Guang, 84, a retired professor at the Central Party School, said he was "cautiously optimistic" about the country's future but believed the nation's hopes lay not so much with the party but with the ordinary people. Even though China's internet was policed and censored, the public could still have unprecedented access to news and information from non-official channels and were increasingly aware of their rights.

"I'm optimistic in the people," said Du Guang, who helped found a semi-official think tank that analysed reform issues in 1988 but was forced to close after Tiananmen. "With the internet's popularisation, grassroots power will influence the people in the upper echelon."

The elder added that government officials starting to open their own microblogs to communicate with the public was also a positive sign. "The power of ordinary people is getting stronger. It's not obvious but it's subtly having an impact on society. It's a struggle between democracy and authoritarian [systems]; we need people and government to work together."

For these party veterans, who had hoped to see their dreams for democracy, equality and freedom fulfilled within their lifetimes, their call for political reform before the 18th party congress was particularly poignant, as many would probably not live to see another leadership transition. They warned that the party's days would be numbered if its leaders continued to ignore the demands for political reform, emphasising that this was not something they wished to see. After all, in their youth, many of them left behind anxious parents, assumed a different identity and risked being arrested, all to join the underground Communist Party to pursue their dreams of a free and equal China. "We old comrades are extremely anxious," Zhong said. "Many people have placed a lot of hope in the 18th party congress; if they don't seize this opportunity to change the authoritarian way, the regime could fall at any time."

Du Daozheng agreed: "If the country doesn't embark on the road of constitutional governance, it [the party] will have to step down for sure ... it won't survive for very long."

*   *   *

At 95, Still Bent on Party Reform

by **Verna Yu**

The wave of democracy cannot be resisted, says Mao's former secretary.

Li Rui has written to the leaders before every Communist Party congress since 1997, urging the party he joined seven decades ago to take on political reform. In 2012 Li, aged 95, the former secretary to Mao Zedong, made yet another plea for reform. But he had to contend with the fact that he probably would not see his dream come true in his lifetime.

"I have done this for the past three congresses," said Li, one of the few remaining reformist party elders. "Now the 18th congress is coming up, I still have to say the same thing. We need political reform, because we still have one-party rule, there is no separation of party and government powers, and there is still a Political and Legal Affairs Committee — this system is a big problem," Li sighed. The judiciary and the police in China are controlled by the Communist Party through the Political and Legal Affairs Committee.

Li knew better than just about anyone the problems of the system. He joined the underground Communist Party at the age of 20 and co-founded a clandestine branch while a student at Wuhan University, driven by his youthful dream of freedom and democracy to fight the corrupt and authoritarian Kuomintang regime.

Despite such revolutionary credentials, Li was punished time and again during his long party career. He was tortured and jailed for more than a year in 1943 at the Communist Party base in Yanan during the Rectification Movement, an internal purge of intellectuals and others that cost some 10,000 lives. He was stripped of his party membership and sacked from his positions as Mao's secretary and vice-minister for water resources and electric power for his criticism of the disastrous

Great Leap Forward. After that, he was sent to a labour camp, where he nearly starved to death. He was jailed again, for eight years, during the Cultural Revolution.

Li, a one-time Central Committee member and deputy head of the party's Organisation Department, had warned repeatedly against the dangers of one-party rule and unchecked power. Instead, he said, constitutional democracy and the rule of law were the only ways to prevent such abuses of power. "The Communist Party's revolution triumphed because it opposed Chiang Kai-shek's fascist rule but advocated freedom, democracy and self-reliance in new China. But after it gained power it pursued the opposite and contradicted its principles."

In the reform and opening era, paramount leader Deng Xiaoping advocated political reform in 1980 and in 1986, resulting in a consensus at the 13th Communist Party Congress in 1987 to separate the functions of the party and government. But the reform push was abandoned after the crackdown on the Tiananmen pro-democracy movement in 1989.

Although economic reform proceeded, resulting in China's breakneck economic development, the lack of checks and balances on official powers also ushered in rampant corruption, social inequality and one of the widest wealth gaps in the world. "My worry is: when will constitutional governance finally come?" Li said.

In a meeting with other liberal party elders in 2012, Li reiterated that the party should embark on political reform by implementing "intra-party democracy", allowing ordinary party members to elect political representatives, separating party and government functions, removing party authority over the judiciary and police and letting party members freely express their political views. His rhetoric, published in the liberal magazine *Yanhuang Chunqiu*, was said to have been criticised by the authorities.

Li said the reformist policies of liberal party leaders Hu Yaobang and Zhao Ziyang in the 1980s that sought more official transparency, a greater public say in policies and a more open media were on the right track in bringing the country to "follow the world trend". But with the crackdown in 1989 on the pro-democracy movement, Li said, the party abandoned universal values such as democracy and rule of law. The death of Hu, purged in 1987 for his liberal stance, in April 1989 triggered the Tiananmen pro-democracy movement, and Zhao, who sympathised with the students, was ousted and kept under house arrest for nearly 16 years until his death in 2005.

"The Communist Party held up the flag of democracy, otherwise it couldn't have toppled Chiang Kai-shek, but in the end it changed and became even worse than Chiang. We couldn't foresee this at the time," Li said. He also blamed a deeply ingrained mass political culture among ordinary Chinese for their lack of modern ideas about nationhood. "This is basically still a peasant nation and Mao is the peasant leader, and our country's problems stem from here," Li said, with a rueful smile. "The peasant tradition is that people want to be ruled, there is no tradition of human rights, democracy, or science [in this country]."

The vast business interests enjoyed by the privileged class of powerful officials and their relatives made them a strong counterforce to reform, Li said. Corruption was rife in the government, and officials from top to bottom exploited their power and influence for financial gain. Many had stashed millions of dollars in overseas bank accounts and sent their children and wives abroad. They feared that if political reforms were implemented, measures that introduced transparency, rule of law and freedom of expression would threaten their privileged positions and the party's survival.

"The Communist Party elite has so many vested interests, so on ideology matters they still need to cling to Mao's image. Otherwise their reign has no foundation and the people will ask, 'Where is your legitimacy?'" But he still saw "a glimmer of hope" when the party purged the flamboyant Chongqing party chief Bo Xilai after Bo and his wife became embroiled in scandal in the months leading up to the 18th party congress.

"The handling of Bo Xilai's case is a warning to the elite," Li said. However, it was the regime's lack of openness and transparency that bred cadres like Bo: "If the party doesn't carry out [political] reform there will be many more like him." Li said the Bo affair indicated an ideological struggle — Bo's popular support base was among people nostalgic for the perceived social equality of Mao's days — but also a power struggle within the party.

Li described new President Xi Jinping as "an honest, down-to-earth person". He stopped short of predicting Xi's future but said he expected the new generation of leaders to be less indoctrinated by party orthodoxy. "There won't be huge changes [under the new leadership], but it won't be worse than the past."

Whether the new leadership pushed for reform or not, Li said he believed the country could not resist the inevitable in the long term. The wave of democracy, he said, simply could not be resisted. "The global situation is changing so fast. Look at North Africa, look at the fall of [Libyan dictator Muammar] Gaddafi and [Egyptian president Hosni] Mubarak after 40 years of rule. With globalisation and the internet, you can no longer hide things from people. It is impossible not to move forward. Could China afford to remain stagnant? That's impossible."

CHAPTER 10

New Leaders Seek China's Renewal

Bold words about reform marked the early days of China's leaders taking over the reins of power at the 18th Communist Party Congress and the subsequent session of the National People's Congress legislature. But the question remained: could the new power brokers at party and government levels free themselves from the legacy of growth for growth's sake and stability at all costs bequeathed by their predecessors and tackle the nation's gnawing social and economic ills? Could they turn talk into action and go down in history as transformative policy makers? We review the pronouncements of newly empowered party and state chief Xi Jinping and Premier Li Keqiang, made as the once-a-decade power transfer concluded, and profile key members of the incoming government tasked with realising the new leadership's goals and dreams.

"Renaissance" Within Reach

by *Jane Cai and Verna Yu*

At the conclusion of the transfer of power in China at the 18th Communist Party Congress and the National People's Congress legislature, the country's new leaders vowed to maintain sustainable growth for the world's second biggest economy and "pursue a renaissance of the Chinese nation". In his maiden speech as head of state, Xi Jinping invoked his favourite concept of the "China dream" and laid out a vision of a stronger nation with a higher standard of living for its 1.3 billion people during his administration.

New Premier Li Keqiang, speaking at a news conference that wrapped up the session of the National People's Congress, gave assurances that the new government's top priority would be to maintain stable growth and that his administration was up to the task, a message likely to be applauded by investors and the market.

Both Xi and Li stressed the necessity of deepening reform to deliver sustained growth but neither mentioned systematic political reform. Painting his vision of a great renaissance of the nation, Xi stressed that the "China dream" could only be realised by seeking "China's own path", cultivating patriotism and following the Communist Party's leadership. "We must continue to strive to achieve the China dream and the nation's great revival," he said. Analysts said Xi's speech outlined lofty goals but stopped short of mentioning initiatives that would have real impact.

Zhang Lifan, a Beijing-based historian, said: "It stressed that everyone should rally around the Communist Party: follow us, then we'll have a bright future." On a more down-to-earth note, Li defined the areas of reform for his cabinet in his 107-minute-long debut press conference as premier. These areas focused on administrative streamlining to make governance more efficient, and included transforming government roles and functions, simplifying bureaucratic procedures and delegating power.

"Right now, there are more than 1,700 items that still require the approval of State Council departments ... We're determined to cut that figure by at least one third," Li promised. In an effort to show his determination to tackle the obstacles blocking economic reform, he said: "Sometimes stirring vested interests may be more difficult than stirring the soul. But however deep the water may be, we will wade into the water. This is because we have no alternative. Reform concerns the destiny of our country and the future of our nation."

Lu Ting, an economist at Bank of America Merrill Lynch, welcomed Li's remarks. "He understood very well that key barriers for reforms are vested interests rather than ideology, or 'soul' in his words, and he promised to tread uncharted waters."

Zhang Ming, a political science professor at Renmin University in Beijing, said such goals indicated China would not see radical changes in the near future. "Political reform was omitted. The new government will probably make no structural or radical change."

Li, the first Chinese premier with a doctorate in economics, said China still had a lot to gain from deepening market-oriented reforms. "I have often said that reform pays the biggest dividend for China. This is because there is still room for improvement in our socialist market economy. There is great space for the further unleashing of productivity through reform and there is great potential for making sure the benefits of reform will reach the entire population."

The key to gaining bigger dividends from reform, he suggested, was to combine the potential of domestic demand and the vitality of creativity to form the new drivers of economic growth. "We need to enhance the quality and efficiency of economic growth, raise employment rates and people's income and enhance environmental protection and the saving of resources so that we will fully upgrade the Chinese economy."

Li outlined three priorities for his cabinet: transformation of the economic model; improving people's livelihoods; and enhancing social justice. He promised to make full use of "fiscal, financing, pricing and other policy instruments" and to "pursue reform of the budgetary system" to make the Chinese economy more open, transparent, standardised and inclusive. "We will drive economic transformation through opening up. The important thing is to further open up the services sector."

In the financial sector, his cabinet would "pursue market-oriented reform of interest and exchange rates. We will develop a multi-tiered capital market and raise the share of direct financing. We will also protect the lawful rights and interests of investors, especially small and medium investors."

Li also said the government needed to pay attention to income distribution. "We need to confront the two biggest gaps in Chinese society — the gap between urban and rural areas and the gap between different regions. In particular, we need to confront the former gap as it involves more than 800 million rural residents and 500 million urban residents." His administration would aim to narrow these disparities by improving the social security system and enhancing vertical mobility among different classes. "We will reform the social sector to promote upward mobility. In some universities in China, the ratio of rural students is quite low. We need to gradually raise that to give hardworking rural students hope." These initiatives could help promote social fairness.

*   *   *

Premier Li: Strong or Just Moderate?

by *Wang Xiangwei*

The premier's news conference on the closing day of "the two meetings" — the annual plenary sessions of the National People's Congress and the Chinese People's Political Consultative Conference — is an important date on the calendar, not only for journalists but also ordinary Chinese. The event is the only time in a year when the premier meets the domestic and foreign media and pontificates on a wide range of issues, unvarnished and live on national television.

The March 17, 2013, event was watched even more closely than usual at home and abroad as Li Keqiang made his debut as the new premier in front of the international media. He came across as being confident and pragmatic in dealing with questions on what he intends to achieve in the next five years ranging from pollution and urbanisation through to Sino-US and Sino-Russian relations.

Whereas his predecessor, Wen Jiabao, relished peppering his replies with poems and quotes from Chinese and foreign philosophers and urging Chinese to look at stars in the sky, Li avoided the high-sounding rhetoric and instead chose popular slang to illustrate his points.

Already billed by the state media as the reform-minded premier, Li vowed to push forward with necessary reforms to make China's economic growth more sustainable, boost spending on improving Chinese people's livelihoods, build up a cleaner government and safeguard social justice.

Highlighting his continuous plan to streamline government and fight corruption, he promised to cut an existing 1,700 administrative approval items by at least one third in the coming five years, after acknowledging that Chinese were faced with having to get approval from dozens of departments in order to start a new business.

Li also vowed to tackle pollution and food safety problems with an "iron fist and firm resolution".

As the news conference is highly choreographed with moderators carefully selecting journalists to raise questions, it was interesting to note that Li was spared hot-issue questions covering China's frosty ties with Japan, the tense situation over North Korea, soaring property prices, how to undertake further financial reforms and the internationalisation of the yuan.

To the disappointment of many Hong Kong journalists, a reporter from Phoenix TV, the only Hong Kong-based media given the opportunity to raise questions, failed to engage Li over rising tension between

Hong Kong and mainland China and the future of the city's political development.

Another question reporters should have raised with Li was whether he would make a stronger premier than Wen. After Wen was chosen as premier 10 years previously, there were concerns over his ability to take on the big challenges and responsibilities of a premier, with some cynics suggesting that his surname, Wen, which rhymed with the word "moderate", signalled he was unlikely to undertake necessary tough reforms.

Ten years later, those cynics were not wide of the mark as many Chinese complained about a lack of meaningful economic and political reforms over the previous decade. By contrast, Li's given name includes the word "Qiang", which means powerful or strong. Let us hope he delivers what his name promises.

* * *

Central Bank

Zhou Xiaochuan

by *Ray Chan and Victoria Ruan*

China's central bank would normally have expected to undergo a personnel reshuffle at the big annual political event in Beijing in March 2013, the National People's Congress. But in a departure from the usual game of musical chairs among China's political circle, People's Bank of China Governor Zhou Xiaochuan was kept on.

The decision to extend Zhou's decade-long stint at China's central bank was made because policymakers had expressed deep concerns about a surge in credit since the global financial crisis in 2008. The total outstanding credit on the books of the bank had reached more than 180 per cent of the country's gross domestic product, fuelling worries about asset bubbles or over investment, people familiar with the government's thinking told the *South China Morning Post*.

Much of the momentum towards growth in China had been based on credit expansion since 2008, when the country began rolling out a 4 trillion yuan stimulus package, according to people working for a large state-owned bank in Beijing. They added that many economic or financial crises in the past had been linked to explosive credit expansion. That's why Zhou, with his vast experience, was asked to defy convention by staying on beyond the retirement age of 65, despite the fact he was left out of the Communist Party's top leadership in the November 2012 reshuffle at the 18th party congress.

"Four years after China's economy was rescued by a huge loan-fuelled stimulus, its economic growth continues to be shored up by an unsustainable dependence on credit," said Mark Williams, an economist at Capital Economics, an independent macroeconomic research consultancy firm based in London.

Commenting on the post-party congress arrangements among China's senior bankers, Zhang Ming, a professor of politics at Beijing's Renmin University, said: "During a power transition, stability is desired above all else."

The *South China Morning Post* welcomed the retention of Zhou Xiaochuan as central bank governor, saying in an editorial that the news should be welcomed in China and overseas. It would be hard to name another Chinese economic official who could match his experience in monetary affairs or enjoy the respect he had from the international financial community.

Keeping Zhou was a shrewd decision made by new leaders Xi Jinping and Li Keqiang. As Zhou was close to former president Jiang Zemin and premier Zhu Rongji, his stay in office would help gain support from the old guard. Zhou would continue to push for economic reforms. In the previous decade, he had helped to overhaul China's banking sector and its interest rate system, gradually internationalise the yuan and liberalise the country's capital account.

While China's central bank does not have full independence like its counterparts in many Western countries, Zhou's prestige was such that it played a key role in the country's macroeconomic policymaking. Overseas, he helped win greater influence and representation for China at the International Monetary Fund and the World Bank.

He shocked some and won kudos from others during the height of the global financial crisis in 2009 when he proposed replacing the US dollar as the international reserve currency under a new global regime controlled by the IMF. One suggestion he made was to use the IMF's special drawing rights — whose value is based on a basket of currencies — as the new reserve currency.

Zhou's easy rapport with central bankers of other major economies will hopefully help promote better communication at a time of serious policy disagreements among them.

*   *   *

Foreign Policy

Wang Yi

by Teddy Ng

In his career Wang Yi, the 59-year-old son-in-law of late leader Zhou Enlai's secretary Qian Jiadong, established himself not only as a diplomat who could defuse a crisis, but also as an official able to cope with unusual career moves.

Wang's appointment as China's foreign minister as part of China's leadership transition was seen by analysts as reflecting Beijing's desire to improve ties with Japan, increasingly tense due to the dispute over the East China Sea islets known as Diaoyu in China and Senkaku in Japan. A student of Japanese at university, Wang also served as ambassador to Japan.

Many observers in Taiwan and in Beijing were surprised in 2008 when Wang, then deputy foreign minister, was appointed head of the State Council's Taiwan Affairs Office. The move, the first time someone with extensive foreign policy experience had been put in charge of Taiwan affairs, triggered concerns in Japan that better communication between the Taiwan Affairs Office and the Chinese foreign ministry was aimed at undermining the relationship between Tokyo and Taipei. Some pundits said the move reflected Beijing's increased willingness to accommodate Taiwan's desire for a greater international presence, a complicated issue for Beijing.

Wang joined the foreign ministry after graduating from university in 1982. In 1983, Wang wrote the speech given by then Communist Party chief Hu Yaobang on his historic trip to Japan, with the Chinese media reporting that Hu made only two changes to the draft. After that, Wang was mainly responsible for Asian affairs, serving as a counsellor in the embassy in Tokyo and head of Asian affairs for the ministry.

He was made deputy foreign minister in 2001, and posted to Tokyo as ambassador between 2004 and 2007. Wang's job was difficult due to the deterioration in Sino-Japanese ties following then Japanese prime minister Junichiro Koizumi's visits to Tokyo's controversial Yasukuni Shrine, which honours 2.5 million Japanese war dead, including 14 class-A war criminals from the Second World War. Wang showed he could deal with difficult issues in a flexible manner and helped ease tensions by arranging for Koizumi's successor, Shinzo Abe, to visit

Beijing soon after he became prime minister for the first time in 2006, followed by a reciprocal visit by then premier Wen Jiabao in 2007.

A US diplomatic cable dated June 15, 2006, released by WikiLeaks said Wang told then US ambassador to Japan Thomas Scheiffer that China realised it was difficult for Japan to alter its position on Yasukuni in response to Chinese pressure, but that such concerns could be addressed diplomatically and China was willing to negotiate a "soft landing" that would give "face" to Japan.

Wang was also China's representative in the first round of six-party talks on North Korea's nuclear programme in 2003. The other five parties were the United States, Japan, South Korea, Russia and North Korea. North Korea had wanted bilateral talks, but the US insisted on multilateral ones. "China advocated that no matter whether it was bilateral or multilateral, it was important for the nations to engage in talks," said Professor Jia Qingguo, an international relations specialist at Peking University. "Wang is very firm when he talks about China's core interests, but he is very pragmatic and will resort to different ways in dealing with difficult issues. Wang definitely puts a lot of effort into studying the issues facing him, and he can always make the right move at the right time."

In addition to defusing crises, Wang is known as a diplomat open to new ideas and always willing to engage in discussions with academics. One scholar who joined in discussions with Wang said he demanded that young Chinese diplomats enhanced their theoretical knowledge, and focused more on analysing the long-term impact of foreign policies in their reports.

*   *   *

Defence

Chang Wanquan

by Choi Chi-yuk and Minnie Chan

New Defence Minister General Chang Wanquan, the public face of the People's Liberation Army and leader of its diplomatic efforts, was the sole general in the new cabinet headed by Premier Li Keqiang. Chang was named a member of the all-important Central Military Commission (CMC) in the 17th party congress in 2007 and retained the position at the 18th party congress.

Analysts said Chang would enjoy limited military power despite being the third-ranked of 10 military officers on the CMC. "The function of the Chinese defence minister is very different from Western counterparts. Our defence minister only handles ceremonial affairs for external relations and there is no concrete political task," said Xu Guangyu, a former general and senior researcher at the Beijing-based China Arms Control and Disarmament Association.

As the CMC's second youngest member before the reshuffle at the 18th party congress, Chang had long been seen as a front runner to become a CMC vice-chairman and secure membership of the party's Politburo. But he failed to obtain either position.

Chang was perceived as an ally of former president Hu Jintao, who promoted him commander of the Shenyang military command in December 2004, three months after Hu succeeded Jiang Zemin as CMC chairman. Some analysts suspected that Chang ended up with the less powerful defence minister post because he was perceived as being too close to Hu, the biggest loser in the power transition. Others suggested that Chang had been implicated in the downfall of the corrupt deputy head of the PLA's general logistics department, Lieutenant General Gu Junshan, in 2012.

In his new role, Chang represented the PLA in its increasingly important external affairs, notably the rising tension between China and its neighbours in the East and South China seas. "Chang's major tasks include modernisation of China's defence, and contributing to the handling of external affairs to protect China's territorial sovereignty," Xu Guangyu said.

Xu described Chang as knowledgeable and calm, but said it was hard to compare Chang with his predecessor General Liang Guanglie. "Liang began his career as a military officer and a war veteran. He has a very distinctive personality. Chang was born in a time of peace and has no first-hand experience of war."

* * *

Finance

Lou Jiwei

by Daniel Ren

Lou Jiwei, known for his reformist outlook and preference for a market-oriented economy, was a deputy finance minister for 10 years before becoming head of China Investment Corp (CIC), the country's sovereign wealth fund, in 2007. His career turned a full circle with his appointment as finance minister at the March 2013 session of the National People's Congress.

A close ally of former premier Zhu Rongji, Lou is viewed as a no-nonsense official with profound knowledge of China's economy and the inner workings of its financial system. When he was appointed CIC chairman, he was put in charge of investing US$200 billion. When he was appointed finance minister, the fund was valued at US$500 billion thanks to additional capital injections from the government and heavy dividend payouts by the biggest state-owned banks. It had recorded an annualised 5.03 per cent return since its inception.

Lou kept a low profile while CIC chairman, but the sovereign wealth fund became involved in several controversies due to unsuccessful investments and the blocking of some attempts to acquire foreign assets. "He's very intelligent, very quick to learn and very capable of dealing with not only our daily investment matters but also with governments, foreign and Chinese, and the people," CIC President Gao Xiqing said. "Overall, he's probably done more for Chinese reform than anyone I can think of. I think he's definitely one of the most important personalities in this country."

Lou spent five years in the People's Liberation Army from 1968 and then worked for Shougang, a big steel mill in Beijing, as a computer programmer before studying for a computer science degree at Tsinghua University in 1978. Lou earned a bachelor's degree in 1982 and received a master's degree in economics from the Chinese Academy of Social Sciences (CASS), a key think tank, in 1984. Afterwards, he became a civil servant at a monetary policy research institute under the State Council before being transferred to a CASS unit.

Zhu, then mayor of Shanghai, moved Lou to the commercial capital in 1988 to help carry out economic reforms. Lou became a department chief at the State Council Office for Restructuring the Economic System in 1992 before being promoted to deputy governor of Guizhou province in 1995. He returned to Beijing in 1998, after Zhu became premier, and became deputy finance minister. Government officials and scholars said Lou was a fan of economic reforms and of giving free rein to market forces.

*   *   *

Economy

Xu Shaoshi

by **Li Jing**

Xu Shaoshi, a former minister of land and resources and a protégé of former premier Wen Jiabao, was appointed director of the National Development and Reform Commission (NDRC), the top economic planning agency.

Xu takes over an expanded NDRC, the biggest beneficiary of a cabinet overhaul which saw the commission take over population policy and absorb the State Electricity Regulatory Commission. That makes Xu one of China's most powerful ministers.

His appointment as head of the NDRC, nicknamed the "mini-State Council", surprised some sources who expected someone with closer ties to new Premier Li Keqiang. Xu had worked directly under Wen twice.

"With the NDRC becoming so powerful, Li would want someone close to him to oversee the commission, otherwise he may lose control over it," a source said. Analysts said the fact Xu spent five years as land and resources minister chimed with the new leadership's vision of driving economic growth through a massive urbanisation programme to resettle 400 million rural people in cities over the following decade.

Born in Zhejiang province, Xu was sent at 18 to the countryside to live and work in Jilin province. Between 1977 and 1980, Xu studied hydrogeology at the Changchun College of Geology, affiliated with the former Ministry of Geology and Mineral Resources. After graduating, Xu started his political career at the ministry's policy and regulation research department, working as a secretary to the ministerial-level officials and then heading the ministry's general office until 1991.

That period saw his first overlap with Wen, who was trained in geology and engineering. Xu worked as a deputy director of the Guangdong provincial department of geology and mineral resources from 1991 to 1993, and was transferred to the State Council's general office. He was appointed deputy secretary general of the State Council in 2000, when Wen served as a vice-premier.

* * *

Commerce

Gao Hucheng

by *Victoria Ruan*

New Commerce Minister Gao Hucheng, an experienced international negotiator and a former senior business executive, faced tough challenges after the country's trade growth missed the official target in 2012, turning in its worst performance since the global financial crisis. A fluent French-speaker, Gao had been a deputy commerce minister since 2003 and international trade representative since 2010.

His promotion from within the ministry rather than Beijing's usual practice of appointing someone from the vast pool of provincial leaders showed that the central government recognised his ability to run an agency that was crucial to economic development.

Unlike his predecessor as minister, Chen Deming, who climbed the political ladder mostly through provincial and central government positions, Gao had experience in both the government and business sectors, including serving as a deputy general manager at China Resources Enterprise in the 1990s.

Entering his new job, Gao needed to stabilise exports, even as the West remained stuck in a protracted recession, and to cope with rising trade frictions with other countries. He also faced rising domestic calls to boost the services industry and domestic consumption, tasks critical to Beijing's long-term goal of cutting reliance on foreign trade and fixed-asset investment as drivers of the economy.

"As China's export competitiveness shrinks, Gao's ministry will face greater pressures to meet Beijing's trade targets," said Zhang Zhiwei, chief China economist for Nomura. "He will need to find new growth engines through upgrading technologies and boosting services exports."

Over the following decade, China could face international friction from a range of countries, including emerging markets competing with it to attract foreign investment such as Brazil, Argentina and Indonesia, Zhang said. Gao's expertise in trade talks would play an important role in such conflicts.

Born in Shanxi province, Gao studied at Zaire National University's college of literature. After working at China's embassy in the Democratic Republic of Congo, he was a deputy general manager of the French branch of the China National Machinery and Equipment Import Export Corporation from 1982 to 1987, simultaneously earning a doctorate in sociology from the University of Paris in 1985. Gao was appointed a deputy trade minister after serving as a vice-chairman of the Guangxi Zhuang autonomous region from 2002 to 2003.

*   *   *

Health

Li Bin

by Zhuang Pinghui

Li Bin, minister in charge of the newly established Health and Family Planning Commission, has a rich background in both health and national family planning affairs, and there was little surprise at her appointment which made her China's fourth minister of public health, in charge of the tricky issues of health-care reform and the country's controversial birth control policies.

"We always bless people with the blessings that we wish everybody: health and a happy family. You can tell the weight of health care and family in people's hearts," said Li after her appointment was announced. "We have to take our job seriously ... to deepen medical and health-care reform and do a good job with the family planning work."

Li worked in the National Population and Family Planning Commission for more than four years, first as a deputy and then as director, until she was named governor of Anhui province in 2011. Prior to that, Li was in charge of health, social security and labour in her six years as deputy governor of Jilin province, from 2001 to 2007.

Former health minister Dr Chen Zhu has spoken highly of Li, offering praise for her health-care initiatives in Anhui as well as for the important role the province played in national medical reform efforts. Anhui was the only province that had two cities out of 17 in the whole country to pilot difficult public hospital reforms. The province also gained attention for its reform of the system of providing essential drugs as well as for increasing health-care coverage.

Li, from Fushun in Liaoning province, spent more than three decades of her political career in Jilin. After starting out as a teacher at the Changchun Institute of Education in 1974, Li went on to become a junior party official in charge of propaganda in Changchun. She first served as a provincial-level official in 1994, as deputy director of Jilin's Planning Commission. Li was named an assistant governor of Jilin six years later and promoted to deputy governor in 2001.

With her doctoral degree in economics, Li asked the province's statistics department to take measures to prevent the filing of fake figures or reports. Her pragmatic approach to politics also saw her make several inspection visits to welfare projects, such as low-income housing developments, in rural areas.

After being transferred to the National Population and Family Planning Commission in 2007, Li went to several provinces, including Xinjiang and Guangdong, to conduct research, and she spoke openly about problems such as the gender imbalance favouring males, and China's rapidly ageing society. A fellow official in Anhui also praised Li for her charisma and people skills, which she used to "bring officials together to achieve a common goal".

* * *

Taiwan Affairs

Zhang Zhijun

by *Teddy Ng*

Zhang Zhijun, appointed the new chief of the State Council's Taiwan Affairs Office, assumed the position without a strong background in Taiwan affairs. Before being named deputy foreign minister in 2009, Zhang spent most of his time as a relatively unknown official with the International Department of the Communist Party's Central Committee.

"He is a totally new face to the Taiwanese people, and we don't know anything about his personality," said Professor Edward Chen I-hsin, a political analyst at Taiwan's Tamkang University. "Zhang has not made any comments on Taiwan before, and we don't know his views on cross-strait ties."

Zhang was born in Nantong, Jiangsu province, in 1953, and joined the Communist Party when he was 18. He served with the Heilongjiang Production and Construction Corps between 1969 and 1974, and in 1975 he started his career with the International Department, an agency in charge of conducting exchanges with political parties of other countries.

In 1988, he was promoted to director of the department's division responsible for American and North European affairs, and in 1991, he was posted to the Chinese embassy in Britain for three years before returning to the International Department. From 1996 to 1997, he was deputy party secretary of Zibo in Shandong province, before being named research director of the International Department.

In 2000, Zhang was appointed deputy director of the department. In 2009, he moved to the Foreign Ministry as deputy minister.

Some Chinese political observers considered Zhang a low-profile diplomat who seldom made his views public until 2012 when tensions between China and Japan flared up in the territorial dispute involving the Diaoyu Islands, known as Senkaku in Japan.

At a Foreign Ministry forum in December 2012, Zhang said China would not be provocative but also would not be frightened, adding that both countries should resolve the disputes through dialogue.

Taiwanese media reported that Zhang was reluctant to go to the Taiwan Affairs Office but Beijing made the decision as it wanted to continue appointing senior diplomats to head cross-strait affairs, which often involve complex international relations, particularly with the United States and Japan.

*   *   *

Anti-Graft

Huang Shuxian

by **Keith Zhai**

Huang Shuxian, deputy head of the Communist Party's internal anti-graft commission, was named supervision minister to lead the clean-up of government at a time when top leaders saw corruption as the major threat to the party's legitimacy.

The Central Commission for Discipline Inspection (CCDI) is a party body responsible for internal discipline and approves the punishment or expulsion of members for corruption and misconduct. The Ministry of Supervision that Huang heads is its parallel state body. He replaces Ma Wen.

The Ministry of Supervision worked in tandem with the CCDI since 1993, and it was party practice to appoint a CCDI deputy chief as the minister.

Huang graduated from the department of literature, history and philosophy at Nanjing University in 1977. After serving as a junior cultural official and party secretary in Yangzhong county, Jiangsu province, for years, Huang became the provincial secretary of the Communist Youth League in 1985. The job made Huang a member of the *tuanpai* camp, officials who originated from the Youth League, as he established a protégé relationship with Premier Li Keqiang, who entered the leadership of the Youth League in the 1980s.

Huang became the Standing Committee member of the CCDI in 2002, while he was also vice-minister of supervision. He was a strong contender for the minister's job in 2007 following the death of Li Zhijun, but lost out to Ma.

Huang was likely to have other duties in addition to being supervision minister. It was most likely that, like Ma, he would serve as director of the National Bureau of Corruption Prevention and the Correcting Industrial Illegitimate Practice Office of the State Council.

Gu Su, a law professor at Nanjing University, described Huang, his schoolmate, as someone who would keep a low profile while he carried out the instructions of top leaders including CCDI chief Wang Qishan, who projected an image of being tough and outspoken.

"Under Wang's leadership, Huang won't have to think too much about his task but just follow the plan," said Gu. "But, being supervision minister will still be a tough job while the top leaders make the fight against corruption their primary mission."

In a 2009 article in the communist mouthpiece magazine *Qiushi,* Huang took a tough line by saying that all party members, regardless of their position or influence, would be held responsible for violating party discipline and laws.

* * *

Securities Regulation

Xiao Gang

by Daniel Ren

Beijing picked the chairman of the Bank of China, Xiao Gang, to head the China Securities Regulatory Commission (CSRC) at a time when massive reforms were being undertaken to revive the stock market. Veteran banker Xiao was a deputy governor at China's central bank between 1998 and 2003 before becoming the chairman of the Bank of China, the country's largest foreign-exchange lender.

During his 10-year tenure at the Bank of China, Xiao was credited with leading the bank's expansion. He was the first boss of a major state-owned bank to publicly question the wild growth of wealth management products, likening them to the shadow banking system. He won plaudits from investors and bankers for his outspoken style after scandals involving wealth management products.

The reshuffle at the regulatory body came after Xiao's predecessor, Guo Shuqing, a reform-minded technocrat, implemented a series of new policies to overhaul the ailing stock market. Small investors had long suffered from the frothy initial public share offerings, fraudulent earnings reports and rampant insider trading plaguing the market.

News that Guo would be removed from the CSRC post to become governor of Shandong province, first reported by the *South China Morning Post,* sparked an uproar on the internet, with thousands of investors coming out in support of the departing securities regulatory chief. Guo took the helm of the CSRC late in 2011 after a miserable run by the A-share market in 2010 and 2011, when a flood of initial share sales drained liquidity out of existing stocks and left millions of investors high and dry when the new stocks sank one after another below their exaggerated listing prices.

Guo suspended approvals for new listings until further reforms of the offering mechanism. He also tightened delisting rules, called for an increase in cash dividend payouts and tried to direct more capital into the market. Although the market hardly responded to Guo's efforts, he earned the respect and confidence of most institutional and retail investors, who said they believed the reform measures could lead to the healthy growth of the market in the long term. Chen Gong, a retail investor, said: "He was a good and capable securities regulator and gave us hope although we are still stuck in paper losses. We hope his successor will be as good."

* * *

Ethnic Affairs

Wang Zhengwei

by *Minnie Chan*

The appointment of a vice-chairman of China's top political advisory body to head the State Council's ethnic affairs commission will not help Beijing solve its ethnic problems even though the new chief, Wang Zhengwei, hales from the Muslim Hui minority, experts said.

Wang, 55, chairman of the Ningxia Hui Autonomous Region in northwestern China, succeeded Yang Jing as head of the State Ethnic Affairs Commission (SEAC). Wang is also the youngest vice-chairman of the Chinese People's Political Consultative Conference (CPPCC) advisory body and was also promoted as one of five state councillors.

"SEAC has had the lowest political impact among the 25 departments under the State Council since it was set up in 1949, no matter what official rankings its heads have held," said Ilham Tohti, an ethnic Uygur economics professor at the Central Nationalities University in Beijing. "As an ethnic Hui from Ningxia, Wang might be more familiar with Uygurs, but he can't influence China's ethnic policy because the role of CPPCC is just a 'political vase' [for display]."

Ningxia has been dubbed the "Chinese Mecca" since the middle of the Ming Dynasty and boasts a long history of Islamic culture. Located on the upper reaches of the Yellow River, more than 80 per cent of the region's 6.6 million inhabitants are ethnic Hui.

Tohti said that two party officials from ethnic minority back-grounds — Yang Jingren, a Hui from Gansu province and former vice-premier, and Ismail Amat, a Uygur from Xinjiang — ruled the SEAC from 1978 to 1998, but ethnic conflicts between minority Uygurs and Han Chinese who settled there had continued for nearly four decades.

Jiang Zhaoyong, a Beijing-based expert on ethnic issues, said the SEAC had no political role as it was just an organisation involved in research and education concerning ethnic minorities. "It's a fact that Wang can't do anything to influence our country's ethnic affairs. In Xinjiang, all ethnic issues are decided by the party's Political and Legal Affairs Commission, while the United Front Line Department controls Tibetan policies," Jiang said.

* * *

Supreme Court

Zhou Chiang

by Choi Chi-yuk and Keith Zhai

Zhou Chiang, named as president of the Supreme People's Court — China's top judge — during the 2012–13 leadership transition, filled a post that made him a state leader but was also a more symbolic one in a country largely ruled by the Communist Party rather than the law. At the age of 52, Zhou had been viewed as a rising political star until his failure to win a seat on the Communist Party's Politburo at the 18th party congress. Still, given his relative youth among the party elite, Zhou, a former party chief in Hunan province, could still join the Politburo in future.

A source close to Zhou said he would have preferred to become party secretary of a province with robust economic development prospects because that would have given him more real power. "He will enjoy little real power even though he is nominally the head of all judges at different levels across the country," the source said. "When you consider that the wages and benefits of his subordinates are largely provided by regional governments, you will immediately figure out whose orders they will listen to."

Sixteen years ago, when he headed the Communist Youth League, Zhou was considered an important member of the *tuanpai* camp — the power base of departing president Hu Jintao — and was being groomed to become part of one of China's so-called sixth generation of leaders a decade after the 18th party congress in 2022.

Born in April 1960 in Huangmei county, Hubei province, Zhou came from a humble family, his father being a local party official. Zhou was sent to the countryside in Huangmei as an "educated youth" during the 1966–76 Cultural Revolution. He entered the prestigious Southwest University of Political Science and Law in 1978, after taking part in the first university entrance examinations following the Cultural Revolution decade of chaos, and earned a bachelor's degree and a master's degree from its law school.

Chen Zhonglin, head of the law school at Chongqing University who went to university with Zhou, said the students wanted to help to restore order. "For law students at that time, we acted with that sense of stewardship in mind, thinking of what was appropriate for the whole system to get back to the rule of law and not simply what was best for our firm. In addition to his legal background, Zhou also has regional and ministerial experience. In that sense, he may help implement and streamline the rule of law."

Zhou became a clerk and a junior official in the Ministry of Justice after he left university in 1985, and served as deputy director of the general office and director of the office of the minister. After serving as director of the ministry's rule of law department in 1995, he became a member of the

Youth League's secretariat. The many years Zhou spent at the Youth League appeared to help his political career, as he became a protégé of new Premier Li Keqiang, whom he succeeded as League head in 1998.

In 2006 Zhou became one of the youngest provincial governors, in Hunan. His interest in reform of the justice system was apparent when he pledged to create a "Hunan governed by law". Chen Jiping, secretary of the party's leading group at the China Law Society and once secretary to former National People's Congress chairman Qiao Shi, praised Zhou's commitment to legal affairs. "Zhou Qiang is an intelligent person, and is passionate about legal affairs."

Zhou became party secretary of Hunan in 2010 but his commitment to ruling by law was plagued by scandals. Li Wangyang, an activist in the Tiananmen protest movement crushed in 1989, was found dead in mysterious circumstances in a hospital in June 2012, while a woman was sent to a labour camp two months later for petitioning after her daughter was kidnapped, raped and forced into prostitution.

A media source in Hunan who met Zhou a number of times said he was like a gymnast who always performed the compulsory exercises correctly and cautiously, but never attempted any creative moves. "I can't remember a single story about a personal trait that is interesting," the source said. "He doesn't seem to have enough self-confidence. Why else would he maintain a tight grip over the media and fail to do anything significant in Hunan?"

He Weifang, a Peking University legal scholar who also studied with Zhou, jumped to Zhou's defence, saying: "As many things take place in an accidental manner, one should not hold a regional chief fully responsible for all these things. These kinds of unexpected things could hardly all be avoided." He said at least Zhou was "a graduate who studied law", unlike many in China's legal system.

*　　*　　*

Cabinet Revamp Short on Action

by *South China Morning Post Reporters*

In its first overhaul in five years, the State Council, or cabinet, sought to streamline its structure, reducing the number of cabinet-level agencies to 25 from 27. But the changes, which affected the nation's railways, health services, maritime security, energy and the media, fell short of more radical proposals pushed by reform advocates.

In this renewed effort to build a smaller, more efficient government announced at the National People's Congress meeting in March 2013, the powerful but scandal-plagued Railways Ministry was axed. Under the much-anticipated plan, the national railways operator was no longer its own regulator. Day-to-day operations and the planning of future railways were spun off to a new China Railway Corporation, while regulatory oversight was handed over to an expanded Transport Ministry. In addition, a new vice-ministerial-level agency, the State Railway Administration, was established under the ministry to oversee railway safety, service quality and other issues.

Departing Railways Minister Sheng Guangzu said he "had no regrets" being the last person in that post. Sheng was appointed in February 2011 after his predecessor, Liu Zhijun, was ousted amid corruption allegations. Wang Feng, an official involved in drafting the reform proposal, said the new structure was intended to fund the debt-laden railway sector better and boost safety supervision. A high-speed train crash in the eastern city of Wenzhou in July 2011 killed at least 40 people, sparking a torrent of public criticism that authorities had compromised on safety in the rush to expand the railways network. A government report blamed the crash on mismanagement and design flaws, with Liu among the officials held responsible.

The country's massive spending on building high-speed railways in the wake of the 2008–09 financial crisis helped create a huge debt burden for the agency. Beijing announced in March 2013 that the spun-off China Railway Corporation had registered capital of 1.04 trillion yuan but 2.66 trillion yuan worth of outstanding liabilities. "Before the historical debt of the railways ministry is resolved, the state will temporarily not tax the company's profit," the government said.

While most internet users welcomed the plan to dissolve a ministry plagued by corruption allegations, some called it "a strategic mistake" as China could lose the opportunity to build a rail network linking Europe and Asia.

China Railway Corp had a viable capital structure, said Ivan Chung, a senior credit officer at Moody's Investors Service. "The company is technically solvent. It looks like a viable balance sheet for them to start a business with." The company had a debt-asset ratio of 73 per cent, which was comparable to that of most state-owned enterprises, he said. "Its leverage is not low, but acceptable."

Whether and when the company could be floated or some of its subsidiaries listed depended on its profitability, Chung said. "The current railway model is not commercially viable, with its low fares, large workforce and inefficiencies. They need to change their business model. Otherwise, the company cannot attract investors."

Also marked for dismantling was China's National Population and Family Planning Commission — executor of the one-child policy — with most of its portfolio going to a ministry-level health agency. Officials said the decision did not signal any changes in family planning policies or a loosening of birth controls. But the move demonstrated changing attitudes about population control after nearly a half of century of successful — if often brutal — efforts to control China's birth rate, population experts said.

In 1979, the central government implemented its controversial one-child policy. Two years later, family planning was made a basic state policy and the National Family Planning Commission was created. For the next two decades, the commission enforced the country's strict birth targets, encouraging many officials to resort to forced abortions, even late into pregnancy. After 2000, the commission banned the practice, although in reality local officials continued to carry it out.

The effectiveness of the one-child policy has been a matter of great debate. But defenders of the commission said it had prevented more than 400 million births. On the flip side, Chinese society is rapidly greying. By 2000, the number of people aged 60 or over had surpassed 10 per cent of the total population, and almost 7 per cent of the population was aged 65.

In a move that could have implications for China's tense territorial disputes with its neighbours, the State Council announced that the country's National Oceanic Administration (NOA) was to be given consolidated control over the numerous agencies that oversaw coastal security.

The NOA, which already looked after marine surveillance, was also to take over the Public Security Ministry's coastguard patrols, the Agriculture Ministry's fisheries patrols and the General Administration of Customs' anti-smuggling efforts.

Ma Kai, secretary general of the State Council, said that having coastal security forces scattered across several agencies was inadequate. He said the consolidation would better "safeguard the country's maritime rights". The restructuring followed months of angry exchanges between Beijing, Tokyo, Manila and other neighbours about overlapping land claims in the East and South China seas. The dispute with Japan in particular stirred concerns about a possible military confrontation, as both nations conducted rival boat patrols around the Diaoyu, or Senkaku, islands in the East China Sea and even scrambled fighter jets.

The changes announced by the State Council disappointed supporters of more dramatic overhauls called for in recent years. There were no proposals for overarching energy and culture ministries. Instead, control of print and broadcast media was to be consolidated into one agency and the State Electricity Regulatory Commission was to be folded into the National Energy Administration.

Li Jiang, party secretary of the Hunan Provincial People's Congress' Standing Committee and a National People's Congress delegate, said he had hoped for a more radical streamlining plan. He suggested setting up an independent new agency to plan and implement further reform. "It's very difficult for a central government body, which has powers in allocating resources and approving certain matters, to bring forward a plan to reform itself," he said.

Professor Wang Yukai, of the National School of Administration, said there was still room for reform. He cited the merger of the General Administration of Press and Publication and the State Administration of Radio, Film and Television as an example. "There could be a super culture ministry when conditions are ripe," he said.

Wang Feng, deputy director of the State Commission Office for Public Sector Reform, said the National Development and Reform Commission, the State Council's policymaking arm, "really needs to sort out its administrative approval powers carefully and decide which to give to local governments and which to abolish".

CHAPTER 11

Will China Miracle Lose Its Magic?

China's path to economic powerhouse led it to oust Japan as the Asian miracle and became the world's second-largest economy during the "Golden Decade" preceding the leadership transition at the 18th party congress. Whether this phenomenal performance could be continued under the leadership of President Xi Jinping and Premier Li Keqiang in the following decade had immeasurable ramifications not just for China but for the rest of the world as well.

Bulls vs Bears

by Wang Xiangwei

As the 18th party congress convened, uncertainty about the true colours of China's next leaders, coupled with a noticeable economic slowdown, led to sharp debate over the future direction of the world's second-largest economy.

On this issue, there were two camps with starkly opposing views. The optimists believed China's economy would remain on a growth trajectory for the next 20 or 30 years, with gross domestic product growth to average 7 to 8 per cent. That was much slower than the double-digit growth rates achieved for most of the previous 40 years, but still enough to enable China to overtake the US as the world's largest economy.

The optimists generally dismissed the political uncertainty and economic slump as temporary, and expected the new leaders to continue the path of reform and opening up once the transition was

settled. After all, maintaining a strong economy was the most important source of the party's legitimacy, enabling it to cling to power.

On the other hand, a growing number of pessimists believed China
was heading into stormy waters with no relief in sight. They said politically, the party was corrupted to the core, and the scandals involving
disgraced politician Bo Xilai and his wife showed the party risked an
implosion at the highest level. And, at the same time, the leadership
was grappling with widespread social unrest at home and a nationalisti-
cally charged war of words over territorial disputes.

Economically, the growth model was unbalanced, uncoordinated,
and unsustainable. In many ways, the pessimists contended, China's
leadership faced challenges similar to those that toppled the Qing
dynasty (1644–1911) and the Kuomintang.

Whether the optimists or pessimists are proved right will have
global ramifications. At stake is whether China will have a strong
leader in President Xi Jinping and a strong government to tackle the
next decade of challenges.

There were also two schools of thoughts on Xi's leadership. The
pessimists believed that Xi was unlikely to undertake drastic reforms
needed to rebalance the economy and put the country on a healthier
growth track, at least not in the first few years of his reign. This was
partly because, after growing up in the chaos of the Cultural Revolution,
Xi shared the prevailing leadership wisdom that maintaining stability
should be the top priority.

But optimists held that Xi had the courage to pursue bolder economic and political reforms and tackle corruption. The optimists were
encouraged when, during his first trip outside Beijing following the
party congress, Xi visited the dynamic manufacturing centre of
Shenzhen, where his rhetoric on reform drew comparisons to late
paramount leader Deng Xiaoping's famous southern tour in 1992,
when he was credited with restarting China's reform drive that had

stalled following the government's bloody crackdown on pro-democracy student demonstrations in 1989.

There were other signs of Xi's willingness to take on key economic reforms at an early stage of his leadership. First, the central government proposed a two-year trial period allowing private businesses to provide domestic mobile phone services, a step to help the private sector enter strategic industries previously restricted to state-owned firms.

The announcement stood in sharp contrast to the empty talk over the previous 10 years that was typical of the regime under president Hu Jintao and premier Wen Jiabao who talked about eliminating barriers to the private sector while never implementing concrete measures to achieve it.

Further evidence that Beijing was intensifying efforts to open up its capital markets came in January 2013 when Guo Shuqing, chairman of the China Securities Regulatory Commission, announced at a financial forum in Hong Kong that the quota for foreign investments in China's financial markets could rise by up to tenfold. "For our capital markets to mature, they must open more in future," said Guo. Shares in Shanghai leapt 3.1 per cent after Guo's comments.

* * *

Old Plans Tie New Hands

by *Cary Huang*

> *The forbidding catalogue of economic and social woes facing China may hold up reform moves.*

China's new economic team led by Premier Li Keqiang was confronted with multiple and daunting challenges, both domestically and internationally. Internally, they had to deal with deep-rooted flaws in China's wobbly economic system and worsening structural problems. They included the market-distorting powers of state monopolies, rampant official graft, an unbalanced industrial structure, an ageing workforce and widening wealth gaps between regions and individuals. Together, they pointed to deepening social tensions that could conceivably threaten the Communist Party's rule.

Analysts and economists expressed the hope that the new leadership that emerged from the 18th party congress would revive long stalled market-oriented reform, but doubted this would happen rapidly or in the near term.

Some analysts said China's phenomenal growth — sinking below 10 per cent in only four of the 10 years leading up to the congress — had been achieved at excessive cost, which all sectors of the economy, including workers, businesses and the state, would have to bear for years to come. Structural problems had worsened in the previous decade, with China's economy less balanced and growth less sustainable.

Hao Hong, head of China research at the Bank of Communications in Hong Kong, said at the time of the congress the economy was at a critical juncture and "it is time for reform". But, citing Chinese philosophy's attachment to the doctrine of the mean (*zhongyong*) and non-action (*wuwei*), Hong ruled out any immediate revamp. "The old leaders' thinking and economic management is likely to continue to exert its influence on the new leadership."

Most China watchers and economists agreed that the new leadership would follow their predecessors' policy prescriptions for some time, with the primary goal of ensuring stability before they consolidated their power and sought new breakthroughs. Professor Steve Tsang, director of the China Policy Institute at the University of Nottingham, said "not that much will change. The main partnership represents a forced marriage between incoming President Xi and incoming Premier Li, with each other's default option being to fall back on their backers for support." Xi's main patron was former party chief Jiang Zemin, while Li was a protégé of former president Hu Jintao, who stepped down at the party congress. Tsang said that meant Xi would not be in a position to put a powerful stamp on policy or direct a major policy shift, while Li had shown himself to be more of a "Teflon" politician than a premier who would assert that the buck stopped on his desk.

"He is unlikely to drive policy change much," Tsang said. "Should the economy slow down seriously and cause major social disturbances, the fun will start as the top leaders try to find a consensus on how best to deal with that."

Dr Liao Qun, chief economist at Citic Bank International, said the policy and reform direction of the new leadership would be largely the same as that of the existing one. "But as with any other new leadership, it will seek breakthroughs in new areas." Professor Kerry Brown, head of the China Studies Centre at the University of Sydney, said people could expect policy continuity for the duration of the 12th five-year plan, running until 2015. "That sets out the consensus position on growth targets and macroeconomic objectives, and acts as the bridge between the leadership groups. This document is the result of party- and government-wide consultation, so to disrupt it would be a huge problem." Such disruption would be countenanced only in the event of a massive external shock, like a rapidly worsening global economic slowdown. Then ideas outside the plan would be needed.

Economists said that in the near term, the new administration would have to deal with the weak global economy and slowing demand both overseas and domestically. "It must act to stabilise growth while containing inflation," Hong said. "We are likely to see a series of monetary easing actions and probably fiscal stimulus."

Liao said that regarding short-term macroeconomic policies, the new government would be more responsive to continuing volatility in the external environment. Stronger and more flexible monetary and fiscal policies should be applied to maintain high rates of economic growth, with fiscal policy likely to play a greater role. He said longer-term reforms were likely to focus on five areas: promoting the private economy by improving the financing environment for small and medium-sized enterprises; accelerating the restructuring of state-owned monopolies; upgrading the economic and industrial structure by fostering strategic, emerging industries, promoting innovation and curbing overcapacity; speeding up financial reforms, including interest rate liberalisation, internationalisation of the yuan and further commercialisation of state banks; and reducing the wealth gap by accelerating income growth and raising social security levels for those on lower incomes.

Hong said interest-rate liberalisation was the key to market reform and should top the new government's agenda. Interest rates in China had been abnormally low because they had not been set by the market, he said. That led to over-investment and the misallocation of resources. He also expected that making the yuan a more international currency and opening up the capital account would be given higher priority in the coming decade. He had already seen traces of such reforms, including asymmetric cuts to interest rates and the sealing of offshore yuan settlement agreements. They were the first steps in a long march towards the final reform, he said, but "the train has left the station".

"These changes will lead to a revaluation of the Chinese currency and a rise in capital costs," Hong said. "It is the reason why capital-intensive industries may be facing a persistent, long-term decline. Meanwhile, together with these reforms, there will be financial innovations and dramatic growth of the capital market." Hong said industrial policies would focus on new sectors — hi-tech, services, health care, the environment, new materials and new energy — many of which were not capital-intensive. "These policy changes are likely to be implemented over the coming years, and their effect on economic restructuring will gradually become evident."

Advice for China's new economic team came two months after the party congress from a senior International Monetary Fund official, Zhu Min, who said at a forum in Hong Kong that China's financial system needed a new approach, playing a more active role in helping its real economy become more resilient to external shocks. Financial reform would make it easier for Chinese consumers to save and borrow, boosting domestic consumption. Apart from supportive financial measures for large state-owned enterprises, Beijing should create preferential policies to support small private businesses as a way to create jobs and increase wages, added Zhu, a former deputy governor of the People's Bank of China.

Analysts said that an unstable backdrop might force the new leadership to make hard choices on whether to revive market reform because the legitimacy of party rule rested on its ability to maintain growth, spread prosperity and achieve social stability. That would involve tackling scores of issues, including corruption, land-rights conflicts, a lack of investment in education, housing and medical care, and pollution.

But Harley Seyedin, president of the American Chamber of Commerce in South China, said he was confident that China's new leadership could overcome such challenges. "I am supremely confident that both gentlemen [Xi and Li] will help build a future characterised by sustainable economic growth, increased integration with the global economy and a continuation of the opening up that has been a cornerstone of China's success for the past 30 years."

* * *

Rough Road to Change

by *Victoria Ruan and Jane Cai*

A new policy blueprint is broad and promising in scope, but implementation remains key.

In a more than 8,000-word document issued in February 2013, the State Council, or cabinet, approved long-delayed and sweeping reform guidelines that included easing the nation's widening income gap by raising wages, cutting taxes for the poor, and allowing them to share more of the state's growth.

Despite the alarming proportions of China's social inequality, the guidelines were held up for about eight years, after being amended half a dozen times amid strong objections from interest groups related to state-owned enterprises (SOEs) and some government bodies.

According to the guidelines, the government aimed to double average urban and rural per capita individual income by 2020 from 2010, and make more rural migrant workers city dwellers. In addition, by 2015, enterprises owned by the central government would be required to surrender a greater share of profits — five percentage points over existing levels — to the government, with part of the funds slated for "improving people's livelihoods".

"The guidelines are about the goals, direction, and major principles of the reform," said Li Shi, a professor at Beijing Normal University. "The broad ideas are correct. However, the key is how to implement them. That will be something left to the new generation of leaders to worry about."

To broaden its channels of income, the government also planned to further develop the capital market; push forward interest-rate liberalisation reforms; widen the range of deposit and lending rates that banks could set themselves; and roll out more bond and currency products.

The plan to ease the income gap, issued just before the 2013 week-long Chinese New Year holiday, was cheered by the public. "It's good timing to roll out the guidelines," said Su Hainan, a vice-chairman of the China Association for Labour Studies. "They will lay a foundation for the new administration to deepen the reforms." Société Generale China economist Yao Wei said: "The plan covers all the bases. Any policy that is generally accepted as being useful in improving income distribution is included in the proposal." But she cautioned that the strategy might not be easy to implement, probably because it was "too comprehensive".

In 2012 the United Nations said 13 per cent of people in China lived on less than US$1.25 a day, while the *Hurun Report*, best known for its "China Rich List" ranking of the wealthiest individuals in China, said the country had 2.7 million US dollar millionaires. Real estate prices had soared tenfold in major cities over the previous decade, despite government measures designed to cool the market.

Shen Jianguang, Mizuho Securities chief economist for Greater China, said reducing tax burdens for households, raising dividend payments by SOEs, and boosting deposit interest rates were good ideas. He estimated in 2010 that these steps could contribute to household income by at least 4 trillion yuan over the years to 2015.

Still, Shen and Yao, along with other researchers, believed the guidelines were too general and lacked concrete measures or measurable targets. For example, the guidelines pledged to cap SOE managers' salaries, but failed to offer any quantifiable guidance. Shen also said a plan to ask SOEs to submit 5 percentage points more of their profits to the government was "a bit too modest", given that the state sector generated more than 2 trillion yuan worth of profits every year. Under existing policies, SOEs submitted 5 to 10 per cent of dividends to the state-assets regulator annually.

Probably more importantly, the plan fell short of a specific target about the wealth gap, something that such a reform should not have omitted. Instead, it repeated a goal set by the Communist Party to double per capita income for urban and rural people by 2020 from 2010. "This probably reflects the difficulty the government expects to have in reducing income inequality and the strong resistance from vested interest groups," said Nomura International's chief China economist Zhang Zhiwei.

In the guidelines, the cabinet also said the government would reform property taxes by "improving the taxation system in property ownership and transactions" and "gradually expanding the pilot scheme of individual property tax".

"The leadership seems to be resolved to push ahead with the property tax reform," said Ma Guoxian, director of Shanghai University of Finance and Economics' Public Policy Centre. "But how to do it remains a question, considering expected opposition from corrupt government officials, large real-estate developers, local governments and related ministries."

Analysts said local governments, relying heavily on land sales to make ends meet, tried to sell land at high prices. Developers made profits on top of the unreasonably high land prices. Buyers paid the price of a property and various taxes.

When China's property prices soared, policymakers tried to redesign the taxation system to reduce local governments' incentive to sell land at high prices — but without much success.

Chen Huai, former head of the policy research centre at the Ministry of Housing and Urban-Rural Development, said the individual property tax would be levied nationwide "for sure", but it was hard to predict whether it would be introduced in a year or two.

Government officials, heads of state firms and bank executives were key holders of property. Mainland media gave big coverage to reports of corrupt officials amassing properties.

The reform also touched the interests of the central and local governments. It would reduce tax revenues of the central government, while the small portion of individual property tax gathered was not expected to encourage local governments to reduce land price and rely on the new tax.

Reformists would also have to deal with large developers, which would be relied on to build government-subsidised housing and other facilities in the urbanisation initiatives to compensate for reduced property demand after introducing the tax, economists said.

Beijing also planned to impose a consumption tax on some big-ticket entertainment and luxury goods, according to the guidelines. "Such a new consumption tax might only make Macau and Hong Kong more favourable places for the mainland's new riches," said Lu Ting, an economist at Bank of America Merrill Lynch.

*   *   *

Bleak Outlook for Tough Pollution Laws

by *Li Jing*

Legal measures to curb China's chronic air pollution have proved ineffective — and may remain so.

The extent of China's chronic pollution problems was brought home to China's new leaders in January 2013 when Beijing was blanketed by heavy smog on a total of 26 days during the month and saw air pollution readings hit record levels. But environmental experts warned that a campaign to tackle China's air pollution through legal means looked doomed to fail. Their reasons for the bleak outlook included poor air-quality standards and the attitude of local governments whose priority was still to maximise growth.

Pollution was cited as a factor by the growing number of Chinese white-collar workers leaving the country. So when property tycoon Pan Shiyi called for a Clean Air Act in China, he received overwhelming support. Of the 57,000 microbloggers who registered their opinion, 98.9 per cent agreed that such a law was needed. Such legislation has proved effective in cities once choked by severe smog, including London, Los Angeles and Tokyo.

China already had an Air Pollution Prevention Law, enacted in 1987 and amended in 2000. Thus the proposal by Pan, a deputy to Beijing's municipal people's congress, was a stark reminder of just how ineffective that law was.

Environmental experts and lawyers have pushed for another amendment, but even though a revision was drafted in 2010, sources say it was unlikely to be reviewed by the National People's Congress before 2014. And even if the amendment was passed, some experts were not optimistic it would bring about desired changes because some key principles for improving air quality — which would give teeth to environmental watchdogs — were still absent.

Wang Canfa, a professor at the China University of Political Science and Law, said the biggest problem was that air-quality standards in China were not set to meet public health requirements. For instance, even though China published new air-quality standards in 2012 that for the first time included a recommended maximum level for PM2.5 — tiny particles that can penetrate lungs — it was set about two times higher than safety levels recommended by the World Health Organization.

In response to the lingering smog that blanketed almost a sixth of China early in 2013, Deputy Environmental Minister Wu Xiaoqing advised the public to "get prepared for a prolonged battle", despite the premature deaths and huge economic losses caused by air pollution, because it had taken developed countries three to five decades to come to grips with their own smog problems.

Chinese officials have long argued that as a developing country, in the middle of industrialisation and urbanisation, it could not adopt the strictest standards applied in developed nations. Wang, however, said lax environmental standards would only encourage local governments to shirk their responsibility to address public health problems and continue in their blind pursuit of economic growth.

Elaine Chang, deputy executive of the South Coast Air Quality Management District, in California, said US standards were based purely on scientific findings about the health implications of pollution, without considering the economic cost of meeting them. "There can be different stages to meet the standards, and the result is a continuous improvement over the years," she said.

Wang said another loophole in the law was that it failed to ensure the environment was not deteriorating, especially in some regions that enjoy cleaner air. For instance, in Qinghai and Tibet, the air quality had always been rated Grade I — the best on China's scale — but the law said reaching Grade II was enough, which meant polluting industries could be moved to those areas, he said.

Also, polluters actually benefited from their polluting practices because the economic cost of breaking the law was much lower than the cost of abiding by it. Polluting companies could be fined up to 200,000 yuan for violating emission regulations. However, in other countries, Wang said, polluters could be fined on a daily basis, which could add up to a huge amount, without a cap. And they might also face criminal charges, which could effectively deter polluting behaviour. "But repeated efforts from the environmental protection ministry to increase fines for polluters have all been stalled."

After extensive debate among meteorologists, linguists and environmental experts, China finally came up with an official Chinese name for the tiny airborne pollutants known elsewhere as PM2.5, meaning particles smaller than 2.5 microns.

But the word they chose, *xikeliwu*, which literally translates as "fine particulate manner," promptly ran into sarcastic nicknames from frustrated smog sufferers. They included "GDP particles", "Happiness index" and "Dust with Chinese characteristics".

One blogger commented: "Apparently the authorities attempt to relieve public panic about air pollution by giving a Chinese name that mentions nothing about its hazardous impact, so that they'd face less pressure."

Even Xinhua news agency blasted the eagerness to give PM2.5 a Chinese name. "Does it really matter what the pollutant is called when the public have no place to hide and have to breathe the toxic air?"

* * *

Lifestyle, Career Concerns Drive Out Talent

by **Mandy Zuo**

The army of Chinese leaving their homeland is set to expand.

"Every time Beijing's PM2.5 level hits 300, the desire to leave this country overwhelms me," said Shi Xue, a magazine editor in Beijing.

Saving money to relocate, Shi, in her mid-30s, added: "It's human nature to move to a better place."

Shi was among growing numbers of Chinese heading for the exits, driven not just by pollution worries but by a long list of other lifestyle and career worries. The leavers included many thousands with skills urgently needed to sustain China's economic powerhouse, leaving the world's most populous country with a talent deficit.

It was no longer just the wealthy and powerful who wanted to find a bolt-hole abroad. More white-collar workers like Shi had joined an expanding army of emigrants, according to the Annual Report on Chinese International Migration, released by the Centre for China and Globalisation (CCG) and the Beijing Institute of Technology's law school shortly after the 18th party congress.

In 2011 alone, more than 150,000 mainland Chinese became permanent residents of the world's major immigration countries, it said. Of them, more than 100,000 acquired skilled worker visas, the most common form of immigration for middle-class professionals, while more than 10,000 obtained investor visas. More than 87,000 of them obtained a US visa, making the United States the most popular destination. Canada, Australia and New Zealand followed, according to the report.

Phil Wang, a Chinese immigrant in Toronto providing immigration services to Chinese, said nearly half of his clients were rich business owners and half were middle class. Among the latter, 60 per cent were middle and senior-level managers at foreign or state-owned companies, and the rest were professionals who were resorting to investment immigration after failing to obtain a skilled-worker visa after Canada tightened the criteria.

"Emigration is becoming something reachable for more mainlanders," he said. "In order to stimulate the economy, some small provinces in Canada require only a two million yuan investment, including real estate, for Chinese who want to immigrate." Such were

China's property prices that anyone who owned one or two apartments in Beijing or Shanghai could afford such a sum.

Zheng Ran, a manager at a foreign publishing firm in Beijing who applied for a Canadian visa, gave two reasons for leaving: "First, society is in great disorder and morality has sunk. Second, I want my daughter to receive a different education." The 36-year-old father said he made up his mind when a friend emigrated to the US, and his daughter was about to start primary school.

Dr Wang Huiyao, director of the CCG and co-author of the report, said worries about society and education were two main reasons why people left. "Pollution and food safety scandals make people feel their health is at risk. Fierce competition, busy working lives and high inflation make life stressful. The newly rich class also feels unhappy because of a low quality of life owing to an underdeveloped social security system and dissatisfying public services."

Many professionals also sought a better working environment. "In China, science and technology are still at a low level. It lacks a system of encouraging creativity," Wang said, "At colleges, academic cheating and government intervention over academic studies are rampant. Small and medium-sized enterprises are struggling for financial support and talent."

Yang Du, a manager at an advertising company in Sydney, said that as long as Chinese immigrants had a good education and no language problems, they could have a better life and career in Australia. He obtained a master's degree in Beijing and taught in Hangzhou before earning a second master's in Sydney. He applied for an Australian visa under an employer-sponsored migration programme.

Sydney was his city of choice. "In Beijing I can make 100,000 yuan a year and in Hangzhou maybe just 50,000. My wife and I would need to save up all our salaries if we wanted to buy an apartment in these cities," he said. "Though property prices are also high in Sydney, an average home costs about 3 million yuan. It would be more realistic to buy one there because our income is higher and other daily costs, such as driving, are lower. We like living a quiet life. [In Sydney] we keep work and personal life separate, and unlike in China, we needn't engage in job-related activities after work."

Another important advantage of being an Australian citizen was the convenience in travelling to the rest of the world. He recalled an e-mail from a friend who grew up in China and moved to the US aged 11. "She wrote to me, saying: 'A US passport opens the world for me'. I was somewhat hurt — we grew up in the same environment but we saw a different world because of different passports we held." Under existing policies, only a dozen developing countries and no developed countries provided visa-free access for citizens of the world's second-largest economy.

Wang said the exodus of the middle class could to some extent prevent China moving from a pyramid-shaped society — a huge middle- and low-income population — to an olive-shaped one, where the middle class makes up the major portion of the population.

While many rich emigrants — mainly successful business people — would stay in China for business after acquiring a foreign passport, the middle-class emigrants were leaving. Wang said those who obtained an investor visa would have spent nearly all their money and were financially incapable of investing in China again. Those who acquired a skilled-worker visa wouldn't need to return to China since they could earn a comfortable wage and enjoy a better-quality life outside of their home country.

This brain drain would hurt domestic companies and affect the development of the real economy, Wang said. While most countries that suffered brain drains had immigrants to fill their talent pool, China had a huge deficit in talent. According to the report, only 4,752 foreigners held permanent residency in China by the end of 2011.

An emigration wave occurred as China started its economic reform in the late 1970s, when people who had relatives overseas left for family reunions or study, Wang said. A second wave came between the 1980s and 1990s as many developed countries loosened immigration requirements to attract Chinese investors and skilled workers. The third wave began at the beginning of this century.

Over the three decades, the number of overseas Chinese grew to more than 45 million, Xu Yousheng, deputy director of the Overseas Chinese Affairs Office of the State Council, was quoted by state media as saying in 2010.

This army is set to keep expanding. According to the report, the number of migration agents in China grew by 8.5 per cent every year between 2006 and 2011. The report predicted there would be more than 1,000 such agents by 2015.

"The background of potential emigrants is changing. For example, more lawyers and doctors have applied in recent years besides business owners and executives," Wang said. "At the same time, we're seeing a group of younger emigrants."

But for many middle-class professionals, leaving China is not the end of their problems. Yang said what worries him most now is how to support his parents when they get old. "They wouldn't live [in Sydney] because there are no relatives or friends. And it's not possible for me to frequently visit them when I get busy with work."

Shi says it's a hard decision to make for people at her age — not young enough to start from scratch yet not old enough to have earned enough money to ensure an idyllic retirement life in a new country. She likened emigration to a luxury item: "Everybody wishes to own it but not everybody can afford it."

But at least it's getting affordable for more ordinary people.

* * *

Red Alert for Greying China

by *Victoria Ruan*

The ageing of China's population is set to have a profound economic and social impact.

One of the huge tasks facing the new Chinese leadership was providing care for its ageing population. A nursing home located in a prosperous district near a diplomatic area in Beijing cared for 26 people aged between 60 and 92. "We have 26 beds. But it's far from being enough," said Liu Yuqin, head of the Dongzhimen Street Senior Home, set up in 1986. "Nearly 100 people applied for beds but left disappointed. We have to give priority to those who live nearby."

Inmates of the government-aided nursing home were charged 1,850 yuan a month for meals, utilities, bed space and other services. The cost was lower than that of many private institutions and was affordable for elderly residents of the capital city where the minimum wage had been raised to 1,400 yuan a month.

"In this prosperous area, every inch of land is valued like gold. It's not easy to find a good nursing home here," said Liu. "The local government is planning to expand the service to new sites, but no decision has been made yet." According to a Xinhua report, welfare institutions in the district offered 1,500 beds for the care of seniors, well short of an estimated need of 8,000 beds.

The nation's working-age population of 15- to 59-year-olds fell for the first time in 2012, Ma Jiantang, chief of the National Bureau of Statistics said, calling attention to the mounting challenge. Working-age citizens who must support the elderly dropped by 3.45 million to 937 million, according to Ma, and was expected to continue to fall steadily until at least 2030.

"The impact will be profound," said HSBC economists Frederic Neumann and Julia Wang in a research report. "Ageing populations mean that fewer workers are around, slowing growth unless productivity gains can be dramatically increased." The trend would also add strains to public finances and cause a shift in household spending and savings as older people "are keener to build a nest egg for retirement", they said.

Ma Jun, Deutsche Bank's chief economist for Greater China, said pension and health-care costs would be the biggest financial risks facing the country. If timely reforms were not carried out, the nation would face a huge gap in pension fund payments equivalent to 83 per cent of its 2011 gross domestic product. It took three income earners to support the needs of one retired person, but as the nation got older, Ma said there would be just one earner to support one retired person by 2050.

According to the International Monetary Fund, spending on pension funds in China would rise by more than 3 per cent of GDP over the two decades to 2030, the third sharpest increase among emerging markets, after Turkey and Egypt. Over the next decade, Ma said, Beijing should replenish the national pension fund by allocating more state-owned assets to the pool, set up an insurance system for nursing the elderly, and develop a local government debt market to reduce financial risks. "If the reforms aren't carried out in a timely manner, the debt crisis emerging in China in a few decades will be no 'Tales of Arabian Nights'," he warned.

Du Peng, the head of the Institute of Gerontology at Renmin University in Beijing, also called for improvements to the social welfare system and health-care services. The government should establish a long-term nursing insurance system, just as Japan and South Korea had done, he said. In Japan, people aged above 40 were required to set aside a portion of their income each month as a fund for health-care and nursing costs after they turned 65, he said. "China's long-term sustainability and growth will be endangered if Beijing doesn't take action quickly."

Andrew Colquhoun, head of Asia-Pacific sovereigns at Fitch Ratings, shared the concerns. China's demographic outlook was unfavourable compared with other emerging markets or even many higher-income countries, although rising pension costs were not yet "a material concern", he said.

*   *   *

Fat Cats Feel the Squeeze

by Victoria Ruan, George Chen and Daniel Ren

China may join the global push to cut bloated pay packages.

Sickened by years of financial crises and reports of huge salaries and bonuses for executives and bankers, governments and voters around the world have moved to put the fat cats on a pay diet. The European Union edged closer to imposing strict limits on bank bonuses, while even in Switzerland, traditionally Europe's staunchest bastion of free-market capitalism, voters backed pay curbs in a referendum held in March 2013.

But while European governments warned of an exodus of talent and capital to Asia, those looking to restrict executive pay might have a new ally rising in the East: China. Departing premier Wen Jiabao left his successors a gift on the eve of his retirement in 2013 — directives designed to ease social inequality in part through raising wages for the poor but also by limiting incomes of senior managers at state-owned monopolies.

It might sound odd to compare the initiatives in China, Switzerland and the EU given their sharply different economic structures, as well as the different root causes of their problems. And economists said the reasons for the initiatives had subtle but significant differences. "The Swiss vote was triggered by widespread anger at banks rather than a general desire to tackle income inequality", unlike the case in China, said Mark Williams, chief Asia economist at Capital Economics.

The possible victims also differed: in Switzerland, it was the top executives in the private sector — at banks and multinational businesses like UBS and Nestlé — that would suffer. In China, the campaign, were it to be successfully introduced, would focus on officials from state and government sectors.

By Swiss standards the executives Beijing had in its sights would be no more than middle-income earners. Daniel Vasella, head of pharmaceuticals giant Novartis, made 15 million Swiss francs in 2011, while Severin Schwan, boss of pharmaceutical powerhouse Roche, earned 12.5 million Swiss francs. It was salaries like those that prompted Dr Marc Laperrouza, a lecturer at the University of Lausanne, to say the Swiss vote was "not about anti-rich sentiment but rather about anti-über-rich".

In contrast, top leaders at Chinese state-owned banks, such as Jiang Jianqing, chairman of Industrial and Commercial Bank of China, the world's largest bank, earned a package of less than 2 million yuan in 2011. That said, Jiang and his industry peers' incomes still sounded astronomical to those living at the bottom of Chinese society, where a monthly income of less than 1,000 yuan was not unusual.

Despite the differences, however, there was at least one similarity between the two countries, analysts said — a distorted market that benefited the privileged. Bankers were seen as taking advantage of a skewed system that allowed them to earn vast amounts without facing the consequences of bad decisions, said Williams.

Despite existing government limits on salaries, senior executives in China's state-owned-enterprise enjoyed big bonuses and benefits, as well as other forms of hidden income, thanks to a system that allowed them to obtain resources more easily than others and which left loopholes to exploit.

A China National Coal official said the high remuneration of executives fostered bribery and corruption as lower-level officials struggled to climb the corporate ladder. "The widening wealth gap was the root cause for nasty behaviour at some of the state-owned enterprises," he said. Ordinary workers and lower-level managers would rather spend 100,000 yuan to bribe their bosses to seek a promotion. A hefty pay rise in line with promotion would be more than enough to cover the cost of bribery.

At a typical state-owned enterprise, a section manager would normally earn an annual salary of between 100,000 to 200,000 yuan while a higher-level official could pocket as much as 1 million yuan.

Professor Yu Yongding, of the Chinese Academy of Social Sciences, urged Beijing to push ahead with income distribution reform. He said that top officials' pay packages "have become too high to be acceptable by ordinary people".

But China's campaign might be more complicated "given the huge size of grey consumption", said Shen Jianguang, a chief economist at Mizuho Securities who previously worked for the European Central Bank. China still lacked official data about grey income — off-the-book gains that became a source of official corruption — due to the difficulty in collecting data. Wang Xiaolu, a well-known academic at the China Reform Foundation, and Professor Wing Thye Woo of the University of California, issued a report in 2010 that estimated China's grey income might have reached 5.4 trillion yuan in 2008.

Alastair Newton, a senior analyst at Nomura, expected that public anger toward inequality would push Beijing to overhaul the income distribution system. "The outcome of the [Swiss] referendum is via a popular vote. It would be true to say that China's leaders are responding to popular pressure [albeit without the benefit of a plebiscite] to which they are certainly not immune."

The clampdowns in Switzerland and the EU would have implications as far away as Hong Kong, with the banks' operations in the city covered by the laws. Kelvin Wong Tin-yau, chairman of the Hong Kong Institute of Directors, praised the initiatives but said there was no need for Hong Kong to follow suit. "This is a good move as it prevents excessive pay to bankers and prevents them from eyeing short-term profits for their companies to boost their bonus payment."

But he added: "I do not think Hong Kong companies need to follow Switzerland or Europe as the pay level in Hong Kong is reasonable and not excessive. Many chief executives receive about HK$2 million to HK$10 million, which is far below some Western bankers who have a pay package as high as HK$100 million or so."

Wong said he did not believe Chinese executives were overpaid — instead, some benefited from corruption. "I would rather think mainland China should increase the salary of executives as a way to discourage them from taking bribes or other illegal payments."

CHAPTER 12

The Media Genie

One of the key issues the new generation of China's leaders will have to face is how to handle the new social media, which has become a major force behind China's social, cultural and political development. How the government copes with the rising power of new media may come to define the tenure of President Xi Jinping.

New Technology, New Voice

by *Raymond Li*

Citizen journalist Wen Yunchao recalled how difficult it was using his now-obsolete Palm Treo mobile phone to cover the huge uprising against a planned chemical plant in Xiamen in June 2007.

There were no microblogs back then on which citizen journalists like Wen — or Bei Feng, as he's more widely known — could instantly share news and pictures across the globe. So Wen devised a way of using text messages and internet bulletin board systems (BBS), an early form of internet forum.

"I had to send the text messages to a friend's mobile and then he relayed them on to the BBS and blogs," said Wen. "It's a shame that I couldn't send pictures back then." Despite those technological short-comings, the dispatches by Wen and others helped mobilise public opposition to the paraxylene plant and earned Chinese activists one of their first victories of the new media age.

The Xiamen government ultimately backed down after more than 20,000 protesters filled the streets of the city in Fujian province for two days. The plant project was called off, the first of several defeated by mass protests aided by social media.

Even in a country that has seen as much change as China over the past decade, few advances have had as much impact as the emergence of the internet. The internet and its ubiquitous microblogs not only allowed unprecedented access to foreign news and culture. They also provided a forum for Chinese to organise protests, debate issues and spread rumours — all with far less government influence and interference than the Communist Party would like.

It was not surprising, then, that former president Hu Jintao's government took steps to rein in the internet and strengthen China's "Great Firewall". But events around the world suggested that the new media genie — once free — was hard to put back in the bottle. "In the age of new media, everyone could be a potential source of news or information and everyone can make an impact by having their voices heard," said Xia Xueluan, a sociologist at Peking University.

Social media's increasing influence may be inevitable as smartphones put internet access in the palm of everyone's hands.

Since 2009, an increasing share of internet traffic took place on weibo — microblogs modelled on global social-networking site Twitter. The most prominent site, Sina Weibo reported in 2012 having 300 million registered users alone, quickly closing in on Twitter's estimated 500 million. China's population of internet users rose to 564 million in 2012, adding 51 million, a number bigger than the population of Spain. The China Internet Network Information Center said the number of Chinese web surfers who went online from mobile phones, tablet computers and other wireless devices rose 18.1 per cent to 420 million.

While weibo accounts allowed some activists to organise illegal protests, they also revolutionised other more innocuous forms of public outreach in China, such as charitable fundraising and recruiting drives after disasters.

Xia, of Peking University, pointed to the unprecedented outpouring of volunteerism after the devastating Sichuan earthquake in 2008 as an example of how social media was changing Chinese society. There were smaller examples, too. In April 2010, Deng Fei, a journalist for the China-based *Phoenix Weekly*, started a weibo-based campaign to raise money for school lunches after learning about an impoverished school in Qianxi county, Guizhou province, which was serving pupils nothing but cold water.

The campaign raised more than 30 million yuan to help feed 16,000 pupils at 200 rural schools. It also helped prod the central government into allocating 16 billion yuan annually to fund a lunch programme for 26 million rural students. Deng was empowered as well. He saw his number of weibo followers grow to 2.3 million from about 160,000 before he launched his campaign. He then used that platform to raise money to buy medical insurance for rural pupils. "How could an individual like me possibly have so much power and appeal without weibo?" Deng said.

That was the beauty of social media, said Wen, the citizen journalist involved in the Xiamen protest. It gave people strength in numbers and encouraged more of them to speak up and stand up to the authorities. Correspondingly, it weakened the government's ability to control public opinion and intimidate those who step out of line. "A relatively free flow of information, which is guaranteed by new media technologies, will certainly lead to an awakening to equality and rights as well as ensuing action to secure them," Wen said.

In particular, he noted the grassroots effort to free blind lawyer Chen Guangcheng from his months-long house arrest in Linyi village, Shandong province. Chen fell foul of the local authorities by exposing forced abortions used to enforce the one-child policy. Organised online, droves of civil activists, academics and ordinary citizens tried to break the security blockade near his home. Eventually, even Batman star Christian Bale got in on the act, drawing global headlines. After Chen ultimately escaped and received sanctuary at the US embassy in Beijing, the public support for his plight was so strong that the central government decided to grant his request to accept an academic fellowship in New York.

"This represented a significant shift in the civil movement on the mainland — a shift from a mere struggle for material rights to [broader] human rights and a shift from a fight for people's own rights to the rights of others," Wen said.

In some cases, the government responded to the pressure in a positive way, with agencies, particularly at the lower levels, becoming more transparent and more responsive to public complaints. But they also took steps to weaken the weibos, such as compelling companies to shut down the accounts of bloggers who became a problem. In March 2012, weibo providers began enforcing a government order requiring weibo users to register their real names, removing the protection of anonymity.

It remains to be seen how much such restrictions will limit the political strength of social media. Weibo accounts overflow with messages criticising government officials and urging people to speak up.

Professor Wu Hui, of the Central Party School, acknowledged that social media had improved free speech and access to information, and argued that some regulation was necessary to prevent rumour-mongering and attacks on the government. But he said the government's best approach for dealing with social media was to use it to interact with people. "While the new media technologies certainly need to improve, the governments also have their own imperfections. If the governments can improve their governance, the chance of negative news spreading via new media technologies is smaller."

Michael Anti, a China-based commentator specialising in new media, said he believed government efforts to blunt the impact of internet activism were succeeding more than people realized. Speaking near the convening of the 18th party congress, he said he had seen a marked drop in the scale and frequency of rights-related civil campaigns. He attributed the drop to crackdowns against activists who crossed the line and caused too much trouble, including dissident artist Ai Weiwei, environmental campaigner Tan Zuoren and civil-rights lawyer Xu Zhiyong.

The weibo accounts for many prominent activists and opinion leaders were also subject to frequent censorship, suspension and closure, Anti said. Wen Yunchao, for example, estimated that he had had more than 40 weibo accounts closed.

Anti said that he would rather self-censor his own microblog and save the hassle of having to open one account after another. "Don't forget they have the control of the servers and they could always do something if they feel it's necessary," he said. "It's as simple as that."

*   *   *

Surprise in Social Media Findings

by *Alan Wong*

The targets in the crosshairs of China's censors have shifted, a study shows.

Beijing was more likely to censor online comments that spurred social movements than those that criticised the government, stated a Harvard University study released in June 2012, suggesting that Beijing's most important objective was maintaining social stability. "Contrary to previous understandings, posts with negative, even vitriolic, criticism of the state, its leaders and its policies are not more likely to be censored," it said. "Instead, we show the censorship programme is aimed at curtailing collective action by silencing comments that represent, reinforce, or spur social mobilisation, regardless of content."

For example, a post on the Sina Weibo microblog that criticised government officials for having mistresses, being shameless, immoral and greedy, was not removed, nor were thousands like it. Such posts were neither exceptions nor unusual, the researchers said, and that indicated that Beijing had no intention of stopping them. However, posts about a rumour that iodised salt would protect people from radiation exposure after the Fukushima nuclear disaster in Japan were heavily censored, the study said.

The study claimed to offer the first large-scale, multiple-source analysis of the outcome of Beijing's extensive censorship of social media. The researchers devised a system to locate, download and analyse the content of millions of social media posts on more than 1,000 different social media websites in China before the authorities could find and censor them.

Beijing routinely censors internet posts that contain sensitive keywords but China's bloggers are ingenious in inventing ways to get around the censorship. With the use of analogies, metaphors, homophones, satire and other evasions, they can express sensitive meanings without touching upon sensitive keywords.

Ng Chi-sum, a veteran Hong Kong-based journalist and columnist, said: "It's like a cat-and-mouse game." For example, a few days before the sensitive June 4 anniversary of the 1989 Tiananmen crackdown on the pro-democracy movement, the authorities even censored the word "tomorrow". "But bloggers came up with clever expressions such as May 35, or images of tears and candles to express themselves."

The study said there were estimated to be between 20,000 and 50,000 internet police in China, plus a further 250,000 to 300,000 members of the *wumao dang* (50 cent party) — party members paid to post favourable comments online and steer discussion away from sensitive topics. It also said that all levels of government — central, provincial and local — took part in the huge effort to censor and shape online discussion, describing this as a "stunning organisational accomplishment" that required "large scale, military-like precision".

*   *   *

Chilling History Lesson for China's "No" Voter

by *Amy Li*

> *Netizens ponder a surprise — and, lonely — vote.*

China's hyperactive social media leapt into action when Xi Jinping was voted China's president. Why? Not because an overwhelming 2,952 delegates at the National People's Congress voted "yes" for Xi. It was because one delegate had the temerity to vote "no". Who was the mystery voter?

Following the election, authorities censored the word for "no vote" on social media, but discussions then resumed on Sina Weibo.

For some commentators, it brought to mind the fate of a past delegate widely believed to have voted "no" in Mao Zedong's election as head of the new communist government in 1949. According to some historical accounts, Zhang Dongsun, a philosopher and former delegate to China's top advisory body, the Chinese People's Political Consultative Conference, was later destroyed by Mao for his alleged actions. He was accused of selling national secrets a few years after Mao's election, and expelled from the CPPCC.

Zhang was arrested at the age of 82 in 1968, two years into the Cultural Revolution. His family didn't know where he was locked up until 1973, when they were notified by authorities that Zhang had died in prison. Of Zhang's three sons, two committed suicide during the Cultural Revolution, while his eldest son was arrested and tortured, according to some accounts. "Zhang paid a high price for a no vote," commented a blogger. "Let's hope this time the person will not be prosecuted."

Other netizens shared differing theories. "Did Xi vote 'no' himself?" wrote a blogger, "Or was it just a show?"

"This is some progress for China's democracy," wrote journalist Zhang Lifen on Weibo. Zhang is a senior editor at the *Financial Times*, and editor-in-chief of its Chinese language website. Zhang said he didn't understand why state media intentionally left out the tally in their coverage, "Were they embarrassed because the percentage was too high?" he wrote, "Or was it still not high enough for them?"

CHAPTER 13

Lost, Found, and Still Searching

China safely gathered in its colonised territories of Hong Kong, in 1997 from Britain, and Macau, in 1999 from Portugal. But Taiwan, regarded as a renegade Chinese province, remained frustratingly beyond the reach of the motherland's embrace despite a quickening pace of trade, investment and people exchanges across the Taiwan Strait. And the initial indications following the 18th party congress were that reconciliation was still a distant prospect. While Hong Kong is securely established as part of China as a Special Administrative Region, friction is rising between Hong Kong and mainland Chinese people that, in Hong Kong at least, threatened to command as much popular attention as the leadership transition in Beijing. *South China Morning Post* reporters also took an in-depth look at China's much-vaunted experimental zone, Qianhai, across the border from Hong Kong. Can it live up to its billing as the future "Manhattan of the Pearl River Delta"?

Still Waters Run Deep in Taiwan Strait

by Lawrence Chung

The frosty wind that blew across the Taiwan Strait for decades had warmed considerably by the time the 18th party congress was held as both Beijing and Taipei focused on areas of agreement rather than dispute. Since the landmark meeting of then-Kuomintang leader Lien Chan with then-president Hu Jintao in 2005, the two governments signed numerous co-operation pacts allowing more people and capital to flow across the strait even as they remained military foes.

But such deals just scratched the surface of any potential reconciliation. And, as President Xi Jinping took the helm in Beijing, Taiwanese experts agreed that cross-strait talks were nearing a "deep water zone" where more vexing problems would become increasingly unavoidable.

While the two sides had signed many co-operation agreements on economic and other non-political issues, they would have to face the thornier political issues, said Wang Kung-yi, a professor at the Institute of International Relations and Strategic Studies at Tamkang University in Taipei. These deeper waters included beginning to confront political and ideological rifts that fuelled the Chinese civil war and led Chiang Kai-shek's Kuomintang to flee to Taiwan in 1949. Beijing still regards Taiwan as a breakaway province and has said it would be willing to take it back by force if necessary. While Taiwanese overwhelmingly oppose reunification they have generally supported warming policies advanced by President Ma Ying-jeou.

Following China's 18th party congress, Lien made a further closely watched visit to Beijing during which Xi, in his highest-level cross-strait meeting since he succeeded Hu Jintao as party chief, said his team would continue to build cross-strait ties and strive for "peaceful reunification" with the island. He also called on people on both sides of the Taiwan Strait to work together to achieve "Chinese dreams" of "China's renaissance". Analysts saw this as a new approach by the Chinese party's new leadership, designed to make the prospect of cross-strait political talks more accessible.

"Nothing can cut the blood bond between mainland and Taiwan compatriots and nothing can change the fact that both sides belong to one China," Xi said. "Realising the great rejuvenation of the Chinese nation — the greatest dream in the country's modern history — requires the joint efforts of people from the two sides," he said, adding that "if brothers are of the same mind, their sharp strength can cut through metal".

He also said it would take time and patience from both sides to resolve tough issues. Analysts said that by resorting to nationalism and images of blood brotherhood, Xi hoped to build a bridge for the two sides to cross political boundaries and make political dialogue a real possibility in the next decade. "Rather than just clichéd appeals, like his predecessors used, Xi's call for 'blood brotherhood' co-operation contains a clearer direction on how the two sides can co-operate," said Professor George Tsai Wei, a political analyst at the Chinese Culture University in Taipei. Such co-operation could be made possible through gradual deepening of cross-strait political, economic, cultural and social exchanges, Tsai said.

During their meeting, Xi told Lien that "unremitting efforts will be made to consolidate and strengthen a political, economic, cultural and social foundation for the peaceful development of cross-strait relations". In response, Lien said people from the two sides should promote brotherhood and mutual understanding, as well as join hands to resist separatism.

"Cross-strait relations can be deepened from a new starting point," Xinhua quoted Lien as saying. Fan Liqing, a spokeswoman for the mainland State Council's Taiwan Affairs Office, was quoted by Taiwan's Central News Agency as saying that there was a need to "create the conditions" for the two sides to resolve thorny political issues and that could start with political issues being discussed by think tanks from the two sides.

Analysts said Fan's remarks reflected the new Chinese leadership's current cross-strait policy. "Discussions of relevant topics by academics and think tanks from the two sides are expected to increase sharply in the future," said Professor Yang Kai-huang, a specialist in cross-strait affairs at Ming Chuan University in Taipei.

In addition to increasing academic dialogue on such topics, Beijing was also expected to strengthen contacts with Taiwan's pro-independence camp, Yang said. But pundits said the attitude of Taiwanese President Ma towards political contact remained the decisive factor in whether political dialogue could take place before Ma's second four-year term ended in 2016.

He had pledged not to have political talks and was lukewarm in his response to the Xi-Lien meeting, saying it was just a "meeting in a private capacity". Ma has committed only to beefing up cross-strait exchanges, the establishment of reciprocal representative offices in major cities and a review of the Act Governing Relations between Peoples of the Taiwan Area and the Mainland Area.

Ma placed particular emphasis on Xi's familiarity with cross-strait issues. The Communist Party's leader served 17 years as an official in nearby Fujian province. "His understanding of Taiwan is very deep," Ma said.

By the time of the 18th party congress more than one million Taiwanese were estimated to be living and working on the mainland, and more than 4.14 million mainlanders had visited the island since Taipei started allowing travel in July 2008. The mainland had become Taiwan's top trading partner, accounting for some 40 per cent of its exports in 2011 compared with 15 per cent for the United States. Trade between the two totalled more than US$100 billion in 2011.

Chao Chung-shan, president of the Foundation on Asia-Pacific Peace Studies, said Beijing had adopted a more patient approach after decades of demanding immediate reunification. "Instead of taking it in a big mouthful, it is swallowing it bit by bit."

Lien had previously proposed using a "building-block approach" to work towards more politically sensitive issues, such as a potential peace deal. He said the two sides could start with peripheral issues and build up to a mutual trust. In the meantime, academics and think tanks from both sides could hold regular peace forums to brainstorm solutions.

As Beijing tried to bring Taiwan closer to the mainland, many Taiwanese hoped Beijing would enact political reform to bring it closer to Taipei. During a visit to Taiwan in July 2012, former US ambassador to China Jon Huntsman said Beijing's next leaders understood that "change is inevitable, but they would not proceed to it quickly for concerns about instability".

*   *   *

Hong Kong Wary of Beijing Intentions

by *South China Morning Post Reporters*

Will restive Hong Kong benefit or suffer under the new Chinese leadership?

Just as opinion among Hong Kong people has become increasingly polarised and heated over a raft of political, economic and social issues since the former British colony reverted to China's control in 1997, so were views sharply divided on what the change in the Chinese leadership would mean for this city of seven million.

Among the pessimists, veteran China watcher Johnny Lau Yui-siu forecast that Beijing would impose tighter control on Hong Kong regardless of the personnel reshuffle at the 18th party congress, saying the central government was losing patience with the restive city, where demands for reforms of Hong Kong's limited form of democracy had become more strident, and vocal anti-mainland sentiment had risen on a host of social, cultural and political issues.

Lau said China's leaders had an "antagonistic mentality" towards Hong Kong. There would be persistent pressure from Beijing for Hong Kong schools to introduce a Beijing-friendly "national education" curriculum, despite immense local opposition to such a step, as expressed in major street demonstrations in 2012. Lau also said Beijing would strip Hong Kong of its much-valued press freedom.

What's more, the city's political and economic influence was on the wane. "The city is no longer a role model for Taiwan in terms of demonstrating the principle of 'one country, two systems'," Lau said, referring to the arrangement under which Beijing accords substantial autonomy to Hong Kong while the city remains part of China as a Special Administrative Region. "Economically, China can do what it was unable to do [in 1997], while Hong Kong's residual significance is its international financial status."

One issue that did infuriate mainland Chinese commentators in the months leading up to the 18th party congress was the appearance in Hong Kong of activists waving British colonial flags at demonstrations. At the March 2013 meeting of the National People's Congress which completed China's transition of power, Yu Zhengsheng of the Politburo Standing Committee raised the issue, denouncing the flag-wavers and warning that "opposition" and "centrifugal forces" would not be allowed to rule the city after its citizens had attained universal suffrage. Hong Kong's activists were unrepentant, saying Yu's comments infringed on their freedom of speech and could stir further conflict.

Despite the Hong Kong-mainland frictions, many observers were sanguine about Beijing's intentions towards the city, saying they expected Beijing's approach to Hong Kong would by and large remain stable. They took heart from comments made at the NPC meeting by a second Standing Committee member, Zhang Dejiang, who spoke to Hong Kong delegates at a closed-door meeting. He used the meeting to show that Beijing's policy on Hong Kong remained unchanged, said Rita Fan, one of the Hong Kong representatives at the meeting.

However Zhang and other leaders touched on a raw nerve in Hong Kong when they reiterated a long-standing dictum that whoever leads Hong Kong had to be able to able to work with Beijing. This rekindled

a debate in Hong Kong over what constituted patriotism and the criteria for choosing the city's next chief executive and lawmakers. The
remarks were perceived as an attempt to tamper with the fundamentals
of universal suffrage, promised for the election of Hong Kong's chief
executive in 2017 and for the Legislative Council in 2020.

The *South China Morning Post,* commenting in an editorial entitled
"Patriotic appeal states the obvious", said there was nothing untoward
about these statements; they were simply reminding Hongkongers of a
reality that could be easily ignored in the heat of politicking. "We need
open public discussion, but not centred only on patriotism. The focus
has to be the process for choosing our chief executive under a democratic electoral system. There are important details to be worked out
and the effort has to be all-encompassing. The process will allay worries and concerns."

According to NPC deputy Wong Kwok-kin, Beijing's approach to
Hong Kong might not alter much. He did not foresee any changes,
despite the shaky start made by the administration of Hong Kong Chief
Executive Leung Chun-ying in 2012. "Under 'one country, two systems'
there is not much Beijing can do about the problems facing Hong Kong.
The most the central government can pursue is to keep the city's economy vibrant to minimise ill will arising from livelihood issues."

Further soothing words came from Zhang Xiaoming, the incoming
head of Beijing's liaison office in Hong Kong, speaking two months
after the party congress closed. He said speculation that Beijing might
dump Chief Executive Leung was "unfounded talk and should be put
to rest".

The Beijing liaison office had earlier faced bipartisan calls in Hong
Kong to tone down its approach to local affairs, with advocates for full
democracy repeating the criticism that "Western District", the location
of the office, "is ruling Hong Kong". Zhang countered: "'Western
District' doesn't rule Hong Kong, but 'Western District' must do its job

and fulfil the tasks the central government has given us." He flatly denied that Beijing had tightened its grip on Hong Kong.

Zhang had stoked alarm among Hong Kong democrats with an article in which he called on the city to pass tough national security laws. Attempts to implement such legislation in 2003 prompted a massive street demonstration of some 500,000 people, and the law was promptly shelved. Zhang's comment was seen as possibly indicating a harder line by Beijing towards dissent in the city. But Zhang said it would be wrong to conclude from the article he was a hardliner. "I'm a person of principle, but I'm also benevolent and willing to befriend others." He also seemed to soften his tone on the controversial security legislation, saying it should be passed when the Hong Kong government deemed appropriate, but it should not be regarded as a taboo.

In a departure from the low profile of his predecessors, Zhang disclosed that he had travelled on Hong Kong's Mass Transit Railway and had visited poor families living in tiny subdivided quarters. However, the Hong Kong Democratic Party's forthright leader Emily Lau Wai-hing commented: "Whether you travel on the MTR or in a car, or whether you see subdivided flats or luxurious mansions on The Peak, don't come out and make irresponsible comments."

*　*　*

Hong Kong–Mainland Sore Points

by *Colleen Lee and He Huifeng*

The huge influx of mainland Chinese visitors to Hong Kong may have been a welcome boost to the city's economy. But it has also given rise to a lengthy catalogue of gripes from Hongkongers over the practices and habits of their mainland brothers and sisters.

"Hong Kong was called a shopping paradise. I would say it's a shopping hell now." So said Raye Long from mainland China about buying infant formula in Hong Kong for her 18-month-old son. She was frustrated by the city's limit imposed on exports of baby milk powder introduced to crack down on parallel-goods traders and to protect local consumers. Her complaint reflected the tip of the iceberg. A plethora of issues had brought mainland Chinese and Hong Kong residents into conflict — a problem for governments on both sides of the border.

Parallel-goods traders, who buy goods in Hong Kong for sale across the border, taking advantage of lower prices and tariffs in the city, became the target of popular anger in 2012, especially in the northern New Territories close to the Chinese border. Protesters waved banners with the slogan "Chinese people, go back to China", which left many mainland Chinese disgruntled. The war of words intensified, particularly after Hong Kong prevented travellers leaving the city from carrying more than two cans, or 1.8 kg, of infant formula across the city in 24 hours, except with a licence. It left mainland mothers, many of whom doubted the quality of the infant formula available at home, struggling to get supplies.

Long said taking the family on a shopping trip to Hong Kong was exhausting, and she was considering weaning her son on to solid food. "We just shop for milk powder and we are not drug dealers. Why is it so insulting and prejudiced [in Hong Kong]? I regret having to wean my son so early."

But the milk powder row was only the most visible sign of tension between Hong Kong and the nation of which it became part in 1997. The heat of the debate on mainland-Hong Kong integration turned up, due in part to an influx to Hong Kong of mainland Chinese giving birth, swamping tourist attractions, crowding public camp sites and snapping up goods and even properties in the city.

How to tackle the booming number of babies born to mainland Chinese parents became a hot issue in the 2012 election campaign for Hong Kong's chief executive, won by Leung Chun-ying. Leung proposed that public hospitals cease admissions of non-local expectant mothers from 2013, and suggested the government stop allowing heavily pregnant women to cross the border to give birth in private hospitals. He lived up to his pledge, announcing the so-called zero-quota policy even before taking office.

In 2000 the number of babies born in Hong Kong to mainland Chinese parents accounted for 1.3 per cent of births in the city, but that figure increased to about 30 per cent by the time measures were brought in to curb the trend. The boom strained local obstetrics services, making it difficult for Hong Kong mothers to book a place in hospitals, and led to worries over the long-term burden on the city's education, health and welfare services.

In 2012, 26,715 babies were locally born to mainland parents, a quarter fewer than in 2011. Leung's policy won applause from local mothers, but disappointed mainland Chinese parents — in particular those who sought to have a second child in Hong Kong to circumvent China's one-child policy, and mainland mothers married to Hong Kong husbands. It was also a blow to Hong Kong's private hospitals, which had invested heavily in maternity services.

Hong Kong-mainland tension spilled over on to the streets. In January 2012, a Dolce & Gabbana shop security guard allegedly prevented a local photographer from taking pictures of the shopfront of its Hong Kong store, and said that only mainlanders were allowed to do so. The incident infuriated Hongkongers, and hundreds of people rallied outside the shop to protest.

Later that month, remarks by Peking University professor Kong Qingdong, who branded Hongkongers "running dogs for the British government" stirred up another controversy. He was commenting on footage that appeared on the internet of Hong Kong Mass Transit Railway passengers berating a mainland family for allowing a child to eat in a train carriage, which is banned. While the academic denied making the comment, some internet users reacted by labelling visitors from across the border "locusts", implying that they sapped Hong Kong's resources.

In March 2012, a long-delayed plan to make it easier for mainland drivers to bring their cars to Hong Kong — and vice versa — hit setbacks after some Hongkongers raised concerns about more accidents, worse air quality and heavier road congestion.

Meanwhile, hot money from China flooded into Hong Kong's already inflated property market. The Hong Kong government imposed an extra 15 per cent tax on all home purchases by companies and non-permanent residents, adding to earlier steps including tightening mortgage lending. The government also doubled the sales tax on properties costing more than HK$2 million and targeted commercial real estate as the potential for a bubble spread from homes to parking spaces, shops and hotels.

While mainland-Hong Kong integration was the aim of both governments, some measures Leung's administration rolled out — from the milk-powder export limit to "Hong Kong properties for Hong Kong people" — led observers to ask if he was driving the two sides further apart.

Dr Chung Kim-wah, assistant professor in the Hong Kong Polytechnic University's department of applied social sciences, said Leung's approach was understandable. "Except where there are conflicts, Hong Kong should work for the nation's integration. But at a time of conflict, what he did was necessary. It might not be easily acceptable [to those affected] in the short run. But in the long run, it could ease bilateral conflicts. Say there was no export restriction and the problem of parallel-goods traders snapping up milk powder worsened. The [anti-mainland] sentiment might further heat up."

Chung added: "Irrespective of whether his moves are for pushing up his popularity, it is good to set out the rules in a timely way and prevent the problems from worsening."

Leung, meanwhile, pledged to improve cross-border communication and seek a better understanding of the export rule. The government should "step up our communication measures to make sure that all, including residents on the mainland, understand the motives behind this, or the intent behind this piece of legislation, and also the content of legislation, so that there is no misunderstanding".

As for Long, even though it had become a pain to shop in Hong Kong, she said she would put up with it instead of feeding her son mainland-made baby formula. "I trust and admire the Hong Kong government on food supervision. I appreciate it no matter how awful it is now for mainland shoppers."

*   *   *

What's in China's "Manhattan" for Hong Kong?

by *Enoch Yiu*

> *An ambitious pilot project in southern China may benefit international and mainland Chinese banks more than neighbouring Hong Kong, industry leaders fear.*

Qianhai, a patch of reclaimed land west of the booming southern city of Shenzhen and within easy reach of Hong Kong, is being touted as a future "Manhattan of the Pearl River Delta". However, while Hong Kong's banking community is bullish about Qianhai's prospects as a

financial hub, others are sceptical about whether it will benefit the
Hong Kong economy as a whole.

The 15-square kilometre Qianhai experimental zone, which has
been mooted since 2010 as a testing ground for economic liberalisation, was given a top-level seal of approval by Xi Jinping soon after he
became Communist Party chief at the 18th party congress.

It was also praised by, among others, HSBC Hong Kong chief executive Anita Fung Yuen-mei, who said the Qianhai project was a milestone for the opportunities it presented. "It will allow banks in Hong
Kong to offer cross-border yuan loans to Qianhai companies. This is a
breakthrough development that will benefit not just the banks, but it
also marks an important step forward in the internationalisation of the
yuan."

In December 2012, the People's Bank of China's Shenzhen branch
announced provisional regulations allowing firms registered in Qianhai
to take out yuan-denominated loans from Hong Kong banks. The following month, HSBC was among 15 Hong Kong banks given permis-
sion to offer a combined 2 billion yuan in loans to companies that
based themselves in Qianhai.

Banks like HSBC took Qianhai seriously, not just because it is an
hour's drive from Hong Kong. More importantly, China's National
Development and Reform Commission confirmed Qianhai would act as
a testing ground for freer convertibility of the yuan.

HSBC was one of 37 financial firms that signed non-binding agreements to pour investments worth more than 300 billion yuan into
Qianhai. Under China's capital controls, all fund transfers in and out of
the country needed official approval. But since 2009, Beijing gradually
amended rules to allow the yuan to be used for international trade settlement and investment purposes.

The liberalisation of the yuan went some way to explain why the 15
banks, including HSBC and fellow big players Hang Seng Bank, Standard

Chartered Bank and Bank of East Asia, were quick to sign up to the 2 billion yuan in loans covering 26 projects in Qianhai. The banks were equally quick to hail their roles in the deal for marketing purposes.

But some analysts questioned the real benefits of the loans, as the sums involved were relatively small. In addition, the cross-border loans could only be used by companies basing themselves in Qianhai and used only in Qianhai projects, helping to build a city with only 800,000 residents. In addition, while banks in Hong Kong could freely negotiate the structure, terms and interest rates of loans, the overall level of lending would be subject to approval by PBOC's Shenzhen branch.

But HSBC's Fung thought differently. "The 2 billion yuan loan amount looks small, but the business will grow bigger in the long term." She added that the cross-border lending experiment would mean that banks could directly use yuan deposits raised in Hong Kong to lend to Qianhai-based companies. Under existing regulations, Chinese or foreign companies that borrowed in yuan from banks in Hong Kong had to seek official approval to transfer the funds across the border, in line with other foreign direct investment.

Another big step forward, Fung said, was that Hong Kong banks would be able to negotiate lending rates with borrowers. This was seen as an experiment in liberalising interest-rate regulations in China, where other banks had to adopt the official lending rate.

John Tan, head of global markets at Standard Chartered Bank in Hong Kong, said Qianhai was important to Hong Kong and the city's banking industry as it gave banks another alternative to deploy their surplus liquidity. "It will also help the development of an offshore yuan yield curve, fixing as well as interest-rate hedging instruments. The scheme will also help invigorate the flow of yuan between Hong Kong and Qianhai, taking internationalisation of the yuan a step further as China slowly opens up its capital account. The move will boost Hong Kong's leading position as an offshore yuan centre as it enjoys its first-mover advantage."

The scheme would benefit Chinese companies, Tan said, because the offshore yuan lending rate was cheaper than the interest rate for borrowing from Chinese banks.

Tan felt that cross-border lending was only the first step in growing cross-border co-operation. "We expect more flexibility in future for companies in Qianhai to deal with banks in Hong Kong on different financial products. Such banking relationships could see new benefits for clients and banks down the road."

Tan also believed the overall level of lending would be increased. "According to past experience, Beijing will relax the policies after the pilot schemes when it feels they are progressing in the right direction ... we believe China will gradually raise the quota under the Qianhai cross-border loan scheme when the time is ripe."

Tan pointed to the fact that when Beijing first allowed yuan trade in mid-2009, only 365 companies were allowed to do so. It had since been opened up to all companies in the country.

He was also optimistic about the overall impact of Qianhai on Hong Kong. "Qianhai can turn into something big. It could become a window linking yuan fund flows with the offshore market. Shanghai's financial district of Lujiazui evolved from undeveloped farmland in the 1990s. Hence, Qianhai, in our perspective, also offers huge potential."

Hang Seng Bank executive director Andrew Fung Hau-chung said Qianhai could play a key future role in yuan liquidity between Hong Kong and mainland China. "The Hong Kong banking sector can borrow onshore via the Qianhai operation if offshore market liquidity is tight and vice versa if offshore liquidity is excessive. If effective, there will be no issue with the size of the liquidity pool in the future."

Among the sceptics about Qianhai's prospects and its benefits for Hong Kong, some wondered whether Qianhai, like the many rounds of the Hong Kong-China Closer Economic Partnership Arrangement (Cepa) agreed since Hong Kong returned to Chinese control in 1997, would benefit global banks and Chinese businesses rather than Hong Kong brokers, fund houses and insurers.

A local broker, who preferred to remain anonymous, commented: "Like the many rounds of Cepa, it mainly benefits the international banks and the mainland financial firms. I do not see how Cepa nor Qianhai will greatly benefit the overall Hong Kong economy or financial services sector."

He pointed out that while Cepa had proposed allowing Hong Kong-based futures brokers to set up joint ventures in China, only a few such ventures were approved. By contrast, many Chinese brokerages and fund houses had been allowed to set up in Hong Kong. "Qianhai ... benefits only the 15 banks involved, and the real purpose is to promote the internationalisation of the yuan. I do not see Beijing wanting to use Qianhai to help Hong Kong brokers or other financial firms develop in China," he added.

The broker believed Qianhai would ultimately become a property project, and that the companies that bought property there to set up offices would benefit from rising property prices rather than by developing their businesses.

But some brokers were fighting more aggressively for a slice of Qianhai's opportunities. In January 2013, the Hong Kong Securities Professionals Association signed an agreement with the Authority of the Qianhai Shenzhen-Hong Kong Modern Service Industry Co-operation Zone of Shenzhen for the two sides to work out proposals to attract Hong Kong and international financial firms to invest in Qianhai.

Christopher Cheung Wah-fung, the Hong Kong financial services sector legislator who led the association's delegation to the signing, said it was submitting a wish list to Qianhai. "Hong Kong brokers would like to set up offices in Qianhai if they will be allowed to sell shares to mainlanders." While Hong Kong lenders were able to offer loans only to Qianhai companies, but not to other Chinese firms, Cheung hoped brokers could have a wider scope. "If Hong Kong brokers or other financial firms can serve only Qianhai residents, it is not very attractive as Qianhai will have a population of only 800,000," Cheung said.

Cheung said brokers would like their Qianhai offices to be able to serve other parts of Guangdong province and the rest of China to tap into a bigger pool of clients. "This is how we can turn Qianhai into a city like Hong Kong."

*   *   *

Qianhai — Seedbed for Reform?

by *He Huifeng*

While new Chinese leader Xi Jinping has endorsed the experimental zone of Qianhai, local officials appear reluctant to take risks.

The pace of development in the ambitious experimental zone of Qianhai across the border from Hong Kong was expected to pick up following Beijing's approval of its blueprint in February 2013. But experts remained divided on whether Qianhai would meet its lofty goal of helping to transform China like the first special economic zones (SEZs) in Shenzhen and Zhuhai did.

While support for the Qianhai project was not in doubt after Xi Jinping made Qianhai a stop on his first tour after taking over as Communist Party chief, questions remained whether political leaders in the now more prosperous China shared the drive and willingness to take a big gamble that their predecessors did in the 1980s.

Xi's trip was widely seen as a nod to the past — after all, his father, Xi Zhongxun, pioneered the SEZs whose success provided models for the changes that drove China's economic reforms.

When the younger Xi toured Qianhai, he was looking at a 15-square-kilometre strip of empty land. But he must have hoped that in the next decade or so, this could do for China what the little fishing village of Shenzhen did for the country. A meeting in February 2013 of officials from two dozen central ministries and institutes, led by the powerful National Development and Reform Commission, discussed and approved the next step for Qianhai. They agreed to speed up the building of infrastructure of the experimental zone and approved a slew of projects proposed by the local authorities. These included allowing Hong Kong investors to set up international schools in Qianhai, operate hospitals solely managed and run by professionals from Hong Kong, and set up a cross-border digital data centre. Shenzhen mayor Xu Qin pledged to spend as much as 10 billion yuan in 2013 on infrastructure in Qianhai.

"By 2015, the GDP of Qianhai will reach 50 billion yuan," Xu told local media, "10 times more than the current level." The bullish comments and the strong start resurrected many people's hope in the Qianhai project. The initial idea was bold. Some suggested that Qianhai should not simply be an experimental economic zone — it should also be used as a laboratory where China could pilot administrative and legal reforms based on the Hong Kong model.

There was talk of a new graft watchdog along similar lines to Hong Kong's Independent Commission Against Corruption, as well as changes to the legal system borrowed from across the border.

But by July 2012, when Beijing's State Council finally approved the policies that would be used to develop Qianhai, all such ideas were dropped. Instead, the new policies focused exclusively on the economic side, covering six fields: finance, taxation, human resources, education, health care and telecommunications.

Xi's visit raised hopes that the administrative and legal side of the experiment would be revived. While in Qianhai, Xi told local officials: "Please carry out reform boldly. The central government has granted you very special policies. Qianhai will be a place for renewal of the service industries." And even though economic issues continued to dominate discussion of Qianhai, hopes still flickered that administrative and legal reforms would follow.

"I'm sorry to say the room for reform in Shenzhen has been shrinking. The idea to set up an ICAC-type of anti-corruption agent has been quickly put on hold," said Guo Wanda, vice-president of the Shenzhen-based China Development Institute, a municipal think tank. "But Xi's visit to Shenzhen has encouraged people to be bold again. We should seize this opportunity and calls for more reforms."

Ding Li, an economist at the Guangdong Academy of Social Science, also said Shenzhen leaders should introduce more daring reforms in Qianhai. "The future vision of Qianhai should be an improved version of Hong Kong — a Hong Kong-like system but under the leadership of the Communist Party," he said.

Ding said Qianhai could be a testing ground that embraced the advantages of the two different systems and overcame their shortcomings. "Qianhai should look for more space for trial and reform while retaining governance by the party," he added. "For example, Qianhai could have a free market and a clean and efficient legal system and administration like Hong Kong, while avoiding the great wealth gap of capitalism."

He said that after 30 years of economic reform, China had to rethink its growth model to sustain its development. Xi and his new leadership had to come up with fresh ideas to rejuvenate China's reform efforts. "A good special zone should not passively wait for Beijing's instructions. Its leaders should actively think what they can contribute to this new governing philosophy."

Ding and Guo believed Xi would not explicitly give Qianhai instructions on how to carry out the next stage of reform. Instead,

Beijing would give the local officials a mandate to experiment. But many experts were pessimistic as to whether Qianhai could be the next Shenzhen. For one thing, after three decades of reform, many leaders had lost the appetite, while entrenched interests had become too powerful.

"I don't really believe Qianhai can breathe new life into the Shenzhen leadership," Guo said. "They are so comfortable with their success, nobody wants to take risks any more. Thirty years ago, they had nothing to lose and a lot to gain. Now Shenzhen is so rich and comfortable. The local leaders have a lot to lose. Who will want to risk their career trying new things? All this so-called studying Hong Kong is just a show to pacify their superiors."

CHAPTER 14

Who to Watch

Even as China ushered in a new leadership at the 18th party congress, eyes were not only on new President Xi Jinping and his colleagues in the so-called fifth generation of the Communist Party leadership but also on the chosen few expected to come to power a decade hence.

Seven Tipped for Sixth Generation

by *Keith Zhai*

As the 18th party congress closed, observers had already broadly identified seven up-and-coming party officials who could be among those presented to the Great Hall of the People when the sixth generation takes the helm after the 20th party congress in 2022.

Prior to the 2012 party conclave, these rising stars, who include Hu Chunhua, appointed party chief of Guangdong province shortly after the 18th congress closed, and Sun Zhengcai, who was sent to run the scandal-plagued municipality of Chongqing, were largely unknown outside their relatively small spheres of influence. But that changed as fourth-generation party leaders used the reshuffle to position them for future advancement.

The seven have different backgrounds, but they share much in common. All were children in the 1960s amid the fear and chaos of Mao Zedong's Cultural Revolution, and came of age amid the optimism of the boom times created by second-generation leader Deng Xiaoping's "opening up" in the late 1970s.

They were among the first to seek higher education after the Cultural Revolution subsided and the universities reopened. All seven hold master's degrees from top Chinese universities. Where many of their predecessors were trained as engineers, the sixth-generation prospects include a lawyer, an economist and an agronomist.

Four of the seven came up through the Communist Youth League, a key base of support and a talent training ground for ex-president Hu Jintao. While they did not travel abroad for education — as is now common for young Chinese — the sixth generation has had more exposure to Western ideas than their predecessors and are more comfortable with the capitalistic practices once shunned by party doctrine.

"Those born in the 60s have a broader and deeper knowledge base," said Professor Wang Yukai of the Chinese Academy of Governance. "It shows the trend. China changed from being ruled by revolutionaries to scientists and now the social scientists. The younger generation has brought innovative ideas and energy to the party, which could also enhance the governance of the party," Wang said, adding that movers and shakers of the sixth generation seemed more liberal and open to new ideas.

As such, some analysts felt the sixth generation could be the one that finally delivers the political reform that Hu and leaders of the fourth generation spoke about only in abstract terms. Others, such as Professor Wu Hui of the Central Party School's party-building department, were not so sure. Wu said that changes from within were slow because the party was the ultimate authority. "Many presidents in the US and European countries are also very young, but they don't make too many stupid mistakes because their society is supervised by law. But in China, the party is powerful but the law is weak and the party is superior to law."

Also, despite occasional talk about increasing the diversity of party leadership, the top sixth-generation prospects are all men, meaning that if other contenders don't emerge, Beijing will be ruled exclusively by men for 20 years.

Hu Chunhua

Sun Zhengcai

Lu Hao

Zhou Qiang

Aside from Hu and Sun, the sixth generation's cast of rising stars comprises: Lu Hao, the Youth League's first secretary; Fujian province governor Su Shulin; Hebei province governor Zhang Qingwei; Xinjiang party chairman Nur Bekri; and Hunan province party boss Zhou Qiang. In appearance, the seven look much like their party predecessors: dark suits and jet-black pompadours. They are nonetheless part of a wave of younger, better-educated cadres getting leadership posts as the central government seeks to bolster its reserves of candidates for higher office.

Some 29 per cent of the roughly 400 people sitting on the party's provincial standing committees were born in the 1960s, according to figures reported by state media in July 2012. That was more than three times the number selected from that decade five years earlier, a greater increase than one would expect due to age alone. Of the group, 37 were women, four more than five years previously.

Unlike those who reached adulthood during the Cultural Revolution, few children born in the 1960s were "sent down" to work in factories and farms. Still, many felt the effects of Mao's movement, suffering through purges, famine and other manifestations of the chairman's actions and personality cult.

They were among those best positioned to profit when Deng's policies suddenly brought business back to life, relaxed social control and opened the country to foreigners and foreign investment. Liu Junsheng, a professor of public administration at the China University of Political Science and Law who has researched the 1960s generation at length, described its members as "more familiar with economic development theory than communist theory. The 1960s generation has very little understanding of the party's revolutionary tradition, as they haven't been through that era. Instead they grew up in the era of change."

Liu's research into the latest party personnel figures released in July 2012 showed they were, as a rule, highly educated. All of the more than 170 ministry-level officials born in the 1960s had university degrees. Nearly 90 per cent had master's degrees.

The seven rising stars were selected in part because the praise they received in the state-run media suggested they had support for future appointments. The official press routinely described them as down-to-earth, honest, diligent and frugal.

But analysts were quick to point out that the entire 1960s generation of party officials had come up through a time of seemingly omnipresent corruption, as powerful cadres sought a larger share of the country's rapidly growing wealth. Party disciplinary authorities reported penalising 136,670 officials for corruption in 2011 — up from 106,626 people in 2009. Analysts said most party officials were involved in some level of corruption in the previous 30 years.

"It's a problem for the entire generation," Liu said. "It's a generation of people who were born in the years of famine in the 1960s and lost their soul during the gold rush in the 1980s. They don't have a belief in anything but money."

One political strength for four of the rising stars is their ties to the Communist Youth League. Lu, Hu and Zhou each served terms as the group's first secretary. Nur Bekri led Xinjiang University's Youth League early in his career.

In the Youth League, young officials quickly gain knowledge about internal party decision-making and work closely with powerful officials, such as former Youth League leader Hu Jintao. Such ties have led Chinese to describe such League alumni as the *tuanpai* camp, or "League faction". Promoting officials from the Youth League could also be a positive for citizens who want cleaner public officials. Since League positions have little real power, the group is believed to have less corruption within its ranks.

But having a top leadership made up largely of the *tuanpai* also has drawbacks, analysts said. Youth League jobs are generally not demanding, meaning its officials receive few of the tests and challenges that might best prepare them for high-level posts.

The rush of ambitious young officials looking to use the Youth League as a political stepping stone also risked undercutting its purpose to maintain a connection between the party and the people. And too many promotions for *tuanpai* could hurt morale among officials excluded from the club. "To work in the Youth League is a safe job, and one can easily obtain a high ranking at a relatively young age,"

Wu said. "Their easy promotions could damage the enthusiasm of non-*tuanpai* officials."

Following the 18th party congress, it will be at least a decade before China learns the full potential of the sixth generation and whether they envision the sort of change the country wants. One analyst cautioned that a lot could happen in the next 10 years to change the cast of rising stars, as their fortunes rose and fell.

The first clues may come in the years after the 18th party congress, when the first members of the sixth generation receive some of the country's toughest jobs. Hu Chunhua, appointed Guangdong party chief after the congress, had a baptism of fire when he mediated in a landmark protest by newspaper workers at the outspoken *Southern Weekly* over censorship by propaganda officials. The *South China Morning Post* described Hu's intervention as a sensible move.

"I'm not sure if the 60s generation will push the envelope on political reforms," Liu said. "In China, a leader can only make reform happen by sacrificing himself. But if he could actually make it, he would become a hero."

Glossary of Names

Politburo (25 members)

Xi Jinping 习近平*
Li Keqiang 李克强*
Zhang Dejiang 张德江*
Yu Zhengsheng 俞正声*
Liu Yunshan 刘云山*
Wang Qishan 王岐山*
Zhang Gaoli 张高丽*

Ma Kai 马凯
Wang Huning 王沪宁
Liu Yandong 刘延东
Liu Qibao 刘奇葆
Xu Qiliang 许其亮
Sun Chunlan 孙春兰
Sun Zhengcai 孙政才
Li Jianguo 李建国
Li Yuanchao 李源潮
Wang Yang 汪洋
Zhang Chunxian 张春贤
Fan Changlong 范长龙
Meng Jianzhu 孟建柱

Zhao Leji 赵乐际
Hu Chunhua 胡春华
Li Zhanshu 栗战书
Guo Jinlong 郭金龙
Han Zheng 韩正

State Council

Premier Li Keqiang 李克强*

Vice Premier

Zhang Gaoli 张高丽*
Liu Yandong 刘延东
Wang Yang 汪洋
Ma Kai 马凯

State Councillor

Yang Jing 杨晶
Chang Wanquan 常万全
Yang Jiechi 杨洁篪
Guo Shengkun 郭声琨
Wang Yong 王勇

---

* Member of the Politburo Standing Committee.

Secretary General
Yang Jing   杨晶

Ministry of Foreign Affairs
Wang Yi   王毅

Ministry of National Defence
Chang Wanquan   常万全

National Development and Reform Commission

Xu Shaoshi   徐绍史

Ministry of Education
Yuan Guiren   袁贵仁

Ministry of Science and Technology
Wan Gang   万钢

Ministry of Industry and Information Technology

Miao Wei   苗圩

Ministry of Ethnic Affairs
Wang Zhengwei   王正伟

Ministry of State Security
Guo Shengkun   郭声琨

Ministry of Public Security
Geng Huichang   耿惠昌

Ministry of Supervision
Huang Shuxian   黄树贤

Ministry of Civil Affairs
Li Liguo   李立国

Ministry of Justice
Wu Aiying   吴爱英

Ministry of Finance
Lou Jiwei   楼继伟

Ministry of Human Resources and Social Security

Yin Weimin   尹蔚民

Ministry of Land and Resources
Jiang Daming   姜大明

Ministry of Environmental Protection

Zhou Shengxian   周生贤

Ministry of Housing and Urban-Rural Development

Jiang Weixin   姜伟新

Ministry of Transport
Yang Chuantang   杨传堂

Ministry of Water Resources
Chen Lei   陈雷

Ministry of Agriculture
Han Changfu   韩长赋

Ministry of Commerce
Gao Hucheng   高虎城

Ministry of Culture
Cai Wu   蔡武

**Health and Family Planning
  Commission**

Li Bin   李斌

People's Bank of China
Zhou Xiaochuan   周小川

National Audit Office
Liu Jiayi   刘家义